Designing Retail Experience in the 21st Century

Designing Retail Experience in the 21st Century

D. J. Huppatz

BLOOMSBURY VISUAL ARTS
LONDON · NEW YORK · OXFORD · NEW DELHI · SYDNEY

BLOOMSBURY VISUAL ARTS
Bloomsbury Publishing Plc
50 Bedford Square, London, WC1B 3DP, UK
1385 Broadway, New York, NY 10018, USA
29 Earlsfort Terrace, Dublin 2, Ireland

BLOOMSBURY, BLOOMSBURY VISUAL ARTS and the Diana logo are trademarks of Bloomsbury Publishing Plc

First published in Great Britain 2025

Copyright © Daniel Huppatz, 2025

Daniel Huppatz has asserted his right under the Copyright, Designs and Patents Act, 1988, to be identified as author of this work.

For legal purposes the Acknowledgements on p. ix constitute an extension of this copyright page.

Cover design by Louise Dugdale
Cover image: Doha, Qatar. 27th Mar, 2019
Sharil Babu/dpa picture alliance/ Alamy Stock Photo

All rights reserved. No part of this publication may be reproduced or transmitted in any form or by any means, electronic or mechanical, including photocopying, recording, or any information storage or retrieval system, without prior permission in writing from the publishers.

Bloomsbury Publishing Plc does not have any control over, or responsibility for, any third-party websites referred to or in this book. All internet addresses given in this book were correct at the time of going to press. The author and publisher regret any inconvenience caused if addresses have changed or sites have ceased to exist, but can accept no responsibility for any such changes.

A catalogue record for this book is available from the British Library.

Library of Congress Cataloging-in-Publication Data
Names: Huppatz, D. J., author.
Title: Designing retail experience in the 21st century / D.J. Huppatz, Swinburne University of Technology, Australia.
Description: New York : Bloomsbury Visual Arts, 2025. | Includes bibliographical references and index.
Identifiers: LCCN 2024016590 (print) | LCCN 2024016591 (ebook) | ISBN 9781350423299 (paperback) | ISBN 9781350423305 (hardback) | ISBN 9781350423312 (ebook) | ISBN 9781350423329 (pdf)
Subjects: LCSH: Retail trade. | Industrial design coordination.
Classification: LCC HF5429 .H83 2025 (print) | LCC HF5429 (ebook) | DDC 658.8/7–dc23/eng/20240819
LC record available at https://lccn.loc.gov/2024016590
LC ebook record available at https://lccn.loc.gov/2024016591

ISBN:	HB:	978-1-3504-2330-5
	PB:	978-1-3504-2329-9
	ePDF:	978-1-3504-2332-9
	eBook:	978-1-3504-2331-2

Typeset by Integra Software Services Pvt. Ltd.
Printed and bound in India

To find out more about our authors and books visit www.bloomsbury.com and sign up for our newsletters.

Contents

List of Figures   vi
Acknowledgements   ix

Introduction   1

1   Simplicity and Transparency: Apple   15
2   Convenience and Personalization: Amazon Go   37
3   Constructive Play: LEGO   59
4   Lifestyle Assemblage: IKEA   81
5   Performance and Innovation: Nike   103
6   A Sensual Respite: Aesop   125
7   Acceleration and Materiality: Zara   147
8   A Korean Dystopia: Gentle Monster   167

Conclusion   189

Notes   200
Index   236

Figures

1	Apple store, Chicago, designed by Foster + Partners, 2017	16
2	"You are on Potawatomi land" by Andrea Carlson, 2021	17
3	Apple store, Chicago, detail	18
4	Apple store, Chicago, looking down from the mezzanine	19
5	Apple store, Chicago, handrail detail	20
6	Apple store, Chicago, tables	21
7	Amazon Go, Union Station, Chicago, entrance	38
8	Amazon Go, Prudential Plaza, Chicago	39
9	Amazon Go, Prudential Plaza, Chicago, baked goods	40
10	Amazon Go, Union Station, Chicago, shelves	41
11	Amazon Go, Prudential Plaza, Chicago	42
12	Amazon Go, Sixth Avenue, New York	43
13	LEGO store, New York, The Tree of Discovery	60
14	LEGO store, New York, Captain America	60
15	LEGO store, New York, The Statue of Liberty	61
16	LEGO store, New York, subway station	62
17	LEGO store, New York, Build your own Minifigure	63
18	LEGO store, New York, play station	64
19	IKEA Richmond, Melbourne, a view of the ceiling	82
20	IKEA Richmond, Melbourne, QR code	82
21	IKEA Richmond, Melbourne, everyday activities	83
22	IKEA Richmond, Melbourne, Responsibly Sourced Wood	84
23	IKEA Richmond, Melbourne, abundant choice	85

Figures vii

24	IKEA Richmond, Melbourne, Pöang chairs in the Warehouse	86
25	Nike's House of Innovation, New York, exterior	104
26	Nike's House of Innovation, New York, new leggings display	105
27	Nike's House of Innovation, New York, digital interaction	106
28	Nike's House of Innovation, New York, Nike By You	107
29	Nike's House of Innovation, New York, the Sneakerlab	108
30	Nike's House of Innovation, New York, Nike and Apple Watch display	108
31	Aesop store, Flinders Lane, Melbourne, entrance	126
32	Aesop store, Flinders Lane, Melbourne, interior	127
33	Aesop store, Chelsea, New York, ceiling	128
34	Aesop store, Chelsea, New York, teacup	129
35	Aesop store, Upper West Side, New York, exterior	133
36	Aesop store, Upper West Side, New York, interior	134
37	Zara store, Porto, exterior	148
38	Zara store, Porto, the luxury of space	148
39	Zara store, Porto, distressed fashion	149
40	Zara store, Porto, mix and match ensembles	150
41	Zara store, Porto, stone veneer tables	150
42	Zara store, Porto, self-checkout station	151
43	Gentle Monster, Singapore, exterior	168
44	Gentle Monster, Singapore, kinetic sculpture	169
45	Gentle Monster, Singapore, "The Data Addicts"	170
46	Gentle Monster, Singapore, satellite dish and crystals	171
47	Gentle Monster, Singapore, sunglasses and sculptures	171
48	Gentle Monster, Soho, New York, The Visitor	172
49	Gentle Monster, Soho, New York, digital screen and sculptures	173
50	Gentle Monster, Soho, New York, the birth of The Visitor	174
51	Showfields, Manhattan, interior 1	197
52	Showfields, Manhattan, interior 2	198

Acknowledgements

Although written over 2022 and 2023, this book is the result of a much longer engagement with architecture, interiors and retail design. For this, I owe thanks to my students over the past decade at Swinburne University of Technology's School of Architecture and Design.

For advice and encouragement on the initial idea, proposal and manuscript, special thanks are due to Dr Marta Filipová, Professor Grace Lees-Maffei, Dr Sebastian Gurciullo and Dr Kirsten Day. For their careful readings and thoughtful feedback, I'd also like to thank the four anonymous reviewers of the proposal and manuscript. And for a smooth process from proposal to publication, thanks to the Bloomsbury team, particularly Olivia Davies and Louise Baird-Smith.

I trialled some ideas about staging experiences and retail design at the 2019 conference "Experience and Principles of Design", convened by Professor Kaja Tooming Buchanan and Professor Richard Buchanan and hosted at Tongji University, Shanghai. Thanks to the organizers and participants of that conference.

Part of Chapter 6 was first published in a book chapter, D. J. Huppatz, "Aesop's Sensory Experience", in John Potvin, Marie-Ève Marchand and Benoit Beaulieu, eds., *The Senses in Interior Design: Sensorial Expressions and Experiences* (Manchester: Manchester University Press, 2023), pp.232–247. Thanks to the editors of that volume.

Introduction

"I'm not writing a book about shopping", I replied.

"It's a book about how we interact with retail stores, websites and social media feeds. It's a book about how companies design experiences. It's about a seductive stage at the culmination of a supply chain that began in a faraway factory and will end one day in a faraway landfill. It's about …"

"Face it", she interrupted, "you're writing a book about shopping."

She's right, I thought. This book is a study of how, where and why we buy things.

Over the past twenty-five years, how, where and why North Americans and Europeans shop has changed. While media claims about the "death" of bricks-and-mortar shopping and the "retail apocalypse" of 2015–17 proved exaggerations, the rise of online shopping resulted in both store closures and anxiety about physical retail's future.[1] A further disruption, precipitated by the 2020 Covid-19 pandemic, resulted in well-known American retail chains, including Neiman Marcus, JC Penny, Lord & Taylor, and J.Crew, filing for bankruptcy. The same year, the United Kingdom's oldest retail chain, Debenhams, also shuttered 124 stores. But, despite this trajectory, some retailers have not only survived but expanded their physical stores.

This book comprises case studies of these retail success stories. Readers will recognize names such as Apple, Amazon, Nike, LEGO, IKEA and Zara, while Aesop and Gentle Monster are less well known. I chose these cases for three reasons. First, they have all thrived in a world dominated by digital connectivity, each of them opening more – and larger – stores. Even in an era of online shopping, these corporations have designed physical spaces seductive enough to entice and engage customers. Second, they all design retail experiences that combine the physical and digital realms in distinctive ways. Third, they all utilize a global design language to appeal to customers of varying cultures, languages and customs.

Neither high-end luxury nor low-end discount stores, my cases lie somewhere in the middle. I assume North American and European readers are familiar with most of these brands, and some – such as Nike, Apple and LEGO – are familiar to Asian and South American readers. Despite documenting *my* experiences throughout the book, I am ultimately interested in common retail experiences – a shared experience – although I will also consider regional and cultural differences. And, although these cases are specific, I hope readers can substitute (with a little modification) stores that utilize the same strategies, so you may note similarities between the Nike store analysed in Chapter 5 and your local Adidas store, for example.

I believe this collection of stores encapsulates a new retail paradigm that differs from earlier paradigms (such as the department store or shopping mall). Glittering surfaces and attentive service are no longer enough to entice customers into a store – physical and digital interaction are the keys to designing twenty-first-century retail experiences. But location is also important. All are products of large, relatively wealthy economies, located in global cities. My case studies are drawn from Chicago, New York, Singapore, Melbourne and Porto. But I assume readers in many other cities are familiar with these experiences and strategies, especially as these companies open more stores around the world.

Retail experience is a vague expression. Is a shopping experience something we can assess or measure? If so, where does it occur and when does it begin and end? I am particularly interested in how stores and their accompanying digital strategies evoke sensory responses and provoke customer interaction and participation both in-store and online. Sensory responses include not only the traditional "five senses" (sight, sound, smell, touch and taste) but also spatial reactions, emotions and memories. Interaction and participation include in-store relationships between customers and staff as well as between customers and products, websites and social media.

While some designers still quote the maxim "form follows function", designing retail experiences is better embodied by "form follows feeling". By form, I mean a term malleable enough to incorporate physical stores and products, packaging, graphics, websites, social media feeds and service design. And by feeling, I mean the full range of responses and emotions evoked in customers in-store and online. Ultimately, I am interested in how and why some stores thrive in a digital culture. How do they design experiences? What desires do they appeal to? And, if these retail experiences reveal something about how we shop today, what do they conceal?

What is an Experience?

The word "experience" permeates contemporary life, yet its precise meaning is elusive. It typically refers to either knowledge accumulated over time ("She has years of teaching experience") or to an immediate, sensory event ("Wow, that rollercoaster ride was an intense experience"). In *Keywords*, Raymond Williams distinguished between these two. He defined experience as: "(i) knowledge gathered from past events, whether by conscious observation or by consideration and reflection; and (ii) a particular kind of consciousness, which can in some contexts be distinguished from 'reason' or 'knowledge'."[2] He referred to the first – accumulated knowledge – as "experience past", and the second – the ongoing rush of sensations in our consciousness – as "experience present".

Although Williams understood both as individual, we can also consider experience as collective. We refer to "women's experience" or "the human experience", for example, as markers of shared conditions. To Williams' "experience past" and "experience present", we therefore need "shared experience" to capture the idea of a collective experience. For philosopher Martin Jay, experience lies "at the nodal point of the intersection between public language and private subjectivity, between expressible commonalities and the ineffability of the individual interior".[3] This fulcrum between an individual and a shared experience is central to my analyses below.

Another difficulty in discussing experience is the gap between the rush of sensory input and what we process, comprehend and remember. Psychologist Daniel Kahneman usefully differentiated between the experiencing, present self and the remembering self.[4] In reconstructing experiences into a coherent narrative, Kahneman argues, we forget or ignore most moment-to-moment details. To comprehend our ongoing rush of perceptions, feelings and sensory input, this "reflected narrative" highlights significant moments, beginnings and endings. We best remember extraordinary events that disrupt or change our everyday lives.

To complicate our definition, qualifiers such as "genuine" or "authentic" imply complementary "fake" or "inauthentic" experiences. In tourism, for example, an "authentic experience" refers to an unscripted, raw and engaging event, while in retail industries, a "genuine experience" typically describes a local, particular or idiosyncratic one.[5] Both suggest engagements with people, places or situations beyond our daily life that challenge or disrupt our expectations, understandings or beliefs. Some tourism scholars suggest a model in which authentic experience is in a dialectical relationship with alienation, with tourism understood as a search for an (unreachable) authentic experience.[6]

For twentieth-century thinkers as diverse as Walter Benjamin and James Dewey, the fragmentation and alienation that characterizes modern life results in a longing for a renewed collective experience. For Benjamin, the "poverty" of experience was a fundamental modern condition resulting from the loss of traditional communities.[7] New technologies and the speed of urban life, he argued, shattered modern experience into fragments, alienating us with ever-more immediate and intense sensory inputs that erase collective traditions and modes of experience. Similarly, Dewey wrote that "shared experience is the greatest of human goods".[8] To Benjamin's urban alienation, Dewey added our alienation from nature. Both thinkers identified a transformation brought about by modernity and argued – in different ways – for a renewal of shared experience.

But, in "The Evidence of Experience", historian Joan Scott highlighted a problem in understanding shared experience. She asked how individual experience can become a foundation (authoritative evidence) for collective knowledge and shared experience. She stressed that our experience is only meaningful through language (or through reflective narratives). For Scott, "experience is a linguistic event (it doesn't happen outside established meanings) but neither is it confined to a fixed order of meaning. Since discourse is by definition shared, experience is collective as well as individual."[9] Importantly, Scott reminds us to consider the contested nature of "experience shared", what we include and exclude when analysing it, and "the politics of its production".[10]

It is tempting to depict experience as a temporal progression. That is, from experience present (my ongoing rush of sensations) to experience past (my reflection on the ongoing rush of sensations) to experience shared (I communicate my experience to others). But, as Scott argues, my individual experience only makes sense through reflected narrative and conceptual categories that are *already shared*. Mediated by a common language and conceptual categories, even personal experiences are already collective. Our contemporary condition is characterized by this paradoxical relationship between modes of experience, individual and shared, and this issue will recur in the case studies that follow.

Staging Experiences

Twenty-first-century shopping – enticing, entertaining and enveloping – is rarely a simple exchange between customer and company of money for goods. In their 1998 essay, "Welcome to the Experience Economy", Joseph Pine and James Gilmore argued that "staging experiences" is central to every company's future prosperity.[11] Designing a compelling experience, they argued, required a coherent set of "cues", integrated across interior design, product design, packaging, staff uniforms and service scripts. Pine and Gilmore highlighted the need to "sensorialize" every detail of a store and design every interaction to accentuate "the sensations created from its use".[12] Future stores, they argued, should evoke a theatrical or cinematic experience for the customer: immersive, seamless and absorbing.

Unlike goods, which are tangible, and services, which are intangible, experiences "are inherently personal", argued Pine and Gilmore.

> They actually occur within any individual who has been engaged on an emotional, physical, intellectual, or even spiritual level. The result? No two

people can have the same experience – period. Each experience derives from the interaction between the staged event and the individual's prior state of mind and being.[13]

In their definition, an experience is an interaction between customer and company that the customer registers – on reflection – as memorable. The customer's senses play a crucial role, as a retail experience relies on sights, sounds, smells and touches that condense into a memorable impression.

In the wake of their essay and subsequent book, *The Experience Economy*, critics questioned aspects of Pine and Gilmore's account.[14] First, they observed, Pine and Gilmore directed their analysis solely at management and not at the customer, who "is consistently viewed as a more or less passive target for the company".[15] Aimed at a managerial readership, it is hardly surprising that Pine and Gilmore's theory positions the customer solely as a potential revenue source. Second, the customer's status within a staged experience is instrumental, "with interaction between spectators as isolated entities, thereby conceiving experiences as means to reach pre-given ends".[16] Experience is characterized as singular (not shared), and the customer is assured that their interactions have no consequences and that they have no responsibilities other than self-satisfaction.

In a 2011 update, Pine and Gilmore continued to promote the experience economy as inevitable across various industries, they added a further stage. "Once the Experience Economy has run its course in the decades to come", they argued, "the *Transformation Economy* will take over."[17] Though only sketched briefly, Pine and Gilmore distinguished between experiences and transformations:

> With an experience, the employees of a staging company are actors performing parts, creating roles, and building characters to engage guests in entertaining, educational, escapist, and/or esthetic ways. With a transformation, all these experiential realms merely set the stage for helping *the customer* learn to act.[18]

Authenticity is an essential theme in this future economy. Pine and Gilmore note that, "the management of the customer perception of authenticity becomes the primary new source of competitive advantage – the new business imperative".[19] The *perception* of authenticity and how this is managed are important issues we will return to in the case studies below.

Subsequent theorists described authentic, transformative experiences as *meaningful*.[20] Pine and Gilmore argued that transformations are created through increasingly customized experiences, or "'individualization' – creating more and more value for individuals by getting closer and closer to what each individual truly wants and needs, culminating in the individual-changing offerings of transformations".[21] For Pine and Gilmore, the next phase of staged experiences should emphasize the authentic and transformative by appealing to a customer's specific desires. In the case studies that follow, I am not only interested in following these desires, but examining how corporations are "helping the customer learn how to act". I contend that an essential part of the paradigm shift in twenty-first-century retail design involves both the management of perceptions and a shift from customer manipulation to customer training.

Designing Experiences

Over the past twenty-five years, designers have also embraced the word "experience". Practitioners, critics and academics have written numerous books, articles and how-to guides devoted to "user experience" (UX), "product experience" and "service experience". In the twentieth century, designers and theorists, enamoured with mass production and functionalism or styling and symbolism, rarely addressed how people experienced products. In contrast, today's designers aim to develop products, services and systems that are not only useful, but meaningful, desirable and engrossing. For Marc Hassenzahl, "… User Experience is not about good industrial design, multi-touch, or fancy interfaces. It is about transcending the material. It is about creating an experience through a device."[22] If a twentieth-century modernist chair was a machine for sitting, for example, my twenty-first-century lounge chair is a stylish accessory designed to enhance my lifestyle.

Beginning in the 1990s, designers began to shift from simply designing functional or beautiful products to designing for user interaction and participation. A new problem was that many products – particularly digital devices – were more complex than their predecessors. The growing computer industry spawned new fields such as interaction design, interface design and Human-Computer Interaction (HCI). User experience (UX) emerged as a specialist field within this mix. Donald Norman, in the field's seminal publication, *The Psychology of Everyday Things* (better known in its later edition, *The Design of Everyday Things*) argued:

> Designers need to make things that satisfy people's needs, in terms of function, in terms of being understandable and usable, and in terms of their ability to deliver emotional satisfaction, pride and delight. In other words, the design must be thought of as a total experience.[23]

UX designers assimilated insights from cognitive science, psychology and anthropology to better understand how users interact and engage with designed products.

Researchers Paul Hekkert and Hendrik Schifferstein, for example, identified three main components of user experience.[24] First, an aesthetic response based on a user's sensory perception of a product (its look, sound, feel, smell); second, its function, based on which actions a product affords; and third, its expressive, symbolic or mythological associations. They also noted the importance of where we interact with products and the atmosphere in which our interactions occur. To return to my example of the chair, I experience my lounge chair aesthetically as colourful and comfortable; functionally as a seat to watch TV; and symbolically as an expression of my personality – modern, stylish and sophisticated.

Brenda Laurel, in an alternative approach to early interaction and interface design, *Computers as Theatre* (originally published in 1991), used terms derived from theatre:

> This confusion over the nature of human-computer activity can be alleviated by thinking about it in terms of theatre, where the special relationship between representation and reality is already comfortably established, not only in theoretical terms, but also in the way that people design and experience theatrical works. Both domains employ representations as contexts for thought. Both attempt to amplify and orchestrate experience. Both have the capacity to represent actions and situations that typically do not and cannot exist in the real world, in ways that invite us to extend our minds, feelings, and senses to envelop them.[25]

Interestingly, although it aligns neatly with Pine and Gilmore's model, later theorists did not adopt Laurel's dramaturgical model. She noted that theatre is not a realm considered "serious" enough for computer scientists (nor subsequent UX designers and theorists).[26]

Instead, Experience Design emerged as a field of research and practice with specialist studios and publications.[27] In the 1980s and 1990s, design consultancies such as Frog Design and IDEO pioneered this new field. They combined older practices such as graphic, interior and industrial design, with interface design, HCI and other digital design fields.[28] CEO of IDEO Tim Brown summed up the new, cross-disciplinary practice:

> As more of our basic needs are met, we increasingly expect sophisticated experiences that are emotionally satisfying and meaningful. These experiences will not be simple products. They will be complex combinations of products, services, spaces and information.[29]

Such a holistic approach to design practice resulted in consultancies devoted to Experience Design and to scholarly work on how designers can design for experiences.[30]

Some practitioners and scholars used terms such as Experience Design and User Experience as shorthand for post-materialism. By focusing on experiences – particularly digital ones – designers often assume the physical realm remains unaffected. But every digital interaction relies on a hidden material infrastructure and energy expenditure (from hardware and cabling to distant data centres). These new approaches also tended to ignore politics and power relationships. UX emerged within the context of technology companies devoted to profit rather than the common good. Design could "magic away" unpalatable aspects of products, systems or services and distract users from issues like sustainability, equity and social justice.

The rise of service design contributed to this mix. At the intersection of marketing, graphic, product and interaction design – a combination of tangible and intangible elements – the idea of designing services began in the 1980s with G. Lynn Shostack's "service blueprint".[31] Shostack proposed a graphic map of a "journey" comprising a series of interaction points (later called "touchpoints") between the customer and the company. These include the retail store, products and advertisements, as well as interactions between customers and staff.[32] In the early 2000s, design consultancies began to specialize in service design. With considerable overlap, both service and experience designers inaugurated a shift from standardized, mass-produced services to personalized, heterogeneous ones.

The theatrical model proposed by Laurel has also been applied to service design. Youngsoo Lee and Miso Kim, for example, posit "storytelling" as central to the discipline. Derived from Aristotle's analysis of drama in his *Poetics*, they propose the sequential flow of interactions in a service is analogous to a dramatic plot. As in ancient Greek drama, so "service similarly fulfills the ritualistic role of supporting individuals' daily lives and providing them opportunities to participate in collective action. Service storytelling ties these two aspects together, contributing to design by proposing a framework that views making as a collective and ongoing human collaboration".[33] This dramatic aspect will be important to my analyses, but Lee and Kim's optimistic vision of shared experience and collaboration will look rather different in the case studies to come.

Although the theatre metaphor is useful for understanding retail experiences, it has limits. A play has a beginning and end. Its action occurs in a bounded space. Unlike a play, the retail experiences I consider have less definitive beginnings and ends, and are not bounded in space or time. Another difference is in the audience member's expectations and understanding. As an audience viewing a play, we know the performers on stage are actors and understand the play is a representation. In contrast, our immersion in a retail experience blurs the boundaries between actors and audience and between representation and reality.

A final idea worth reiterating from recent design theorists is that designed objects shape human action and behavior. Numerous theorists have noted the ways design "designs us".[34] Some scholars argue that designed products contain a "script" that shapes its users' behavior.[35] This script extends beyond a singular use to imply an entire lifestyle or world-view. Richard Buchanan explains this phenomenon via rhetoric:

> In approaching design from a rhetorical perspective, our hypothesis should be that all products – digital and analog, tangible and intangible – are vivid arguments about how we should lead our lives.[36]

The earlier chair example illustrates how this works. My lounge chair directs me towards the TV. Relaxed and comfortable, I face away from my friend, turning awkwardly to answer her before I return to a posture shaped by the chair. While I designed my room, now my behavior, habits and rituals are – to some extent – "designed" by the chair, the TV and other furniture.

This rhetorical power of designed products, interiors and services is central to my analyses. How are we shaped by our shopping experiences? What are their implicit arguments about how to live? How do we absorb the mythologies enacted in these experiences – Simplicity, Convenience or Creativity? How do designers script our retail experiences?[37] Here, I envisage a retail experience within a "fluid assemblage" of physical and digital components that includes the store, its products, the company's website, social media feeds and advertising, as well as the customer's aspirations, imagination and memories.[38]

Analysing Retail Experience

Each chapter that follows begins with a first-person description of a store. I've done this for three reasons. First, to situate the reader in the position of a customer. Second, to describe a customer's experience in terms of sensory input, engagement and perception. This helps "flesh out" the accompanying photos with sounds, smells and other tactile impressions in an attempt to describe each store's atmosphere. Third, by providing a "generic" experience as a starting point, I can reflect upon alternative experiences beyond my own.

Here, I am building upon an established phenomenological tradition. Phenomenologists seek to describe and understand the world – objects, events, places, people, nature – *as experienced*. Although philosopher Edmund Husserl initiated phenomenological analysis, Maurice Merleau-Ponty's version has proved most useful to architects and designers.[39] Architects such as Juhani Pallasmaa and Peter Zumthor have used Merleau-Ponty's ideas in both their writings and practice to highlight our sensory perception of the built environment.[40] In the last decade or so, in addition to understanding the sensory interaction we have with buildings, architectural theorists have also sought to understand how designers create "atmosphere" and "mood" in architectural spaces.[41]

Although such an approach – describing and understanding phenomena – may strike some readers as unscientific, experience is, after all, first-hand knowledge gained by observation. Architectural theorist Harry Francis Mallgrave argued that "… architecture is at heart a phenomenal experience, one in which the built environment can no longer be considered *apart from the user's experience of it*".[42] Having said this, my interest is not in my particular experiences but understanding how elements of the material realm – the architecture, interior, furniture, fixtures and products – combine to evoke a shared experience.

The first-person narratives also set these spaces within their urban context. As these stores are designed to be immersive, self-contained spaces, their contrast with neighbouring stores and their surrounding city is important. Upon crossing the threshold and entering a LEGO store, for example, or entering the IKEA store from the parking lot, you immediately sense (if subconsciously) a change. You are no longer in the chaotic city or busy mall but immersed in a carefully designed and controlled environment. In most cases, these stores are placeless, designed to generate the same – or at least a similar – experience in any global location.

But placing too much emphasis on the personal nature of experience can be problematic. Emotional responses are subjective. As opposing fans in a football stadium experience the same game differently, each person will experience a store and its products differently. Individual reactions and interactions differ according to age, gender, education, cultural and social background. Entering a store as a particular type of body – a female person of colour, for example, or a young, disabled person – might evoke discomfort, anxiety or fear. As a white, able-bodied, middle-aged male, I fit the generic customer mould. And, of course, this results in a particular experience of these retail spaces.

I acknowledge this limitation in advance. Feminist theorists have long noted differences in the way women experience architectural spaces.[43] More recently, Sara Ahmed stressed the role race plays in experiencing space:

> … whiteness may function as a form of public comfort *by allowing bodies to extend into spaces that have already taken their shape*. Those spaces are lived as comfortable as they allow bodies to fit in; the surfaces of social space are already impressed upon by the shape of such bodies.[44]

My body fits comfortably into these retail spaces. All I can do to compensate is to emphasize a "generic" experience and try to understand its "politics of production" (as Scott advised). At the same time, these stores have been designed by global corporations to appeal to the widest possible demographic.

But, in the end, my experience is simply a starting point and I hope readers integrate their own into these case studies.

Another criticism often levelled at the phenomenological method relates to how to describe the immediacy of experience. The key phenomenological method involves not simply a description but involves a "bracketing" – in which experience is placed in quotation marks – and this necessarily entails a break with the unmediated world.[45] Consider this like entering an experience temporarily, then stepping back to reflect on it. In the analyses that follow, after a brief first-person description of the store, I dig into the history of the company, its products, marketing and aims, as well as connecting the physical store with the company's online presence. An initial experience is only the starting point for an archaeological process that exposes sedimented layers that I piece together into a bigger picture.

Although the stores I analyse below are contemporary, there is some historical material to consider, particularly as some stores embody long-standing brand associations. After the phenomenological analysis of the store at the start of each chapter, I consider the company's history in terms of products, branding and marketing, and continuities or changes in the latest iterations of their retail experience. For some of the larger companies, there was considerable literature to sift through and, again, I approached this in an archaeological manner, highlighting key moments, quotes, statistics and other evidence that contributes to our understanding of each store's design of a particular retail experience.

To consider retail experience solely from a design or architectural perspective is limiting. Academic scholarship tends to be specialized. Traditionally, such an approach would tell us a great deal about a store's physical structure, interiors, fixtures and furniture, but little on its contents or the store's connections to services, systems and digital platforms.[46] To achieve a holistic sense of designing contemporary retail experience, my method in compiling this book resembled bricolage.[47] That is, each chapter combines resources from design and architectural theory, cultural studies, retail history, marketing and business scholarship, as well as psychology, philosophy and sociology. Such an approach, rather than focusing on a singular designer, structure or process, allows us to see design in a broader context.

From Spectacle to Experience

Finally, my study builds upon the work of many scholars of retail history and consumption, marketing, sociology and cultural studies. Scholars have adopted various approaches, including detailed histories of retail architecture and interiors, consumerism and issues such as the construction of social and cultural identities through shopping, and how credit, governance and regulations affect retail experiences.[48] Of all of these, I found studies of the department store and the mall to be the most useful as a historical backdrop.

The department store stands out as the paradigm of the first modern retail experience.[49] Developed in Paris and London from the mid-nineteenth century, the department store's theatrical windows, dazzling interiors of marble, mirrors and artificial lighting, as well as innovations such as fixed prices and attentive service, transformed shopping habits and customer expectations. Walter Benjamin wrote that within the grand Parisian department stores, the "circus-like and theatrical element of commerce is quite extraordinarily heightened".[50] The nineteenth-century department store designers sought to engage customers with spectacular interiors, expansive shop windows on the street and new technologies such as the elevator.

But more than simply impressive architecture and interiors, department stores offered a range of activities beyond shopping. These included musical and theatrical performances, demonstrations, lectures and exhibitions. Customers could eat and drink in the department store's café or restaurant. Department store designers, who developed model interiors, display windows and theatrical sets to display mannequins and props, pioneered the "architecture of display".[51] Department stores were also spaces for mediating modernity, mass production and new domestic technologies, and some of their strategies are still used today.

Developed in the United States in the 1950s, the shopping mall was the next significant paradigm of modern retail experience.[52] Opened in 1956, architect Victor Gruen's Southdale mall in Minnesota refined the template that was rolled out in malls across the country. Surrounded by parking lots, Gruen brought together a collection of stores into one huge complex – heated in winter and air-conditioned in summer – in which customers could buy everything from clothes to groceries. The mall redefined retail in the second half of the twentieth century and, like the department store, spread globally, adapting to different cultures and contexts.[53]

Malls too, despite their bland reputation, sheltered many activities beyond shopping. Food courts, amusement parlours, mini-golf and even indoor ski slopes and artificial beaches enticed customers to stay for a day. No less than department stores, mall designers appealed to customers through an array of sensual delights in carefully controlled interiors which included sound (Muzak), temperature control, landscaping, fountains and public art. In Jon Jerde's Californian malls of the 1980s, the mall took a theatrical turn. Inspired by Disney's theme parks, Jerde aimed to create an immersive, entertaining retail experience.[54] But, by the first decade of the twenty-first century, the mall – at least in the United States – seemed in decline, with many either closing or struggling to survive.[55]

Beyond the department store and the mall, in the 1990s and 2000s, luxury fashion boutiques shifted towards more immersive environments, particularly as high-profile architects such as Rem Koolhaas and Herzog & de Meuron designed flagship stores for global brands like Prada and Louis Vuitton.[56] While scholars have written books and articles on the architecture of luxury retail stores, at the other end of the scale, there has been little interest in the design of discount stores, "big box" stores or $2 stores. In the early twenty-first century, theorists began to consider retail as a proliferation of stores across a dispersed context, with neither department store nor mall as the dominant model.[57]

It is no coincidence that Experience Design and the new paradigm of retail experience arose in the United States in the 2000s. The dot-com boom of the late 1990s inspired the idea of an economy based in finance, computing and services, while manufacturing moved offshore, suggesting a future of increasingly immaterial experiences. Here, scholarly work on "brandscapes" and branded spaces emerged to describe new types of retail experience.[58] Precedents such as McDonalds, Starbucks, the Hard Rock café chain, Disney's theme parks and the carefully calibrated environments of casinos all developed experience design strategies that continued in the stores of the early twenty-first century.[59] And it is here that I will begin, just after the turn of the millennium, where the digital meets the physical in one of contemporary retail's most successful stories.

Chapter 1
Simplicity and Transparency: Apple

Chicago's Apple store is easy to miss. On a bright, cold morning, as I walked across the Du Sable Bridge, it was the Wrigley Building, that gleaming white edifice of Chicago's chewing gum king, that first drew my eyes, then the Chicago Tribune tower opposite it. Finally, my eyes dropped to an empty plaza and there, below a modern office building, stood a modest glass pavilion (Figure 1). In a city renowned for iconic architecture, Chicago's Michigan Avenue Apple store seemed – at least from a distance – underwhelming. Opened in 2017, the store is one of Apple's new generation flagship stores that reinforce the brand's minimal aesthetic and aim to become a new type of public space. This winter's morning, while the surrounding plaza was deserted, I spotted movement in the store. I just hoped it was warm inside.

The Apple store sits near where the Chicago River empties into Lake Michigan. Here, sometime before 1790, Jean Baptiste Pointe du Sable constructed a farm and trading post.[1] While the Potawatomi and other First Nations peoples had camped by the river for centuries, du Sable's farm was reputedly the first permanent dwelling in the area. On the bridge named after him stands his bronze bust with a sign below claiming him as the "Founder of Chicago". Of West African and French ancestry, du Sable married a Potawatomi woman and had two children here, but he and his family left in 1800, presumably due to the westward expansion of American settlers. In 1847, Cyrus McCormick bought the site and built a factory to produce his mechanical reapers, essential tools for new settlers to plough up the prairies.[2]

As I paused on the Bridge to admire the Apple store, I noticed a sign in large red letters on the Chicago River's opposite bank. "Bodéwadmikik ėthë yéyék", it read, "You are on Potawatomi land" (Figure 2). The statement – 15 feet high and 266 feet long – is an installation by Andrea Carlson, an artist of Ojibwe ancestry. Her 2021 work reminds me that long before this site was a hub of modern trade and industry, it was home to the Potawatomi people.[3] They were displaced after the 1833 Treaty of Chicago, a result of the American colonial policy of forcibly removing Native Americans from their homelands. But for Carlson's sign, the Potawatomi's presence and relationship to this place have been erased by the modern city.

Figure 1 Apple store, Chicago, designed by Foster + Partners, 2017. Author photo.

The mute indifference of the Apple store to this history is not unusual: the site as a *tabula rasa* is a foundation of modern design and architecture. As Wrigley and the Chicago Tribune before it, Apple simply built a new structure on a prime lot of riverside real estate at the start of Chicago's premier shopping strip. Why would Apple or its architects engage with the site's history? After all, Apple is renowned for innovation, progress and newness: its products signify the future, not the past. Yet Carlson's work on the opposite bank provokes me – if only for a moment – to reflect on the site's significance and the Apple store's neutral, universal aesthetic. This store could be anywhere.

Figure 2 "You are on Potawatomi land" by Andrea Carlson, 2021. Author photo.

As well as this place-lessness, transparency seemed another defining feature of the Apple store. It stands alone in an empty plaza yet almost disappears into the background due to its expansive glass walls. As I approached, a slender roof materialized, gently sloping like a closed MacBook (Figure 3). Only when closer did I spot the white logo, modestly glowing on an interior wall. Then the exquisite details: the smooth curve of its glass wall recalls that of an iPhone; the store's stairs continue outside to serve as seating for an outdoor stage; and the store's front is perfectly symmetrical, its glass panes aligned, a revolving glass door on each side.

Figure 3 Apple store, Chicago, detail. Author photo.

I entered one of these into an airy mezzanine level. Here, tiered steps overlook a huge, free-standing video wall on the floor below, and, beyond this, the Chicago River and Carlson's installation (Figure 4). Pop music filled the space, which curiously didn't echo despite the stone floors and hard surfaces. The colour palette was neutral: grey and beige, though the light-yellow timber ceiling brightened up the space a little. A few customers sat on the tiered seating, chatting with a red-jacketed Apple employee. Their conversation turned to the music. It's a familiar song but no one can name it. Luckily, "there's an app for that", says the employee showing them his iPad.

I sat and watched the video on screen for a while (a reel of advertising for Apple products), then walked down the granite staircase to the lower level.

Figure 4 Apple store, Chicago, looking down from the mezzanine. Author photo.

The handrail seemed magically stuck onto the glass wall, the inside handrail mirrored by an identical one outside. Like a long metal sculpture floating in space, it cast a distinctive shadow on the steps (Figure 5). At the bottom of the stairs, the two slim, stainless-steel pillars that support the roof were cool to the touch. All the lines in the store – where granite meets glass, where steel meets granite, where granite meets limestone – are crisp, clean and clear. I imagine Mies van der Rohe, that modernist master of refined detailing, would be impressed.

On the river level, a scatter of wooden cubes sat between four potted trees, and finally, tucked under the mezzanine I found the familiar tables lined with

Figure 5 Apple store, Chicago, handrail detail. Author photo.

iPhones, iPads, MacBooks and Apple Watches. The retail section – the place where you buy things – occupies less than half the floorspace (Figure 6). It was not busy, so a dozen red-shirted Apple employees milled around aimlessly. All were friendly and asked if I needed any help. When I replied that I was here to admire the architecture, I was told that I was welcome to "just hang out". I asked a red shirt if it gets hot in summer, and he pointed to a vent on the inside of the glass wall and said the temperature's always perfect. "The architects", he assured me, "thought of everything."

Figure 6 Apple store, Chicago, tables. Author photo.

I'd chosen a quiet morning to explore the store: great for taking photographs but perhaps not the best time to experience an Apple store. More than simply a shop, an Apple store is a space for events: lectures by creatives, coding workshops, educators' classes and live music performances. Given none of these were on, I quickly realized there was nothing to do. The store's aesthetic neutrality highlights the only interesting objects: the products themselves. And this is what "hanging out" really means – an interactive experience with Apple's products. But, given I'm already familiar with iPhones and iPads, it's time to go. Before I leave, I notice a woman cleaning glass on the mezzanine level above. She isn't wearing a red shirt. I wonder what her experience of the Apple store is like.

The Apple Store Experience

With his trademark flair for publicity, Steve Jobs informed the media only two days before he opened Apple's first retail stores on 21 May 2001 at Tysons Corner Center, Virginia, and an almost identical store in Glendale, California. Located in wealthy suburban malls, both were clean, open and bright. Unlike in a typical electronics store, Apple divided the interior into eight sections defined by experiences.[4] "Movies", "Music", "Photos" and "Kids" featured internet-ready iMacs connected to cameras and headphones on which customers could shoot and edit movies or photos, listen to music and play games. In the "Genius" section, technical staff helped customers, while "Home" and "Pro" delineated price and processing power, and "Etc" housed accessories. The Tysons Corner store featured posters of artists and musicians, including a prominent one of John Lennon and Yoko Ono.[5] Instead of referring to spreadsheets or documents, the posters reinforced Apple's ongoing association with creativity and self-expression rather than work.

At the time, industry experts noted Apple's folly in opening stores that sold very few products. Yet the retail team, which included Ron Johnson (former vice-president of merchandising at Target), Micky Drexler (former CEO of Gap) and Michael Fisher (former visual merchandiser at Bloomingdale's), proved that a retail store devoted to interactive experiences could be successful. On the opening weekend, over 7,700 people visited the two stores, and many more visited the other twenty-three Apple stores that opened in cities around the United States that year. Overseen by Johnson (Senior Vice President of Retail Operations from 2001 until 2011), Apple stores also expanded globally, beginning with stores in Tokyo (2003) and London (2004). In its first decade of operation, Apple claimed that its 326 stores contributed almost $10 billion in annual sales.[6]

While the first two stores generated Apple's mall store template – simplicity, openness, and product organization via interactive experiences – architects Bohlin Cywinski Jackson developed a more distinctive aesthetic and material palette for the flagship stores.[7] Their first Apple store, in a former post office in New York's Soho (2001), featured what would become Apple's signature maple tables, grey limestone, stainless steel and, in collaboration with engineers Eckersley O'Callaghan, a spectacular glass staircase. Bohlin Cywinski Jackson went on to design over seventy Apple stores around the world. Of these, the most famous is New York's Fifth Avenue store (2006), a free-standing glass cube through which customers access the underground store, its transparency a stark contrast to its solid, masonry neighbours. One critic aptly described how the store's "crisp detachment, sitting alone on a travertine plinth … communicates an unmistakable newness and difference".[8]

In the first decade of the twenty-first century, Apple refined its store design. The spacious, orderly interiors contained little furniture – simple timber stools and two rows of plain timber tables – few visible fixtures, and a neutral colour palette. As urban lives became more complex, here was a store that embodied simplicity. Minimal distracting signage and spotlessly clean surfaces offered customers a space of calm respite and a place to play with the latest devices. Apple's store design complemented its products. Apple computers were characterized by their clean, uncluttered interfaces, simple icons and orderly menus, with few buttons or ports. As iMacs gave way to the iPhone (2007) and iPad (2010), each iteration promised to be smaller, simpler and more powerful, ensuring a steady churn of products and in-store experiences.

Despite the minimal fixtures and furniture, Apple convinced the US Patent and Trademark Office in 2013 to register its store design as a trademark.[9] Although Apple is renowned for collecting patents, global media attention on a "fake" Apple store in 2011 was certainly a factor. In Kunming, China, someone had reproduced an Apple store's interior to sell iPhones, iPads and Apple computers. Other "fake" stores in other Chinese cities also reproduced the timber tables, glass staircases and spatial layout, and their staff even wore shirts with Apple logos.[10] Ironically, some sold (or resold) authentic Apple products, shipped directly from Chinese factories.[11]

As well as aesthetics, interaction was essential to the Apple store experience. Apple designed the stores to ensure customers would not only see but touch the products on display. Staff positioned the angle of a laptop screen at 90 degrees, for example, so that its "position forces you to touch the computer, moving the screen to your ideal viewing angle".[12] This tactile experience remains central to the way iPhones are displayed in Apple stores today, their glass screens function as immediate, accessible portals into the virtual realm. Touching also immerses a customer in an ownership experience and enables a feeling of control: anyone can pick up a device and manipulate virtual objects via their fingers.

Service was another essential ingredient. Unlike in many other retail stores, Apple staff were not paid on commission, relieving them of the pressure to sell products. Staff were initially drawn from the company's large fan base, a ready population of brand evangelists motivated by more than just making money. Instead, they believe they are "improving people's lives", or, as the oft-repeated Jobs credo has it, "Enriching Lives". As the original Genius section evolved in the Genius Bar, approachable technicians aimed to understand the customer's problems with "the idea of replicating something between a concierge desk and a bar".[13] This was certainly my experience with the red-shirted staff who welcomed me and seemed happy to chat about almost anything.

Apple designed store interiors to encourage informal staff-customer interaction. Rather than standing behind a counter, staff roam the open space, helping customers experience the products' capabilities. Staff training manuals contain elaborate etiquette guidelines, scripted conversations and roleplays that emphasize empathy and trying to understand a customer's individual needs.[14]

In-store activities such as workshops on shooting and editing movies, making music, cataloguing photos, publishing and video chat encourage customers to feel like they are learning new skills. Again, rather than work, the emphasis is on personal, passion projects that connect the customer intimately to Apple's products and software.

Even Apple's packaging is designed to contribute to the experience. Apple's white boxes feature a crisp photograph of the product on a white background on the top, simple black text on two sides and the logo on the other two sides. Lifting the lid's smooth, satin surface is a distinctive, tactile experience. Each piece of the packaging fits together to ensure that, as the cover slides up, the customer notices the sound of air rushing out. Apple's Chief Design Officer Jonathan Ive stated that Apple "design a ritual of unpacking to make the product feel special. Packaging can be theater, it can create a story."[15] Unboxing even became a popular YouTube genre in the 2010s among Apple fans keen to share their ritual with others.[16]

This consistency of experience extends to Apple's website, which reinforces the brand's minimal aesthetic and ordering. Its menus, organized by products and their accessories, correspond closely to the spatial arrangement of products in the store.[17] Apple's visual language – colours, typefaces, labels and icons – is also consistent between the website and store. In-store, posters and digital screens reproduce online advertising and product descriptions, a seamless experience reinforced by continuous and consistent messages. In 2011, for example, when Steve Jobs launched the iPad 2, the three words he used – "thinner, faster, lighter" – appeared again and again in online and in-store advertising and marketing.

In their first decade, Apple stores also became important sites for new product launches. The ritual of lining up in front of an Apple store for days to be the first to purchase the latest iPhone or iPad became a media event. The frenzy of the doors opening and employees high-fiving and clapping incoming customers, the delirious excitement of unboxing: such rituals grew from Apple's fanatical fan base.[18] The elevation of Steve Jobs as a kind of prophet or messiah-figure, whose keynote addresses and launches were akin to sermons even lent the stores a religious aura.[19] And, with Jobs' death in 2011, Apple stores all around the world became shrines, with fans leaving flowers, candles and Post-it notes on the glass.

New Generation Stores

Despite doubts about its post-Jobs future, Apple grew under CEO Tim Cook to become the world's biggest publicly traded company in 2015 and the first trillion-dollar company in 2018. Cook's specialization was logistics, and his career at Apple began in 1998 by overhauling manufacturing and distribution, including closing down American factories and outsourcing production abroad.[20] After assuming the leadership in 2011, Cook launched Apple Music (2014) and Apple Pay (2014), acquired Beats headphones (2014) and launched the Apple Watch (2015) and Airpods (2016). Apple's interactive experience was no longer restricted to a single product. Now, Apple offers synchronization across an ecosystem comprising computers, phones, wearables and services, unified by a common design language.

In 2014, Cook appointed a new Senior Vice President of Retail, Angela Ahrendts, who, with Chief Design Officer Jonathan Ive and architects Foster + Partners, began a new store design programme. Ahrendts arrived at Apple after a successful term as CEO at fashion house Burberry, where she transformed the company by increasing online sales and integrating new technology into stores. During her Apple tenure (2014–19), she was reportedly the highest-paid employee in the company, a reflection of the value Cook placed on its retail experience. The alliance between Norman Foster and Apple goes back to 2009, when Jobs asked Foster to design Apple's new headquarters in Cupertino, California. Renowned for designing high-tech, minimal structures and an obsession for elegant detailing, Foster's firm, Foster + Partners, seemed a natural fit with Apple's established design language.

The retail redesign brought a renewed emphasis on simplicity and transparency. Apple's new stores featured more glass, more space, less signage and clutter, large video walls and trees or green walls. A new pivot door system comprising black-framed glass panels for the mall stores blurred the boundaries between store and mall. Other changes included the Avenue, an in-store timber shelving display for coloured phone cases. The expanded in-store programming included free music performances, lectures, interviews and the "Today at Apple" programme featuring creative workshops, an educational programme and coding lessons. Beyond an interactive experience with products, Apple promoted the Chicago flagship store I described at the start of this chapter as "a gathering place for the local community".[21]

The first of these "new generation" stores opened in Brussels in 2015. A collaborative effort between Foster + Partners and Jonathan Ive, the store features curved glass structural walls along the street and a clean, sparse interior. Continuing the minimal furniture and fixtures of previous stores, the new generation stores also featured new displays specifically for Apple Watches and Beats headphones. The new tables for the Apple Watches, for example, included a sunken glass cabinet with integrated LED lighting, while portable, moulded timber trays displayed a variety of coloured watch bands. Even more than iPads and iPhones, watches are considered fashion accessories (although Apple also promotes them as "wellness" devices), hence the need for an expanded display.

Cook and Ahrendts stressed the new stores' role as community centres, with some stores featuring an open space called a "Town Square" or an outdoor "Public Plaza". "In my mind", Ahrendts said in an interview, store leaders "are the mayors of their community".[22] A town square traditionally refers to a public space in which citizens can speak and be heard – a place of dialogue, discussion, contestation – a shared place of social and political participation, while a mayor is an official elected by the community. This is not what Ahrendts had in mind. The expanded in-store programming studiously avoids any political or social issues and there is no sense of community apart from one comprising Apple customers (like most US tech companies, Apple is vehemently anti-union).

In-store events function as both marketing and a means to "localize" the placeless stores within their communities. On the surface, a free concert in an Apple store sounds very civic-minded. But musicians, in exchange for in-store "exposure", are paid in Apple products rather than cash. They are also required to do their own promotion. In this way, local musicians – typically young, up-and-coming acts – bring their friends and fans into the store.[23] Although promoted as events supporting the local community, such events are equally the reverse: musicians support Apple by bringing potential customers to the store.

The other important component in the new generation stores is the collaboration with London-based architects Foster + Partners. Founder Norman Foster's architecture has long been described as "high-tech", from early projects such as the Willis, Faber and Dumas offices in Ipswich (1975) and his first major international commission, the HSBC Bank Headquarters in Hong Kong (1986).[24] The firm grew in the 1990s and 2000s, designing skyscrapers, airports and master-planning new cities so by the time they became Foster + Partners in 2007, it comprised over a thousand employees in dozens of offices around the world. Yet Foster + Partners maintained a consistent aesthetic and material sensibility, avoiding narrative and symbolism while eliminating physical barriers to build as lightly and transparently as possible.

The Apple-Foster collaboration began with the Apple Zorlu Centre in Istanbul (2014) and included new stores such as Apple Westlake, Hangzhou (2015), Singapore (2017), Dubai (2017) and Chicago (2017), as well as the renovation of old stores, such as Union Square in San Francisco (2016), Regent Street in London (2016) and New York's Fifth Avenue glass cube (2019). Foster + Partners' headquarters for Apple in California, Apple Park (2017), epitomized the shared vision of the two companies: a building as an autonomous, self-contained machine, its temperature, lighting and ambience all carefully controlled, its every detail – down to precision-milled aluminium door handles – designed for a particular function.

While Foster + Partners designed stand-alone new generation stores (such as the Chicago store), they also designed stores within historic buildings such as Brussels (2015). In these examples, a new Apple store can become a seamless part of the existing urban fabric. Foster + Partners designed the Champs-Élysées Apple store (2018), for example, within a classic nineteenth-century Parisian apartment building, and the Apple Tower Theatre in downtown Los Angeles (2021), inserted into a 1927 movie theatre. These stores retain the original façade and important interior details of the original building, but interior walls and ceilings are typically whitewashed to minimize distraction from the Apple experience.

A good illustration of Apple's new generation stores in a historic building is the Washington DC store (2019), inserted into the Carnegie Library building. Built between 1901 and 1903, the grand Beaux-Arts edifice, once filled with books, now houses an Apple store and a new home for the Historical Society of Washington. Steel magnate Andrew Carnegie famously built over two thousand of these public libraries, not only in the US but in other English-speaking countries too, to make education freely available.[25] Arguably a paternal, wealth-washing gesture, Carnegie – unlike billionaires today – at least felt a moral obligation to fund cultural institutions for the public good.[26]

The Carnegie Library moved to a new location in 1970 and the building remained largely unoccupied. Apple and Foster + Partners upgraded the building, reportedly spending upward of $30 million on the renovation. Along with a meticulous restoration of historic details, the building now features an extensive Apple store interior including an "Experience Room" designed to demonstrate products such as the Apple TV in a home-like environment. According to Ashley Middleton, head of programming for Today at Apple, the intention is to "celebrate the space as a center for learning, but to also give the community a platform to share their stories".[27] Now, community is an essential component of the Apple experience.

But not all cities have embraced the community ideal of a new Apple store. In 2018, for example, both Stockholm and Melbourne rejected flagship Apple stores designed by Foster + Partners. In Stockholm, a public consultation found locals were opposed to the proposed store that would stand adjacent to a historic park.[28] In Melbourne, the city council rejected the insertion of a new Apple store into an already existing public space, Federation Square, on heritage grounds.[29] Even though Federation Square was less than twenty years old, the city thought the Apple store's aesthetic and purpose would clash with the Square's. Changes to public spaces provoke strong feelings, and Apple stores are ultimately carefully controlled spaces designed for customers to interact with products, not each other. Yet Apple's retail experience embodies popular consumer desires, and this chapter's remaining two sections analyse two of these: simplicity and transparency.

Simplicity

"Simplicity", read a 1977 Apple II ad, "is the ultimate sophistication." The statement encapsulates not only the stores and products but also Apple's philosophy. Jobs described the company's approach as: "Very simple ... The way we're running the company, the product design, the advertising, it all comes down to this: Let's make it simple. Really simple."[30] This simplicity extended from Apple's products to their interface and software design, ensuring a consistent and coherent user experience. As the company expanded in the first two decades of the twenty-first century, the spare, refined store design reinforced this mantra of simplicity. More than an aesthetic, simplicity was Apple's key to corporate success.[31] But it is worth examining simplicity further, as it has come to encompass a design philosophy that some believe is synonymous with "integrity, essence, deference, style, and honesty".[32]

In a design sense, simplicity implies paring an object, graphic, interface or building down to its essential elements. Symmetry and balance order what remains, while neutral colours and the least possible components evoke calm and serenity. Apple's products, graphics, software, interfaces and stores encapsulate these characteristics. The company's Chief Designer Officer, Jonathan Ive, stated that simplicity should pervade the design process. "Simplicity is not the absence of clutter", he said, "that's a consequence of simplicity. Simplicity is somehow essentially describing the purpose and place of an object and product. The absence of clutter is just a clutter-free product. That's not simple. The quest for simplicity has to pervade every part of the process."[33] Design, for Ive, is a discipline of refining or editing a product down to what is absolutely necessary, eliminating not only extra features, decorations or colours but even seams and joins.

Simplicity has a long association with "good design". Apple's simplicity follows early twentieth-century modernists' calls for a new style for a new era, beyond the clutter and decorative excess of the previous century's architecture and design. In Adolf Loos' infamous 1908 essay "Ornament and Crime", for example, he condemned the Art Nouveau style as "degenerate" and "regressive", while praising the virtues of "neutral", "pure" and "essential" surfaces. In the twentieth century, "simple" became a routine description of modernist architecture, "but covered anything from the method of design, to structural expression, to perceived effect".[34] Institutions such as MoMA, with its "good design" exhibitions and publications, established modernist simplicity in the popular imagination as both progressive and fashionable.

German industrial designer Dieter Rams' version of simplicity had a significant impact on Apple's design approach.[35] As head of design at Braun from 1961 to 1995, Rams designed calculators, record players, radios and electric shavers. For him, simplicity meant products with few details, plain buttons and flat, block colours. In the 1980s, he distilled his philosophy into ten principles of "good design". The final principle claims good design "is as little design as possible – Less is more. Simple as possible but not simpler." More recently, designers such as Per Mollerup and John Maeda continue to promote simplicity as a strategy to counter our confusing and complex twenty-first-century lives.[36]

Beyond aesthetics, Apple's simplicity also carries a moral connotation. Ken Segall, a former advertising creative director who worked with Apple for many years, noted Apple's "deep, almost religious belief in the power of Simplicity".[37] This Segall opposes to its evil twin, Complexity. Simplicity is a principle that Apple applied, argues Segall, to the design of products, software and its organization, as well as its online and physical retail experiences. And the religious aspect to simplicity – its emphasis on austere, restrained and "pure" products and retail stores – is revealing. Simplicity evokes a modest, honest, good life.[38]

In architecture, European modernists employed simplicity to describe an aesthetic approach as well as an ideal production process.[39] Inspired by Henry Ford's simplified production in the assembly line to create an affordable automobile, modernist architects sought similar means to (mass) produce housing. Yet Apple's simplicity does not seem to include production. Manufacturing Apple products is incredibly complex. An iPhone, for example, is ultimately composed of a vast array of raw materials from all over the planet. Mostly aluminium, iron, lithium and gold, Apple's phones also include a dozen trace elements – from tungsten and cobalt from the Democratic Republic of the Congo to rare earth metals from Inner Mongolia. The process involves coordinating a complex global supply chain.[40]

From these raw materials, global contractors from Japan to Germany design and manufacture components – chips, lenses, cases and cameras – and send them to Shenzhen where Chinese workers in huge factories assemble them by hand into Apple products. The finished iPhones, Watches and iPads are then shipped to the United States and distributed to stores around the world. This vast network, which includes hundreds of suppliers and contractors as well as thousands of workers – from miners to assemblers – is hardly the essence of simplicity. In fact, the simplicity of the finished product conceals the ordering and disciplining of this supply chain.

Like an Apple phone, an Apple store is also a complex assemblage of global materials and components. For the Chicago store, the London-based Foster + Partners used very few local materials. The walls are clad in Tuscan limestone and the floors are Chinese granite. Germany company Sedak manufactured the glass panels, Minnesota-based G&R collaborated with Japanese-based Mitsubishi Electric to design the glass elevator, and a Dubai-based company manufactured the Carbon Fiber Polymer roof. Like Apple, Foster + Partners draw upon resources and supply chains from a complex global network that is concealed by the clarity, purity and restraint presented to the customer.

Both the Apple stores and their products reinforce an image of a simple, autonomous object: placeless, traceless, without history or culture. In this way, the new generation stores continue Jobs' obsession with the seamless casing of iPhones and iPads: there are no visible gaps, joints, bolts or screws. For Jobs, simplicity involved reducing the number of buttons (to the iPhone and iPad's single button), the size of devices and the number of interactions (clicks or swipes).[41] To maintain the image of simplicity in the stores, Foster + Partners carefully conceal the air conditioning, heating, and mechanical systems and hide wires and cables in table legs and wall cavities.

As well as reducing visible parts, clear organization is central to Apple's simplicity. The iPhone's graphic interface, for example, orders apps in balanced, symmetrical columns, each icon an identical size and shape. Similarly, Apple's phones, watches and tablets are arranged in the store in neat rows. Simplicity, attained through a meticulous adherence to design principles, is also about ease of recognition and perception. This is evident in the progressive simplification of icons in Apple's GUI, with the shift from early iOS systems' material-looking icons to more recent "flat" icons (the photo button, formerly a photograph of a sunflower, is now an abstract flower).[42] As well as the simplified shapes, Apple increasingly moved away from metaphors of the desktop (such as the "trash can"). That is, simplification is also a process of abstraction.

Importantly, simplicity is more than eliminating ornament in architecture, visual clutter in interfaces or extraneous parts of products. Simplicity is an ethical imperative. Rams makes this explicit in one of his ten principles: "good design is honest".[43] Here, an apparently "honest" product or store not only attains a human quality, but also reflects its designer: "Honesty indicates that the designer understands what the design is truly for."[44] Simplicity is not just good but honest, an ethical attribute that purifies the designer, brand and customer.

Simplicity is also timeless. Rams also argued that good design is long-lasting. Ironically, the designer has outlived his "timeless" Braun products. Today's Apple products have even shorter life spans than Braun's. Apple's iPhones, for example, are designed to be discarded rather than repaired, upgraded or recycled. The seamless, sealed cases of iPhones and Airpods make repair and upgrade impossible.[45] Apple's design team – capable of such magical simplicity – have consistently resisted even the simplest repairable options such as a removable battery. Simplicity conceals the planned obsolescence of Apple's products.[46]

In the Apple store, the customer encounters Apple's simplicity at the end of a long, complex process. The stores are designed to concentrate all our powers of fetishization on the Apple products. And the word fetishization is apt, as it refers to "the habit humans have of endowing real or imagined objects or entities with self-contained, mysterious, and even magical powers to move and shape the world in distinctive ways".⁴⁷ The magical powers of simplicity embodied in the Apple iPhone not only appear simple, pure and honest, but promise to simplify my chaotic life. But ironically, after decades of Apple's simplification, even my privileged, first-world life doesn't seem to be getting any simpler.

Transparency

Chicago's Apple store almost disappears into its surroundings. Glass staircases and the elimination of details such as door fittings, joints and screws on the glass façades, all reinforce another fundamental Apple concept, transparency. In an Apple store, there are no dark or hidden corners, nothing secret or inaccessible, nothing ambiguous that requires untangling or unveiling. All is exposed. Foster + Partners' new generation stores further emphasize transparency by using the thinnest possible columns that hold up the slimmest possible roof while expansive glass walls push closer to nothingness. Devoid of colour, texture and odour, glass buildings are barely perceivable.

Early modernist architects considered glass an essential modern material and transparency a key signifier of the new era.⁴⁸ Paul Scheerbart, in his visionary 1914 book, *Glass in Architecture*, promised a future of dematerialized buildings. Arthur Korn, the author of an influential 1929 book, *Glass in Modern Architecture*, marvelled at the material's paradoxical condition: "both there and not there", while Walter Gropius emphasized glass's honesty and truth due to its ability to expose the inner workings of modern buildings. Other architects praised glass's healing qualities and its ability to allow natural light and heat to permeate a building.⁴⁹ In 1951, just outside Chicago, Mies van der Rohe designed a glass house for Dr Edith Farnsworth: less a machine than an aquarium for living in.⁵⁰

Philosopher Walter Benjamin also praised the qualities of glass in a 1933 essay, "Experience and Poverty". "Objects made of glass have no 'aura,'" he wrote. "Glass is, in general, the enemy of secrets. It is also the enemy of possession."⁵¹ He associated glass with a *tabula rasa*, a new start beyond the values and traditions of previous generations. A revolutionary material, glass resisted "traces" of the past (in Benjamin's case, traces of bourgeois domestic conformity). We could also ascribe these characteristics to the Apple store: its transparent surface is not only ahistorical but value-free. Yet maintaining such a transparent surface requires constant labour. Recall the cleaner I saw in the Apple store: every fingerprint must be removed, laboriously, by hand.⁵²

Norman Foster's early architecture such as the Carré d'Art in Nîmes, France (1993), Berlin's Reichstag Rotunda (1999) and the British Museum Great Court (2000), continued the modernist enthusiasm for transparency. Yet the adoption of transparency as the signature statement of Apple stores is more holistic than these. The uninterrupted glass walls of Apple stores are emblematic of purity, lightness and dematerialization. For Foster + Partners, such transparency was a foil to postmodern architects' emphasis on narrative, symbolism, decorative surfaces, patterns and colour. Their glass architecture seemed stripped down to essentials, laid bare for all to see, hiding nothing. The firm also pursued the latest techniques in glass bending, thermal qualities and structural innovation. Unlike Mies van der Rohe's steel skeletons filled with glass, the new Apple stores use glass as both structure and skin.[53]

But if modernist designers are devoted to functionalism, it is unclear what an Apple store's function is. A sealed, hermetic space that replicates the iPhones within could be seen as simply a marketing device. Stripped of semiotic intensity, mystery or narrative ambiguity, I can marvel at its simplicity and its weightless transparency. There is nothing to contemplate or reflect upon. All is exposed, there is nowhere to hide. Yet Foster + Partner's design ultimately conceals as much as it reveals. Like the iPhones and Watches, its complexity is hidden. The store's wiring, cables and climate control systems are carefully concealed so that customers focus on the building itself, as if it were an autonomous Apple product. There is likewise no hint of the optic fibres, wi-fi towers, distant data centres and undersea cables that allow the products inside it to function.

Yet the word transparency has shifted in the last two decades to signify something more than a property of glass. In its twenty-first-century sense, transparency has become a key concept in contemporary governance as institutions, companies and social clubs clamber to display their transparency.[54] In a media-saturated, surveillance society, calls for more transparency – of finances, decisions, supply chains or environmental and labour policies – are so common that the term has "become a sign of cultural, political, and moral authenticity and authority".[55] Transparency is "a largely consensual norm today" that evokes a just, progressive and open society.[56] Transparency has also become an ethical imperative on a personal level: only people with something to hide are against it. Like simplicity, transparency has a natural affinity with honesty.

Apple's stores and products seem to be on a trajectory towards increasingly lighter, more transparent devices, as if they will someday disappear altogether. Yet despite this impulse towards disappearance, a material object remains. The rhetoric of transparency asserts that even this will eventually disappear as we become completely immersed in a virtual world. The Apple Watch and digital wearables promise a further elimination of distance between the material and digital realms – the promise to make exercise and health more efficient by monitoring every heartbeat, counting every footstep and tracking our location. In this way, wearables such as the Watch or Airpods integrate the Apple world into our lives.

In the fields of Human-Computer Interaction and interface design, transparency also has been a long-standing goal. The aim of an invisible interface – or at least as minimal as possible – to allow users to manipulate digital objects, tools and data without reference to the material world also suggests a trajectory towards dematerialization.[57] Yet the material barriers between a user and the digital realm remain. The glass walls of the Apple store mirror the glass screen of the iPhone or iPad, with their promise of a transparent interface between me and the virtual realm on the other side of the glass.

There is, ironically, little transparency in Apple's products. Impenetrable glass, aluminium and plastic surfaces conceal the complex inner machinery of an iPhone. Only trained technicians can penetrate beyond the glass, and even they are discouraged from opening Apple products. Technical complexity, restricted access to documentation and intellectual property laws all restrict consumer access to Apple's products. The customer is rendered powerless when it comes to the device they have purchased, except to use it as Apple has designed it, with the company's monopoly of the App Store, propriety software and incompatibility with rival devices.

Despite an emphasis on transparency, Apple's iPhones are assembled by numerous hands far from the customer's view. The 2012 Foxconn scandal brought to light the sweatshop conditions and worker suicides in Shenzhen factories due to stressful conditions, long hours and low pay.[58] While public scrutiny brought a veneer of accountability, factory conditions in China, though hard to ascertain precisely due to secrecy, remain dehumanizing.[59] The reality of iPhone assembly was described by one reporter in this way: "Each iPhone has more than one hundred parts. Every worker specializes in one task and performs repetitive motions at high speed, hourly, daily, ten hours or more on many working days, for months on end."[60] Apple relies not only on cheap labour, but a huge, flexible workforce, capable of round-the-clock production schedules and rapid changes for new models and seasonal fluctuations.

Yet, in the store, the iPhone appears as "a revolutionary and magic product" – magic because it appears fully formed, without any traces of where it came from or how it came to be. Or who ultimately profits. In Apple's complex, global division of labour, American shareholders claim a huge share, Chinese assembly line workers and Congolese miners very little. In 2019, a group of international lawyers representing Congolese families took Apple, Google and other tech companies to court over the death and injury of children who mine for cobalt, an essential element in smartphone batteries.[61] Its extraction in the Democratic Republic of the Congo is linked not only to child labour but also to environmental destruction. Following media exposure, Apple published statements about better transparency in their supply chains and worker conditions, but these have so far had minimal effects.

Returning to the Chicago Apple store, transparency appears as both an optical impression and a metaphoric promise – the promise of neutrality. Glass is an anonymous material, not associated with a particular culture, society, history or religion. The glass of an Apple store is designed to be seen *through* not *at*: you cannot see your reflection in it. The transparent surface diverts attention from itself to the products and our interaction with them. For a generation who grew up with selfies, Big Brother and "reality" TV, such perverse visibility is normal. Two decades of digital living have convinced many people to expose their lives online and freely give away private photos and data. Apple customers are active participants in this digital panopticon.

But the issue of transparency took a turn in 2016 when the FBI demanded Apple unlock the iPhone of a shooter in an ISIS-inspired murder of fourteen people in San Bernardino, California.[62] Apple's battle with the United States government agency over unlocking the killer's phone resulted in a publicity win for Apple. By refusing to unlock the phone, Apple claimed the moral high ground by championing privacy. In an era in which so much of our everyday lives is exposed, Apple proved that it keeps its customers' data secure. Apple then launched an advertising campaign, "Privacy. That's iPhone" (2019) to highlight this as a point of differentiation. Its "App Tracking Transparency" campaign of 2022 further distinguished Apple from the surveillance practices of Google, Facebook and Microsoft.

Beyond the personal, transparency is also a topical subject on a government and corporate level. Following Wikileaks (2006) and the Paradise Papers (2016), governments and corporations have also been subject to calls for transparency over issues such as tax avoidance and other ethical and legal breaches. The Paradise Papers, a trove of over fourteen million documents leaked to a German newspaper in 2016, revealed Apple's tax avoidance strategies via a complex global structure that ensures the company pays little or no tax by shifting profits and patents to offshore tax havens.[63] As Cook had overseen the offshoring of Apple's manufacturing, he too oversaw Apple's financial offshoring. Apple created subsidiary companies in tax havens such as Ireland and Jersey designed to avoid taxes not only in the United States (where value is ultimately created) but in most other countries too. In this global strategy, local communities lose.

Perhaps these latter ideas produced the sense of melancholy I felt while hanging out in the Chicago Apple store. Despite the elegant design and cheery staff, it was lifeless. Every connection with the surrounding city and its people is carefully controlled. Like the Apple ecosystem, the store has no gaps. Transparent yet closed, it reminded me of philosopher Byung-Chul Han's argument that the "society of transparency is not a society of trust, but a society of control".[64] The Apple world – physical and digital – is meticulously controlled via intellectual property documents and patents. The company is so paranoid that Apple's legal team threatens any businesses that feature fruit in their name or logo with trademark lawsuits.[65] In a reversal of what Benjamin predicted, transparency is not the enemy of secrets but the empire of secrets.

Reinforced by the design of Apple's stores, products and systems, both simplicity and transparency suggest progressive ideals: clarity, ease and especially honesty. Yet the Apple experience is predicated upon the individual and designed into a seamless integration of architecture, products, software and interfaces for singular consumption. The simple, transparent stores belong everywhere and yet nowhere, their design abstract enough to include almost everyone. But, enclosed in the Apple store, all we can do is play with Apple products, which use apps from the Apple App Store, pay for goods with Apple Pay, play music through Apple Music and read books on Apple Books. If the Apple store is a new type of public space, it is one built upon a society of individuals who inhabit this Apple world.

Chapter 2
Convenience and Personalization: Amazon Go

My first impression of Amazon's latest retail innovation wasn't excitement but "Really? That's it?" The first Amazon Go store I visited – in Chicago in 2020 – looked utterly conventional. The only novelty was the black, lower-case word "amazon" with the curved yellow arrow below emblazoned on a wall (instead of a cardboard box) plus the word "go". For an e-commerce giant that redefined online retail, opening a chain of physical stores seemed counter-intuitive. Yet in 2018, Amazon opened the first Amazon Go convenience stores in Seattle, San Francisco and New York, hoping their famed "one-click" shopping could make food shopping "friction-less", faster and more convenient.

The entrance, broad and clear, comprised a few silver and white turnstiles that looked more like a train station entry than a retail store (Figure 7). A wall text just before the turnstiles read, "JUST WALK OUT SHOPPING. NO LINES. NO CHECKOUT. (NO, SERIOUSLY)" (Figure 8). Here was my problem – standing in line, waiting to check out grocery items – and Amazon's solution – just walk out. These short, anonymous sentences, informing me of a problem I didn't even know I had, comprised my first interaction with Amazon Go. With no human staff in sight, the wall text sought to allay my hesitation at the idea of simply walking out without a transaction at a checkout counter.

Inside, the neon-strip lighting and neatly stacked shelves resembled a small grocery store, a decent-sized 7-11 or bodega (Figure 9). This particular Amazon Go contained bakery and hot food selections, shelves of frozen and canned foods, sodas, snacks, pre-packaged salads, sandwiches and sushi (Figure 10). Its black shelving with wooden laminate surrounds was conventional, as were the range of popular brands. The store stocked nothing exotic, luxurious or unusual. And this comforting feeling of everydayness is part of Amazon's strategy. With the Amazon Go store, I encountered an ordinary scene – familiar food items laid out conventionally – ready to be integrated seamlessly into my life.

The packaging of Amazon Go's "ready-to-eat" foods is, like the store layout, not especially distinctive. Simple labels with apparently "hand-drawn" fonts emphasize the "hand-made" sandwiches. Their black-and-white simplicity fades into the background to let the food stand out (only words distinguish a turkey

Figure 7 Amazon Go, Union Station, Chicago, entrance. Author photo.

sandwich from a vegetable wrap). Similarly, the walls are plain and relatively unadorned. Unlike in a supermarket, there are no advertisements for specific brands, products or weekly specials: the clean, simple graphics and posters reinforce the idea of speed with straightforward phrases like "Good food fast".

Though I found Amazon Go's conventional appearance reassuring, it took a while to realize where the innovation was. That's because it's hidden, or at least partially hidden. Between the neon strips on the ceiling, black boxes house cameras that fade into the background. Shelves are filled with sensors. They are difficult to spot at first, but if you bend down, you see these are not quite ordinary shelves. Out of sight, cables and wires concealed in the walls and ceiling connect the store to distant data centres. For customers, perhaps the only unusual thing you notice about the Amazon Go store experience is the absence of staff.

Figure 8 Amazon Go, Prudential Plaza, Chicago. Author photo.

While the interior fit-out, spatial layout and product range are not innovative, the stores' technological infrastructure is. Customers first download the Amazon Go app, then tap the app's QR code on their phone onto the top of a turnstile scanner so that the barrier opens (Figure 11). Inside, scores of cameras on the ceiling with facial recognition software register who is in the store and track who is taking which items from the shelves. In some stores, cameras dangle down from the ceiling (Figure 12). Scales, embedded in the shelves, register when an item has been picked up. In-shelf cameras even verify when a customer puts an item back.

As the customer exits, Amazon Go's systems automatically debit their account for the items they take and send a receipt to the app. The Amazon system, designed with rigorous efficiency at every step, aims to keep human

Figure 9 Amazon Go, Prudential Plaza, Chicago, baked goods. Author photo.

intervention to a minimum. While a cash-free, contactless store has some appeal in a post-pandemic society, a grocery store cannot operate without humans. Amazon's surveillance system notifies security guards of theft, for example, or lets staff know when it's time to restock. And who knows how many people monitor, repair and maintain the digital scanners, cameras and infrastructure that keeps the system running?

When the first stores opened, critics noted the irony of the colossus of e-commerce expanding into physical retail, particularly given Amazon's alleged role in the demise of "bricks and mortar" shopping. But Amazon founder Jeff Bezos has always stressed long-term strategies. In 2017, he added the Whole Foods grocery chain to Amazon's growing business portfolio, so Amazon

Convenience and Personalization: Amazon Go

Figure 10 Amazon Go, Union Station, Chicago, shelves. Author photo.

Go is a natural complement to the company's move into food retail. And yet. Amazon has opened retail stores in the past with limited success. In 2022, the company closed its chain of physical bookstores, Amazon Books (sixty-eight in all), after seven years in operation.[1] Amazon Go may prove a similar, short-term experiment.

But Amazon Go differs from the bookstores. The experience is closer to an online "one-click" shopping experience than a trip to a regular grocery store. Founded on the twin Amazon ideals of convenience and automation –

Figure 11 Amazon Go, Prudential Plaza, Chicago. Author photo.

for the customer and the corporation – Amazon Go is a logical extension of the Amazon system. Elimination of human labour, with its associated costs and problems, is only part of it. Self-checkout systems and contactless (and cashless) payment systems were well established before Amazon Go. But a fully automated, staff-less store, a dream of retail entrepreneurs for over a century, is now a reality.

Figure 12 Amazon Go, Sixth Avenue, New York. Author photo.

Designing a New Retail Experience

Amazon Go's design is the result of principles refined by Amazon over thirty years. It is worth briefly reviewing this history to understand how a chain of "bricks and mortar" convenience stores aligns with the long-term strategy of a company that began as an online bookstore. Given the interconnected nature of Amazon's businesses, it is also important to understand Amazon Go as a part of an already existing ecosystem. These insights help us understand how Amazon Go differs from earlier attempts at automated retail stores and other retailers. Rather than low prices, exclusive products or lifestyle aspirations, Amazon's appeal lies in the principles of convenience and personalization.

When he founded Amazon in 1995, Jeff Bezos decided that books would be the best products to sell online. Familiar and predictable, books were standard shapes and easily delivered via the existing postal service. Designing an online platform was the first step. But the first Amazon website, like the Amazon Go store, did not look especially distinctive. It comprised a grey background with black text and bold, blue clickable links. In the top right-hand corner sat the logo: a winding river flowing through a letter A with the words, "Amazon.com, Earth's biggest bookstore", below it. Aesthetically, Amazon's design was like other mid-1990s websites. Colourful book covers only featured in the 1997 iteration.[2] But Bezos was not trying to win design awards: he was designing a new retail platform.

Amazon's first point of difference was convenience. Here, on your home computer, was a bookstore open twenty-four hours a day, every day: a store that fitted into your busy schedule. The next difference was choice: Amazon offered customers a million titles (far more than any physical store could stock) and a simple search box to find them. Importantly, the earliest Amazon websites featured two modes of interaction – personalized notifications and customer reviews. Refined in later iterations, these proved essential to Amazon's success. A notification service would email recommended books to a customer (based on previous purchases), while the website provided space for customers to review books.

Yet, from the beginning, Amazon was not a bookstore, but a different type of retailer. "When we first started Amazon.com, we had very conscious discussions where we talked about the fact that we were not a bookstore", stated Bezos in 1999, "but we were a book service. I do think that is a better way to think about it. Thinking of yourself as a store is limiting. Services can be anything."[3] Not surprisingly, Amazon expanded that year from books to CDs and DVDs. Like books, these were standard shapes and easy to deliver. The new products, soon to include toys and electronics, required a new website with navigation tabs to search the new categories. But Amazon's website design remained sober, readable and easy to navigate.

In 2000, Amazon adopted a new logo, an arched arrow under the word "Amazon". Designed by Turner Duckworth studio, the black, lower-case text in a conventional typeface looked familiar. The golden arrow highlighted speedy delivery. Connecting the A and the Z, the arrow also anticipated Amazon's growth over the next decade to become the "everything store". Importantly, the arrow also suggested a smile. Unchanged since 2000, the Amazon logo proved flexible enough to adopt variations (such as the addition of the blue "Prime") and remained a stable visual identity for a rapidly expanding company.

A further Amazon innovation, launched in 2000, was a free shipping programme. Of course, shipping is incorporated into the price, but rival retailers needed to adopt this model as it shifted customer expectations. For the customer, the term "free" erased the labour and logistics of transporting a package. It simply arrived on your doorstep, as if by magic, in a plain cardboard box. By repetition – the arrow-smile printed on billions of cardboard boxes on doorsteps across America – the Amazon logo soon became ubiquitous. Combined with the website, the Amazon box was a key site of interaction between customer and company, generating a new type of at-home retail experience.[4]

Amazon survived the 2000 dot-com crash to become the dominant online retailer in the United States. Its website underwent multiple iterations as product categories grew but key features remained: the navigation section on the left-hand side, the search bar near the top and the shopping cart on the upper right-hand side. Amazon's primary strategy at this time was to maintain low prices, even if that meant low (or no) profits for select items. Compared to physical stores, they paid little rent, avoided many sales taxes and employed less staff. Initially, Amazon did relatively little advertising, relying on word of mouth and repeat customers.[5] The website also featured prominent reminders of Amazon's low prices (compared to "regular" prices) and free shipping.

Importantly, Amazon refined its interactive, retail experience. Customer reviews proved popular, developing into a kind of conversation-style social network. For Amazon, rather than employ staff to review books (as they did in its early years), now customers reviewed products, voluntarily and without payment. By including both negative and positive reviews, Amazon reinforced its commitment to "customer obsession" and the interactive engagement bypassed both biased promotional material and traditional "gatekeepers" such as critics. Customers perceived Amazon reviews as the unfiltered truth about products written by people just like themselves.[6]

By designing automated systems, Amazon also refined interactions between the company and customers. From the beginning, the website's interface provided no obvious way to contact Amazon staff. Instead, instructions pre-empted customer questions while shipment tracking tools allowed a customer to follow a package from the warehouse to their door. For the customer, interaction with Amazon's systems was instantaneous (a customer did not have to wait for a human to reply). Instantaneous, but not reciprocal. Amazon replied via automated messages. Over time, customers adapted to this new mode of interaction and came to expect instant answers.

Amazon's trajectory with books is a useful case to see how Amazon's retail system works. After selling physical books for over a decade, Amazon launched the e-book reader, Kindle, in 2007. For customers, an e-book could be downloaded (almost) instantly, without waiting days for a physical book to arrive in the mail. And the single device could hold an entire library. Despite the promises of e-readers as improvements on print, the Kindle's designers went to remarkable lengths to replicate the material nature of a book – its size, shape and feel – even designing electronic "ink". Rather than exploit the possibilities of e-books, the Kindle aimed to replicate conventional reading so that Amazon could replace the material book, its costs and shipping, with a digital transfer.

By 2011, e-books outsold print books on Amazon's website. While some proclaimed this the inevitable triumph of digital over print books, it was more accurately a triumph of tethering.[7] More than a discreet electronic device, the Kindle was one of the first successful "tethered appliances", a personal, mobile device connected to – and dependent on – the Amazon network.[8] While simple for the customer to use, it is not a simple device for the customer to repair, alter or customize. Unlike buying a book, buying a Kindle is entering into a longer-term relationship with Amazon, which can alter the software, delete books or change the service terms at any time.

Beyond the Kindle, Amazon expanded its books-as-service concept. In 2008, Amazon purchased the audiobook distributor Audible, and in 2013, Goodreads, a social media-type site dedicated to book reviews. It also purchased the used-book website Abebooks, and founded Amazon Publishing.[9] Finally, the Kindle Unlimited subscription service, launched in 2014, offered customers access to a vast range of e-books and audiobooks for a monthly fee. This shift from selling physical books to selling a variety of reading experiences is a good example of Amazon's retail strategy within a large, integrated ecosystem.

Given Amazon's dominance of the American book retail landscape, physical bookstores seemed redundant. Yet in 2015, Amazon launched a chain of "bricks and mortar" stores. Their template followed that of established bookstore chains and included a café and spaces to hang out. While the stores looked familiar, their stock was "determined by digital metrics such as Goodreads reviews, Amazon sales, and pre-orders, and by input from the curators at Amazon books" – that is, books that were already popular on Amazon's digital platform.[10] In-store, Amazon tried to "repersonalize" the retail experience through differential pricing (savings for Amazon Prime members) and customer reviews and ratings rather than price tags.[11] In 2022, Amazon closed all sixty-eight stores, suggesting a failed experiment.[12]

Despite this, Amazon kept experimenting with other formats and store types, including food provisioning. Amazon Fresh, the company's online grocery delivery service, started in 2007 in Seattle. It was not extended across the United States until 2013 due to problems with warehousing and transporting perishable foods. Another issue was that Amazon customers might purchase two to four books per order, but when grocery shopping, they average fifty items, all from different brands, making supply chains more complex.[13] A further service launched in 2007 was "Subscribe and Save" that generated automated delivery of non-perishable groceries at given intervals: Amazon's first subscription-based grocery service.

Amazon's more visible move into food retail came with the 2017 purchase of Whole Foods. In the first five years, Amazon expanded Whole Foods' delivery services, introduced biometric scanning technology that scans a customer's palm print upon entry and trialled the "Just Walk Out" technology in select stores.[14] Additionally, Amazon offered discounts for Prime members. It is no coincidence that the purchase of Whole Foods occurred while the Amazon Go concept was in development.[15] As with books, now with groceries, Amazon offers Fresh for food delivery, Whole Foods for groceries and Go for convenience – an integrated network of food retail options.

But before we return to the Amazon Go store, it's worth considering Amazon's ecosystem when the first stores opened. In 2018, Amazon became the second trillion-dollar company after Apple. It was much more than an online store. By this time, it had become a multifaceted platform, offering services to a wide range of customers and corporations. For corporations, Amazon Web Services offered cloud-based data storage and software services, while Amazon Robotic and Logistics offered corporate automation services. For consumers, in addition to Amazon's "everything" retail website, services include Amazon Prime (video), Amazon Music, Amazon Pay (finance) and Amazon Care (healthcare).

Importantly, Amazon captures, aggregates and analyses data within and across these services. Data collection on customers allows Amazon to make better predictions about stock, supply and deliveries, but also enables their systems to nudge customers towards the next purchase. Very few of these services have physical stores to visit or staff to interact with. Instead, the customer interacts with various Amazon interfaces designed to replicate the same experience and user journey across different services – from delivering books to buying groceries. Crucially, every step the customer takes feeds data back into the Amazon system.

This is what scholars have termed "surveillance" or "platform" capitalism in which corporations claim "human experience as free raw material for hidden commercial practices of extraction, prediction, and sales".[16] A key strategy for surveillance capitalism is the extraction of "behavioural surplus", that is, personal data gathered by technological means that records and predicts a customer's behaviour, habits and decisions. Amazon's Kindle and Echo devices, for example, extract data from users as well as fulfil customer commands. Then, through reminders, special deals and discounts, and easy means to complete transactions, Amazon nudges customers towards more desirable transactions.

For Amazon's move into physical retail, this has several consequences. An earlier retail world of malls and main street stores comprised staff who served customers and built up an intuitive sense of customer behaviours and patterns. Now, Amazon's data collection can compile ever-more detailed individual customer profiles. As Amazon first aimed to sell a familiar product – the book – via online shopping, then moved into transforming the reading experience so Go (and Whole Foods and Fresh) aim to fulfil food provisioning. By capturing and containing customers within the Amazon ecosystem, the company can better predict customer behaviours and patterns across a wide range of products and services.

While physical retail stores have proven difficult (as Amazon's bookstore foray confirmed), Bezos and his team planned more physical stores as early as 2012, and a secret Amazon team workshopped both what type – department, electronics or grocery – as well as the combination of technology – from robots to conveyor belts.[17] They decided to focus on "the waiting problem" and settled on groceries and computer vision and sensors. While they began with a supermarket and built a mock-up in Seattle, Bezos decided waiting at the meat, seafood and vegetable counters was too slow. The variable weights and sizes of fruit, vegetables and meat proved too difficult for the sensors, so the team shifted to a smaller, convenience-sized store stocking regular-sized items. After staff-only trials in 2016 and 2017, the first Amazon Go store opened in early 2018. Though not as immediately successful as Amazon hoped, five years later, there are over forty stores in New York, Seattle, Chicago, Los Angeles and London.

Convenience

From the beginning, Amazon had no ethical stance, catchy slogan or brand narrative apart from the original logo's ambition to become "Earth's biggest bookstore". While a mission of relentless growth appeals to shareholders, bigness is not especially appealing for customers. Unlike Apple or Nike, whose branding and advertising aspired to emotional states or social distinctions, Amazon focused on "emphasizing a service or overall experience that they provide rather than a specific product or image. For Amazon, that service is defined by the convenience …".[18] If a single word could capture both Amazon's brand and the appeal of Amazon Go, it's "convenience".

But what is convenience? In a retail or broader business context, convenience is "reducing friction", by "taking down as many barriers as possible to buying or using a product or service".[19] Bill Gates, in his 1995 book *The Road Ahead*, popularized the idea of "friction-free" commerce, enabled by the internet:

> The information highway will extend the electronic marketplace and make it the ultimate go-between, the universal middleman. Often the only humans involved in a transaction will be the actual buyer and seller. All the goods for sale in the world will be available for you to examine, compare, and, often, customize. When you want to buy something you'll be able to tell your computer to find it for you at the best price offered by any acceptable

source or ask your computer to "haggle" with the computers of various sellers. Information about vendors and their products and services will be available to any computer connected to the highway. Servers distributed worldwide will accept bids, resolve offers into completed transactions, control authentication and security, and handle all other aspects of the marketplace, including the transfer of funds. This will carry us into a new world of low-friction, low-overhead capitalism, in which market information will be plentiful and transaction costs low.[20]

By the second decade of the twenty-first century, "low friction" shopping became a reality, but not quite as Gates had envisaged. After experimenting with books, Amazon's strategy aimed at becoming the "universal middleman", controlling the information flows between seller and buyer while extracting information from both.

But convenience has a longer history. In the eighteenth century, "conveniences" referred to household technologies – from the eggbeater to the umbrella – designed to make life easier. The word was closely associated with comfort. Historian John Crowley argues that convenience, as "predecessor for what would eventually be known as *comfort* regarding possessions in a consumer society ... had two advantages: it measured usefulness according to 'any purpose,' and it left the purposes themselves morally neutral and open-ended".[21] Comfort and convenience were twin ideas that arose with modern consumer culture in Europe and the United States in the eighteenth and nineteenth centuries.[22]

In the twentieth century, convenience acquired an association with time. Technologies of convenience enabled people to perform daily tasks more efficiently and the term came to be associated with speed. Designers created household technologies such as the fridge, the dishwasher and the vacuum cleaner in order to make housework more efficient. As sociologist Elizabeth Shove argues, "convenience, like that of comfort, legitimized new forms of consumption and located them as self-evident and sensible".[23] From electrified household technologies to fast food and TV dinners, convenience was intimately connected to automation, electrification and liberation. That is, technologies of convenience could free people, specifically middle-class women, from domestic drudgery. Or so they were told.

American life in the twentieth century seemed to be on a trajectory towards more convenient lifestyles thanks to new technological tools. Convenience cut to the heart of contemporary capitalism – making things easier is supposedly a driver of innovation and economic growth. But technologies of convenience did not always live up to their promises. Historian Ruth Schwartz Cowan described the paradox of convenience in the 1920s:

> ... every time-study of affluent housewives during these years (and many such studies were done, as these were the years in which home economists, like

so many other Americans, were fascinated by "efficiency studies") revealed that no matter how many appliances they owned, or how many conveniences were at their command, they were still spending roughly the same number of hours per week at housework as their mothers had.[24]

Additionally, technologies of convenience often create inconvenience: a society built on the convenience of private automobiles, for example, resulted in air pollution, traffic jams and an increased road death toll.

Yet convenience rose as a noble value associated with new technologies. It changed our relationship to technological devices. Beyond a single product, convenience also changed our social practices and patterns of behaviour. Design theorist Cameron Tonkinwise notes that such technologies "offer convenient ways of doing things" not as "neutral tools, but attractors".[25] That is, technologies of convenience attract more technologies of convenience. In this way, we can better understand the appeal of Amazon Go within a lifestyle comprised of interconnected social practices that are increasingly fast-paced, mobile and individualized.

By the twenty-first century, the idea of convenience was embedded in public consciousness: convenience stores, convenience foods and convenient, online retail. As more shopping and services became available 24/7, consumer expectations shifted towards ever-more convenient options. Recall Amazon's transformation of the book-buying experience – before the mid-1990s, to buy a book, you needed to travel to a bookstore within its limited opening hours. With Amazon, you could speed up this experience by ordering from your home computer and reducing the transaction time even more with their "1-click technology",

> that shaves seconds off each purchase, reducing barriers to purchase by removing clicks or seconds during which a customer might change their mind. "1-click" meant that if you had already created an Amazon account and provided a default shipping address and credit card number, you could purchase a product with one click directly from the product page, a feature that still exists today with the button called "Buy Now."[26]

Each new iteration of Amazon's website and every component of the company's infrastructure, including logistics, warehousing and transport systems, are designed to further customer convenience. Amazon's "virtual assistant", Alexa, for example, "constantly available for service", is another extension of the magic of convenience – now, rather than click a button, customers can verbalize instructions to purchase something.[27] For customers, Amazon Go offers the same convenience: an even faster retail experience.

Yet even in food retail, the ideal of a more convenient store has a long history. From this perspective, Amazon Go's roots lie in vending machines, automatic boxes that sell products without human staff.[28] A completely automated store has been an elusive dream for almost a century. In the late 1930s, entrepreneur Clarence Saunders trialled the first "automated" grocery store. Based in Memphis, Saunders began his business ventures with the Piggly Wiggly stores, designed with an innovative store layout and self-service system that eliminated the need for clerks and delivery boys. Saunders franchised his "Piggly Wiggly System" so that, by 1923, there were over a thousand stores across the United States. But Saunders aimed for the next level of automation with Keedoozle.

In 1937, the first Keedoozle store in Memphis presented customers with a vending-machine-style interface of glass boxes. Rather than a coin, the customer inserted a key into a slot that created an electronic printout on ticker tape which they presented to the cashier when finished. The cashier fed this into a machine and groceries fell onto a conveyor belt behind the shelves where a (hidden) staff member bagged the items. Keedoozle required fewer staff, and Saunders believed his "the robot grocery store" would make shopping more convenient.[29] Despite three attempts – in 1937, 1938 and 1948 – Keedoozle's mechanical and electronic systems proved too complex, error-ridden and prone to failure. None of the three iterations lasted more than a year.

Decades later, Saunders' dream of an automated store reappeared with self-checkout systems. Howard Schneider designed the earliest self-checkout system for Price Chopper Supermarkets in New York's Clifton Park in 1992. A Canadian psychiatrist, Schneider patented his machines as "automated point-of-sale machines" or "self-checkout robots". The Kroger supermarket chain adopted these self-checkout robots, and the technology spread in the mid-1990s to other stores across North America, the United Kingdom and Australia.[30] While the Amazon Go store built upon the normalization of self-service, the key Amazon difference was to "… weave the most advanced machine learning, computer vision, and AI into the very fabric of the store …".[31] That is, rather than customers scanning items on a machine, Amazon's vision technology tracks customers as well as items.

This trajectory of retail convenience is premised on several factors. For the store, automation enables better data on inventory, prices and customer preferences. For customers, autonomy and authority appear to be transferred from the store owner and staff to the customer. For customers, convenience implies not only ease, speed and accessibility but greater control.[32] Amazon Go operates at the end of a trajectory of gradual automation in retail stores, particularly in supermarkets, yet has two significant advantages over its competition: an established digital infrastructure and existing customers. By the time Amazon Go arrived in 2018, customers were habituated to the Amazon system, some for as long as twenty years.

Today's heightened status of convenience is an outcome of a society in which shared temporal schedules – the eight-hour working day, the five-day week – have disintegrated. The twentieth-century industrial schedule has disappeared in favour of a personal schedule.[33] A consequence of this fractured temporal order is a customer expectation of constant and continual access to products and services. And, unlike the twentieth-century version of convenience built around a family home – with shared appliances such as the fridge, washing machine and vacuum cleaner – today's convenience is founded on individual practices.

Although the temporal convenience of the Amazon Go store appears relatively small, it is enough to appeal to some busy urbanites. Available all the time, the automated store cuts out the checkout experience – that unknown quantity of time and its random human interactions – so that the customer can better organize their time. In this way, the Amazon Go store parallels other services developed in the early twenty-first century such as Uber. Uber's promise is a car and driver always available to fit into your personal schedule and take you to a precise destination. Automated payment means no cash or physical interactions. When taking public transport, in contrast, you need to fit into the bus or train schedule plus walk to your destination. Convenience can extract a little extra time from a busy personal schedule.

But what are the consequences of convenience? Across various daily activities, convenience "is habituating us to a way of life where the desire to save time trumps the desire to interact with people".[34] New York City's "bodegas", for example, are part of local, neighbourhood culture, social spaces as well as convenience stores. In contrast, Amazon's ecosystem of services is founded upon anonymous interactions with automated response systems. And, as well as eliminating retail staff, Amazon Go goes further to conceal the human labour that grows, packages, delivers and stocks the food, as well as the labour that cleans the store. It also conceals the energy expenditure of its digital infrastructure – the data centres, cell towers, cables and wires – that enables the system to operate.[35]

As with earlier critiques of household technologies, Amazon Go's shift to retail automation carries unintended (and hidden) costs. Consider convenience's aim: making tasks simpler and faster. Convenience technologies change our temporal organization, but in multiple directions rather than one. Even a single convenience technology contributed to a broader, flexible temporal organization. Washing, for example, moved from "laundry days" to fragmented moments of loading and unloading washing machines and thus disrupted collective rhythms: "the contemporary valuing of convenience relates to an increasing intensity of small tasks and to a reliance on individualized modes of co-ordination. This goes hand-in-hand with the weakening of a shared sociotemporal order".[36] That is, convenience degrades formerly shared experiences.

Critiques of the "throwaway society" in the post-war era, such as Vance Packard's *Waste Makers*, linked convenience with disposability and increased waste, particularly with food.[37] This applies even more today. Amazon's Go's single portions and packaged goods are designed for individuals rather than families or groups. Ease and speed trump shared food purchasing and preparation or waste minimization. For both the customer and Amazon, ready-made meals and snacks packaged in plastic may be the most convenient option but, when adopted on a mass scale, have serious environmental consequences.

Finally, convenience across a range of daily activities has a flow-on effect, particularly as customers come to expect ever-faster and more efficient transactions. The pressure of convenience "exerts a pressure on everything else to be easy or get left behind. We are spoiled by immediacy and become annoyed by tasks that remain at the old level of effort and time."[38] Waiting evokes frustration. Amazon's capture of numerous services – from books, movies and music, to healthcare, finance and food – increases expectations among customers that other services, from government to community organizations, should be equally convenient.

Personalization

As well as convenience, Amazon's systems are designed to build a personal relationship with every customer. It does this not by identifying lifestyle aspirations or appealing to emotional states, but by designing interactions around "me". More than the impersonal relationship we had with previous technologies of conveniences, Amazon's automated systems remember your purchasing history and habits. Such personalization reinforces a sense of trust. Of course, the trade-off for the customer is the exchange of personal information:

> Amazon gathers huge amounts of consumer data. According to the company's Privacy Notice, this includes searches, purchases, product wishlists and registries, page clicks, time spent on pages, streamed content, and product ratings and reviews.[39]

Customer experience is touted as an Amazon obsession, embodied by Bezo's often-repeated phrase of aiming to make Amazon "the most customer-centric company on earth".[40] Every interaction is carefully designed to facilitate the customer's needs. In fact, customer experience is an essential piece of Amazon's "flywheel of growth", a diagram that depicts Amazon's corporate strategy.[41] In contrast, Walmart's growth strategy aims only to generate lower prices, while Amazon's aims to use customer experience to drive growth and lower prices. For Amazon, a personalized experience establishes an intimate customer relationship, and, when repeated, becomes an embedded, then essential, part of their daily life.

By placing the customer at the centre of every interaction, Amazon develops not only trust but affection. Such affection is generated by Amazon's reliable and efficient systems. In 2002, for example, Amazon offered customers free shipping for orders over 99 dollars, and, with repeat orders and popularity, launched Prime membership and two-day shipping on many items. Since then, shipping has become even faster, particularly in cities.[42] By renaming its warehouses "fulfilment centres", Amazon further situated even the most prosaic infrastructure in a relationship to customer desires. Amazon's key metric and strategic advantage – its speed – is continually communicated to the customer via delivery tracking tools and notifications that imply not just a delivery service, but a personal one.

As a series of touchpoints, Amazon's automated systems seem to respond instantly to the customer's personal needs and desires. Such interactions on Amazon's website, apps and devices accumulate over time into a relationship – one in which Amazon strives to be consistent and responsive. For the customer, this relationship, premised on predictability and stability as well as speed, can be reassuring in an unstable and unpredictable world. Importantly, each step and every personalized interaction increases the normality of the Amazon system and the customer's dependence on it.

But a customer's interactions with Amazon's systems are limited and the communication is one-way. Customers cannot interact with Amazon's vast army of warehouse workers and only have limited (if any) interaction with delivery drivers. Instead, customer relationships are mediated by Amazon's interface on a smartphone or computer screen. With Amazon Go, this mediation is pushed even further – already within the Amazon ecosystem, all the customer needs to do is take whatever they desire without interacting with any humans at all.

This increased personalization in retail experience results in fewer shared, collective experiences. Amazon Go shopping is designed for individuals rather than a couple, family or group. The solitary shopper is autonomous but must also be self-reliant – there are no staff to offer advice or answer questions. The food stocked in Amazon Go also fits the model of an individualized, just-in-time lifestyle. Food is not packaged for stocking up the pantry and filling the freezer as one might in a weekly supermarket shop. Instead, Amazon's heat-at-home meal kits, grab-and-go lunches, breakfasts and snacks are designed for a customer starved of time as much as food.

One hidden aspect of retail personalization is social discrimination. Not only do stores such as Amazon Go train customers how to shop, but "they also habituate customers to a grab-and-go lifestyle that is predicated upon ever more entrenched forms of technological dependence and *privilege*".[43] Unlike entering a regular convenience store, Amazon Go is based on a membership model whereby you cannot enter the store without having an existing account already linked to a credit card. Although retail stores have never been completely inclusive, Amazon Go is explicitly exclusionary as the stores are not designed to accept cash or food stamps. After a 2019 legal battle against such exclusion, a court forced Amazon to integrate a cash payment option into one of its New York stores.[44]

However, if the relationship between Amazon and its customers is built on trust (or even affection), that between Amazon and its labour force is not. For workers, instead of personalized service, "fear and ruthless discipline. Instead of making life ever more convenient and seamless, as it aims to do for its customers, Amazon ratchets up quotas and micromanages workers' every action."[45] And this relationship is also a personalized one – Amazon has consistently quashed workers' attempts to establish unions. The distributed nature of Amazon's workforce makes collective action difficult, with so many different services – from warehouse workers to delivery drivers – and no common physical space for them to interact.

The human costs of Amazon's systems on its workforce are well documented. A *New York Times* expose from 2015, for example, exposed Amazon's labour conditions: "Just as fulfillment center employees are asked to embrace actual robots as coworkers and emulate their machinic efficiency, employees in the Amazon offices aspire to be 'Amabots,' a term that has come to mean 'you have become at one with the system.'"[46] Amazon's delivery infrastructure also relies upon an army of low-paid warehouse workers and delivery drivers with numbers fluctuating according to the season or market conditions. For Amazon, convenience means an always available pool of cheap labour.

The Covid-19 pandemic accelerated Amazon's delivery services and made the company more profitable and more powerful. Customers previously reluctant to use online retail had little option. Online retail was safe, hygienic and, with lockdowns, the only available option. But the pandemic also highlighted working conditions in Amazon facilities. Just as Amazon collects and uses data from customers, it also does so

> to surveil its fleet of workers, including warehouse workers, delivery drivers, ghost writers, and other high-tech workers, in order to extract valuable information about their work flow that is used to further exploit, discipline, and control workers, increase labor efficiency, and inform the development of workplace automation and other business investments.[47]

Among numerous studies on Amazon's labour practices, two examples highlight its use of personalized, automated systems: warehouse workers and delivery drivers. Amazon warehouses are typically huge, impersonal places, partially automated with conveyor belts and robots, but also reliant on low-wage labour subject to algorithmic management. A 2020 study of warehouse conditions in California detailed how this works:

> Scanners are among the primary tools that management uses to direct, evaluate, and discipline workers in the labor process. As our interviewees

report, the devices at the time of writing are hand-held, mounted to workstations, or carts, and are used to electronically read various kinds of barcodes, worker IDs, or other labels tracking goods and their routes from receipt to storage and shipping. In some tasks, scanners direct workers through digital displays and monitors, and track output digitally to allow management to ensure that workers carry out their designated tasks at a profitable speed, regardless of the distances required to walk, or the volume of goods passing through their hands.[48]

Hiring and scheduling is conducted online, work schedules are precarious and hours fluctuate according to Amazon's seasonal needs. In such a scheme, workers are as interchangeable as robots. Algorithms, interfaces and automated systems retain the knowledge, organize and guide individual workers, as well as dictate their schedules. In Alessandro Delfanti's recent study of Amazon warehouse work regimes, he writes:

> A pervasive surveillance system monitors their productivity at every step. The valuable information generated by their labor is captured and monopolized by Amazon's software systems, and then fed to the machines that run the warehouse and organize fulfillment processes. Employee turnover is high, by design, as the warehouse quickly discards and replaces workers worn out by the dictated pace.[49]

Another recent legal report documented high injury and turnover rates and described Amazon's warehouse labour as "disposable workers".[50] On one face of Amazon, convenience revolves around the customer's personal schedule, but on the other, workers must adjust their schedule to Amazon's temporal rhythms and requirements. Worker obsolescence is designed into the Amazon warehouse system – punishing physical labour, organized by algorithms and captured by productivity scanners is designed to exhaust bodies and replace them with fresh ones.

Amazon subjects its delivery drivers to a similar regime. Drivers use a device known as a "Rabbit", a smartphone that tracks the driver's movements and dictates the delivery route. But drivers are subject to triple surveillance:

> Amazon's subcontracted delivery drivers remain one of the only groups of logistics workers that are simultaneously surveilled by their formal employers (DSPs), the parent company (Amazon), and Amazon's Prime customers, who increasingly keep track of the location of their package via GPS monitoring. This heavy surveillance remains an ongoing source of stress and anxiety for last mile workers.[51]

Such are the consequences of Amazon's convenience and personalization for warehouse and delivery workers. For the customer, such conditions are concealed by the absence of humans or minimal interaction with them.

A final consequence that Amazon has had some difficulty overcoming is a customer's fear of losing privacy. An initial hesitation for customers using Amazon Go was Amazon's use of vision technology, facial recognition and CCTV. In a way, many of us are prepared to accept such technologies. In the large cities in which Amazon Go stores are located, CCTV cameras are routinely positioned atop streetlights, roofs or under eaves. Whether by city authorities or retail stores, the idea of surveillance seems one that was accepted (actively or passively) as cameras spread across cities in the twenty-first century. Despite this, critics raised the issue of Amazon Go's invasion of privacy, and a 2023 lawsuit accused the company of not alerting customers to their biometric surveillance regime.[52] The trade-off – gain convenience, lose privacy – is Amazon's means of decreasing resistance.

Scholars explain this phenomenon as "digital resignation" or "privacy resignation". That is, while most people disapprove of personal data collection and video surveillance, the majority see no point trying to resist – they have resigned themselves to the future Amazon has designed.[53] Surveillance capitalism, in which platform companies such as Amazon (and Google and Meta) extract personal data without our knowledge and consent, has increasingly become normalized.[54] Amazon has built up trust and intimacy with customers over thirty years, and such feelings are an effective means to naturalize its surveillance and data-gathering methods.

But, if Amazon Go store represents the culmination of a century-long quest for the staff-less or robot store, it has not yet proven broadly successful. Other retail chains followed Amazon's lead. Both Walmart and Kroger rolled out "Scan and Go" technologies, for example, in hundreds of stores in 2018, while Apple allows customers to "just walk out" of some stores by scanning a barcode.[55] But the fully automated "vision" technology employed by Amazon Go involves less friction, more convenience and personalization, particularly for customers already in the Amazon ecosystem. Even so, the future of Amazon Go and similar automated retail stores is uncertain. With currently only forty stores in the United States, Amazon Go is not exactly a competitor to 7-11's ten thousand staffed stores. Amazon Go may yet be a failed experiment like its "bricks and mortar" bookstores, but an experiment Amazon will learn from and build upon.

Chapter 3
Constructive Play: LEGO

Stepping into New York's flagship LEGO store on a grey winter's day, I'm overwhelmed by a bright, glossy space filled with colourful sculptures and crowded with people. Built from 880,000 LEGO bricks, the rainbow-coloured "Tree of Discovery" stretches up to the ceiling before me (Figure 13). A LEGO squirrel peers at me from a low branch while a cat stares from a branch above. Beside the Tree of Discovery, tourists line up to pose on a park bench beside the life-sized LEGO Hulk. I try to absorb this alternate universe of trees, animals and comic book heroes composed of plastic bricks.

Clutching his hammer, Thor flies over an almost life-sized yellow cab (Figure 14). Captain America has just alighted on the cab's roof. I consider the complexity of this single sculpture. Originally a 1940s comic book character, Captain America has appeared in numerous books, TV series, films and video games since then. But this sculpture doesn't portray a cartoon or a cinematic Captain America, rather a LEGO minifigure Captain America. Yet it's not minifigure-sized, but a giant minifigure composed of regular-sized LEGO bricks. And it appears on a modern New York cab beside the ancient Norse god of Thunder.

I turn to the opposite wall. Ordered by themes – Marvel, Disney, Star Wars, Creator, Architect – LEGO box sets adorn rows of shelves. Some suggest specific customers: Duplo for toddlers, Friends for girls and Technics for older children. Complex, collectible sets sit under a sign that reads "Adults Welcome". Completed sets sit in Perspex cases within the shelves, so that a City police station with a finished car and policemen sits below its box. Digital screens framed with oversized LEGO bricks flash further information. Staff in bright yellow aprons emblazoned with LEGO's red, white and yellow logo guide customers around.

I consider the LEGO Statue of Liberty nearby. She's a minifigure standing on a podium, surrounded by boxes of LEGO "Architecture" sets of the Statue of Liberty (Figure 15). The photograph on the boxes is a representation of the real Statue of Liberty, not the minifigure that stands above them. Amid my overthinking, she blinks: her face is a digital screen. I turn and consider a life-sized LEGO scene of the Times Square subway station (Figure 16). There's no

Figure 13 LEGO store, New York, The Tree of Discovery. Author photo.

Figure 14 LEGO store, New York, Captain America. Author photo.

Figure 15 LEGO store, New York, The Statue of Liberty. Author photo.

protective screen in front of the minifigure attendant and a huge subway token sits above him. These tokens were phased out two decades ago. As well as space-time compression, slippage between real and fictional, physical and digital, the LEGO store exudes nostalgia.

Walking upstairs, I pass LEGO-brick Broadway-style billboards and posters featuring minifigure characters from popular films. The first floor is equally crowded. Digital screens invite customers to design their own minifigure and then watch it get made in the "Minifigure Factory" (a 3D printer stylized in LEGO). Beside the Factory stands what appears to be an old-fashioned photo booth: the Mosaic workshop. Upon payment, the machine takes your photo and translates it into a LEGO brick mosaic. On this floor, I can customize plastic toys and

Figure 16 LEGO store, New York, subway station. Author photo.

convert myself into plastic bricks so both can inhabit the same LEGO universe as Captain America and the Statue of Liberty.

In the digital Brick Lab, customers can build a (physical) LEGO creation from plastic bricks, scan it, then "play" with it. This involves dragging it (virtually) around the walls of a room onto which a LEGO city is projected. As well as this digital interactivity, there's also a "Pick a Brick" wall where customers can choose their own physical bricks, "Build your own Minifigure" stations (Figure 17) and play tables with "classic" LEGO bricks (Figure 18). I see a free table, so I sit down and play. I recall the familiar feel and satisfying snap as I join two bricks. I imagine how this might become a spaceship or dinosaur. I may be here a while.

Constructive Play: LEGO

Figure 17 LEGO store, New York, Build your own Minifigure. Author photo.

I'm comfortable playing here as adults and children – male and female, people from all over the world – crowd around the minifigure stations and crane to see the 3D printer at work. Although a global chain, LEGO stores feature local landmarks and characters – both real and fictional – to differentiate locations. London's Leicester Square store, for example, features a LEGO Tube carriage in which customers can pose for a photo between life-sized minifigures of William Shakespeare and a Beefeater. Big Ben replaces Lady Liberty and Harry Potter replaces Captain America. But I wonder, as I put the tail fin onto my LEGO spaceship, how we simply accept such a surreal carnival of size-shifting comic book heroes and cultural icons without the slightest hesitation?

Figure 18 LEGO store, New York, play station. Author photo.

A Short History of LEGO

It's difficult to write objectively about LEGO. The faces of my design and architecture students become animated with joy if I mention the word. For them, as for many people around the world, LEGO is infused with memories. I have two distinct sets of LEGO memories: long winter afternoons spent constructing castles and cities on my bedroom floor as a child and more recent memories of cleaning up hundreds of pieces from my child's bedroom floor. Unlike toys that come and go (who today plays with Cabbage Patch Kids, Tickle Me Elmo or Bratz Dolls?), LEGO has remained a stable presence for generations. LEGO seems timeless. But it isn't.

In 1916, in the Danish village of Billund, carpenter Ole Kirk Christensen bought a workshop where he made timber furniture, doors and windows.[1] With the 1930s downturn in construction due to the Depression, he refocused his business on wooden toys. Christensen hand-crafted and hand-painted miniature trucks, buses and airplanes, as well as the now iconic duck pull-toy. In 1934, he named his company LEGO after the Danish phrase "leg godt", meaning "play well". With his son Godtfred, Ole designed over a hundred toys and his attention to detail and quality materials remain ingrained in the company's design principles.

In 1947, Ole purchased a plastic injection moulding machine and a set of "Self-Locking Building Bricks" designed by the English company, Kiddicraft. He and Godtfred copied these plastic bricks and released LEGO's "Automatic Binding Bricks" two years later. While LEGO's first construction toy was a copy, the company's original contribution came in 1958 with its "stud-and-tube" coupling system that comprised internal cylinders within each brick.[2] Designed with regular dimensions, the new bricks had better structural strength. They also allowed for modular construction as interchangeable bricks could interlock in various combinations.

After his father died in 1958, Godtfred took over LEGO and soon ceased wooden toy production to concentrate on mass-producing plastic toys. Injection moulding was cheaper, faster and more precise than hand-crafting wood, and plastic was lighter, longer-lasting and could be any colour. In 1963, LEGO changed its plastic from cellulose acetate, a plastic that could deform and change over time, to acrylonitrile butadiene styrene (ABS). ABS could be moulded more precisely and "the bricks now fitted together more tightly and constructions became more stable".[3] The plastic is so durable and LEGO's production process is so precise that bricks manufactured sixty years ago fit with today's bricks.

Godtfred promoted LEGO as a play system and sold bricks in sets. The popular LEGO Town sets of the 1960s, for example, allowed children to construct houses, shops, vehicles, signposts and trees. LEGO became renowned for a construction play system that was non-violent and non-gender specific. Whereas Ole exported his wooden toys to neighbouring Nordic countries, Godtfred transformed LEGO into a global corporation in the 1960s, opening offices and distributing LEGO across Europe, North America and Asia. A simplified logo projected a consistent image for the now-global brand: the word LEGO in a white, bubble-shaped font, the capital letters outlined in black and yellow against a red background.[4]

LEGO launched two innovations in 1978. The first were the Castle and Space sets. Referencing familiar genres from children's books or television shows, the new sets included step-by-step building instructions and came with already embedded stories: children could defend the castle or explore new galaxies. LEGO's second innovation was the minifigure, miniature human figures designed to inhabit these new sets. After the plastic bricks, minifigures would prove

LEGO's most important design and, combined with the new sets represented a "shift in emphasis from *construction* play to *narrative* play".[5] Children could now build theatrical sets populated by knights and astronauts and create stories around them.

LEGO also designed plastic bricks for more specific market segments. These included the large, chunky bricks of Duplo (1969) for toddlers and the complex Technics sets (1977) for older children. LEGO's differentiation of its product lines both for age groups and subject matter enabled broader market capture and "brand loyalty" among children from toddlers to teenagers.[6] Beyond simply play toys, in the 1980s, CEO Kjeld Kirk Kristiansen – Ole's grandson – promoted LEGO as an *educational* tool. He established an educational research division that distributed materials such as Teacher's Manuals and sets designed to fit with school curricula.

Although generations of children had grown up playing with LEGO, by the mid-1990s, children had access to new toys and alternative modes of play. Hand-held video games, computer games and electronic toys made static construction toys like LEGO seem old-fashioned. In response, LEGO expanded quickly into new fields, including video games, theme parks, clothing and media licensing. LEGO's first (partially) successful video game, *LEGO Island* (1997), was an action-adventure game in which players could explore an island composed of LEGO bricks and complete missions with their minifigure avatars.

But LEGO's diversification spread the company thinly across too many new initiatives, many of them unsuccessful. A record financial loss in 2004 prompted significant changes. LEGO management sold theme parks, halved product lines, cut staff and shifted production facilities from Denmark to the Czech Republic and Mexico.[7] It also refocused on its traditional strength: construction play. Although LEGO's financial turnaround over the next decade was remarkable, the problem of how to bridge the physical-digital play divide remained.

In retrospect, a licensing agreement to produce Star Wars sets in 1998 began a significant shift in LEGO's concept of play. Children no longer played with generic knights or anonymous astronauts but with specific characters, such as Luke Skywalker and Darth Vader. LEGO's "mediatization" in the 2000s entailed a shift from designing physical toys to designing media entertainment toys linked to films, video games and television series.[8] Plastic brick sets became inseparable from their virtual "worlds" such that children could now reconstruct scenes from *Star Wars*, *Harry Potter*, *Indiana Jones* and Marvel movies. LEGO also developed its own fictional world of Bionicles (2001–10) which included comic books, video games, trading cards and LEGO brick sets.

After 2004, LEGO also developed dozens of successful video games. *LEGO Star Wars* (2005), *LEGO Indiana Jones* (2008), *LEGO Batman* (2008) and their sequels combined already established fictional worlds with LEGO minifigure characters. Infused with a sense of irreverent humour, LEGO's video games complemented their other media products. Although video games represented a break from construction play, they served to reinforce the idea of a universe composed of LEGO bricks and populated by minifigures. Of course, physical brick sets accompanied each new game.

Paradoxically, the rise of the internet in the 2000s affected LEGO in some positive ways. Fan web pages and chat rooms, particularly from Adult Fans of LEGO (AFOLs), developed an interest in collecting, building and promoting LEGO among adults. AFOLs also organized in-person fairs, conventions and events. Blogs such as the Brothers Brick (founded in 2005) featured the latest LEGO news and fan activities. LEGO also took advantage of the internet's collaborative potential with the LEGO Factory (launched in 2004) which allowed users to design their own sets and LEGO Idea (launched in 2014) which provided a platform for continual interaction between users and LEGO.[9]

Adults became a significant market, with sets such as the Architecture series (launched in 2008), as well as complex, expensive sets – most famously, the seven-thousand-piece Millennium Falcon set. In previous generations, adults purchased LEGO for their children, but in the twenty-first century, they also purchased LEGO for themselves. LEGO's market now extended from toddlers to pensioners. To progress another underdeveloped market segment, LEGO launched the female-oriented Friends range (2012). This sparked a gender debate – which we will return to below – but proved more long-lived than previous female-oriented LEGO sets.

A series of movies further boosted LEGO's popularity. The 2014 hit, *The LEGO Movie* was followed by *The LEGO Batman Movie*, *The LEGO Ninjago Movie* and the (less popular) 2019 sequel, *The LEGO Movie 2*. Essentially feature-length advertisements, these movies encapsulate the LEGO universe of the store described in this chapter's opening: a mix of real and fictional worlds populated with real historical and contemporary characters as well as fictional ones, all coexisting in a playful realm of humour and nostalgia. Brick sets and video games accompanied each new movie release. By refocusing on key themes across physical and digital media forms, LEGO overtook rivals Mattel and Hasbro to become the world's largest toy manufacturer in 2014.[10]

Yet despite LEGO's long history, its retail stores are relatively recent.[11] The first LEGO brand stores opened in Cologne, London and Moscow in 2002 as test spaces for new retail concepts. At the time, LEGO stated that "the Company wants to examine how it can best inform children and their parents about the values inherent in learning through play products".[12] A dozen more "test stores" opened in 2003 with play tables, "Pick-a-Brick" walls, and "Build your own Minifigure" stations. Over the next fifteen years, LEGO refined a formula for its branded stores based on interactive physical and, eventually, digital play.

Retail expansion doubled from 2018 to 2022, and now the company has over nine hundred branded stores on every continent.[13] Although LEGO became a global giant by creating products across video games, television series and films, the LEGO stores reassert the central role of the physical brick. As well as a space to experience LEGO play and playfulness, LEGO stores have become important event spaces for product launches and promotions. Despite the trans-media proliferation across digital platforms, plastic bricks and minifigures remain the fundamental building blocks of the LEGO universe.

Construction

Studded rectangles are everywhere in the LEGO store. Embedded on the walls, painted on the floors, in ornamental details and on digital screens: LEGO repeats the brick to remind customers of the foundational unit, or atom, of its universe.[14] The fact that the basic, rectangular blocks, precise and right-angled but for the round studs, are called bricks, emphasizes LEGO's fundamental link to construction. One of LEGO's unique characteristics as a physical toy is that its bricks are consistent and compatible, both between sets and over time. Yet LEGO play incorporates construction as both a material and a narrative practice. That is, customers assemble and reassemble physical bricks and stories. This section considers how LEGO's material construction operates first, then turns to its narrative construction.

After the basic brick, LEGO's earliest specialized pieces comprised architectural components such as doors, windows and sloped roof tiles. As early as the 1960s, LEGO's Town Plan set aligned it in the popular imagination with architecture, engineering and urban design. From the Town Plan to today's City sets, LEGO embodied a construction ideal that mirrors design's transformative power. "LEGO worlds", argued one critic, "consist of constantly evolving assemblages of prefabricated parts that reflect modern spaces in the perpetual process of construction and reconstruction."[15]

But, while Town Plan play mats, designed with roads and green spaces, encouraged children to mimic conventional modern planning of the 1960s (centred around the suburb and automobile), today's City sets embody a different urban ideal. City sets no longer focus on constructing and organizing suburbs. Instead, construction centres around urban drama "connected by narrative threads rather than spatial relations."[16] Today's City sets – Fire Command Truck or Police Chase at the Bank – are designed to recreate a miniature scenario involving firefighters or police rather than plan out an ideal city.

Yet the affiliation between LEGO and architecture remains. LEGO's systematic approach to building with modular components, using regular, rectilinear forms has long appealed to modernist architects (and students). Architect Moshe Safdie allegedly used all the LEGO bricks in Montreal to build models for his Habitat 67 apartments, an architectural centrepiece of the 1967 Montreal World's Fair.[17]

More recently, LEGO's Architecture series comprises sets whereby customers can build architectural icons such as the Empire State Building, Fallingwater and the Statue of Liberty. Ironically, these architectural sets lack the openness of a "classic" brick set. Instead, they prompt builders towards a specific, pre-defined end.

This returns me to the store where the Architecture series was located. On the store's ground floor, there are no bricks or minifigures to build with. Instead, customers admire the LEGO sculptures and purchase boxed brick sets. The box sets, adorned with a photograph of the finished build – a completed Fallingwater, Millennium Falcon or Fire Command scene – occupy a great deal of the store's real estate. In fact, it took me a while to find the "classic" brick set: on a side shelf upstairs, not centrally positioned on the ground floor.

A common critique of the boxed sets is that they restrict creativity. A boxed set contains instructions that "script" specific outcomes. The two-dimensional instructions, the photo on the box and the completed model in-store embed a script within the boxed set.[18] Such instructions – like those in an IKEA flat pack – imply LEGO is an assembly toy, with little imagination required. Rather than build an imaginary spaceship, scripts encourage us to build a specific Star Wars spaceship. But do scripts – with the clear end goal of a completed model – restrict creativity more than a "classic" brick set?

Not necessarily. What makes LEGO bricks unique are their interchangeability. Even though the boxes' packaging and instructions provide a script towards a specific end, the pieces within are open to numerous combinations and possibilities. Children often complete a set as instructed, then destroy it and use the pieces to make something else. The interchangeable nature of LEGO bricks enables children to remix the pieces into a new creation: a hybrid or a surreal fragment: Captain America holding Thor's hammer and riding in the Millennium Falcon, for example. Such possibilities make LEGO a powerful and flexible system.

The LEGO Movie highlighted this argument about construction in its central battle between President Business, who tries to fix LEGO bricks permanently with Kragle (glue), and the Master Builders who champion creativity in the form of playful remixing. LEGO reimagined the battle between good and evil as one between scripted and off-script construction. Ultimately, *The LEGO Movie* circumvented the scripting argument by playfully endorsing remixing. Yet in the LEGO store, hybrid sets – Marvel heroes mixed with Star Wars characters – are not available. LEGO keeps its virtual worlds separate and contained.

This argument recurs with the openness of the "classic" rectilinear bricks versus the themed sets, with their preformed pieces, decals and specific symbols. The latter are portrayed as limiting possibilities of LEGO's open-ended system. This becomes ultimately an argument about the nature of children's imagination and creativity: a battle between an imagination moulded by predestined ends versus improvisation and remixing. Yet the LEGO system can accommodate both. The more sets you accumulate, the more pieces you own. The more pieces you own, the more possibilities for more elaborate remixes.

Back in the store, another aspect of construction deserves scrutiny. Recall the Tree of Discovery, a huge sculpture constructed from 880,000 bricks. Expertise in LEGO building was popularized with the television series *LEGO Masters*. Launched first in 2017 in the United Kingdom, it followed a well-worn path of competitive reality shows such as *MasterChef*. In *LEGO Masters*, pairs of "master builders" – typically a mix of males and females, children and adults – compete in "challenges" that include engineering problems, architectural builds and creative builds. The "wow" factor when the Master Builders reveal their LEGO builds is replicated as customers enter the LEGO store. Both are evidence not only of physical construction expertise but also narratives. LEGO builds are embedded with stories.

A single box of plastic construction bricks – no matter how flexible – is not enough to build the world's biggest toy company. This is why the first LEGO a customer confronts in-store are not "classic" bricks, but LEGO sets linked to films, video games and other media, either borrowed (Star Wars) or created by LEGO (Friends). Here, it is useful to understand LEGO as a construction toy designed to build and rebuild narratives. Building with LEGO box sets is not simply constructing with mute, inanimate bricks but a practice already embedded with stories. LEGO bricks are both plastic and semiotic material.

While LEGO began designing sets based on fantasy worlds in the 1970s – astronaut, pirate and knight sets, for example – a significant shift occurred after the licensing agreement with Lucas Entertainment for Star Wars LEGO in 1998. LEGO followed this with a licensing agreement with Warner Brothers to develop Harry Potter (2000) and in the 2000s with Disney, Marvel and DC Comics. Now, children build not just generic fictional worlds but "specific fictional universes that are already promoted – and owned – by other media companies".[19] These ready-made universes come with plots and characters – good (Luke Skywalker) versus evil (Darth Vadar), for example. By the 2010s, such fictional universes were cross-generational in that both adults and children understand these elements of the Star Wars LEGO universe.

Customers can buy and build LEGO sets designed to recreate scenes from films, complete with minifigure characters, vehicles and props.[20] In this way, both bricks and minifigures are already "narrativized" with known characters and plot structures. With the success of Star Wars and Harry Potter, LEGO developed its own fictional universes, Bionicles and Ninjago, with accompanying animated series, films and brick sets.[21] By the 2020s, a visitor to the LEGO store can understand Captain America and Thor in contemporary New York as sculptures that not only display LEGO's physical possibilities but also the narrative remixing possibilities within the LEGO universe.

By understanding LEGO bricks as semiotic as well as material, the connections to other media products become clearer. The sculpture of LEGO Captain America, for example, is multi-layered and cross-generational. Customers may recognize this as Captain America from films or comic books of the twentieth century, from LEGO Avengers video games or recent Marvel films. In this way, LEGO is a flexible, transmedia product. A customer entering the store finds nothing unusual about Captain America on top of a New York cab, Spiderman on the Brooklyn Bridge or Hulk on a park bench. Like LEGO bricks, these various narrative components can be assembled and reassembled seamlessly within the LEGO universe.

Interestingly, LEGO carefully regulates this seamlessness. Take the minifigure, for example. Like video game avatars, minifigures are simplified characters, with exaggerated features, iconic objects (Captain America's shield), and, in the films and video games, characteristic gestures and expressions. But, licensed digital media for video games, movies and television series must conform to physical LEGO's possibilities. Game and animation designers who want to use minifigures must conform to a three-hundred-page rulebook on how to design digital minifigures: ultimately, they need to look and behave like physical ones.[22]

This close integration between LEGO's physical sets and various films, television series and other media products means:

> the customer will see the toy as an artifact belonging to the media narrative. As a consequence, more industries, including toy industries, are becoming dependent on the successful promotion of media products and the general ups and downs of the media industry.[23]

For LEGO, this means continual updates: new brick sets in response to the latest Batman or Star Wars films, television series or video games. In-store, this results in a continually changing range of box sets in response to films customers have already seen or games they have already played.

But constructing narrative worlds can be risky. LEGO's popular Bionicles, for example, launched in 2001, inhabited "the island of Mata Nui, home of the Toa, characterized by a unique cosmology, origin myths, a clan system, tribal alliances and rivalries, ritual practices of storytelling, and sacred iconography".[24] When the sets appeared in New Zealand, a group of lawyers representing Māori groups contacted LEGO claiming that the world of Bionicles appropriated language, names and rituals from living Māori and Polynesian culture. For Māori people, these words, language and stories are not simply neutral material for playsets but essential to cultural being and ways of knowing.

LEGO's gender sets have also proved problematic. Although LEGO marketing in the 1960s and 1970s was gender inclusive, the company's increased emphasis on narrative-based play and licensing in the 1990s – particularly of action-adventure scenarios – led to research that suggested half its potential market had become alienated. In response, LEGO launched a narrative world targeted at girls.[25] The LEGO Friends range, launched in 2012, features a different colour palette and emphasizes role play with interiors, fashion and lifestyle themes.

Friends minifigures also differ from regular minifigures and their accompanying narratives reinforce gender stereotypes:

> Activity within LEGO Friends games predominantly focused on forming social relationships (planning parties, earning money for parties, dressing like your friends), and participating in expensive hobbies and leisure activities such as throwing extravagant pool parties, riding horses, yachting, and water-skiing. The majority of game "play" involved choosing the appropriate style and color of clothing, accessories, food, furniture, or decorations for a given task.[26]

LEGO's violent, action-adventure narratives (such as Star Wars and Indiana Jones) supposedly appealed more to boys. The idea was that boys' toys emphasize action, professional roles, heroes and missions, while girls' toys emphasize domestic, caring and recreational activities, social relationships and grooming.[27] The problem is that toys "marketed to and subsequently favored by girls and boys are designed to be consistent with gendered adult roles".[28] While critics claim such stereotypes are harmful, for LEGO, market segmentation means more sets to sell. The LEGO store offers box sets for boys and girls, younger and older children, adults and collectors; there's a narrative for everyone.

Play

The LEGO store is designed to emphasize a permeable boundary between material bricks and immaterial narratives. Acknowledging both, LEGO emphasizes physical boxes that promote its films, television series and video games. But the reverse is also true, as customers consume films in cinemas and video games at home that function as advertising for brick sets. LEGO describes this movement between physical and virtual realms as "fluid play". While play remains central to LEGO's mission, its meaning – seemingly self-evident – as well as its practices have shifted in the twenty-first century.

In his *Homo ludens*, cultural historian Johan Huizinga outlined a classic definition of play:

> we might call it a free activity standing quite consciously outside "ordinary" life as being "not serious", but at the same time absorbing the player intensely and utterly. It is an activity connected with no material interest, and no profit

can be gained by it. It proceeds within its own proper boundaries of time and space according to fixed rules and in an orderly manner. It promotes the formation of social groupings which tend to surround themselves with secrecy and to stress their difference from the common world by disguise or other means.[29]

First, Huizinga characterized play as a voluntary ("free") and unprofitable activity. Second, he defined play as an unserious activity opposed to "ordinary" life, and associated with fantasy and frivolous activities. Third, he argued, play takes place within a bounded space and limited time in which players suspend daily behaviour and rituals. Fourth, the play world is regulated by rules. And finally, argued Huizinga, play "*is* order. Into an imperfect world and into the confusion of life it brings a temporary, a limited perfection."

Huizinga wrote this in the 1930s, when play (associated with children) was popularly understood as something opposed to work (associated with adults). But, in the past two decades, play has moved to a more central role in adult culture. New forms of play such as video games are no longer designed only for children. More than this, play is not restricted to leisure time or portrayed as frivolous. "Serious" corporate offices incorporate play – Silicon Valley headquarters' video game parlours and ping pong tables, for example – into the world of work. LEGO even launched a programme called "Serious Play" to promote their play sets to corporate executives as "tools for thinking".[30]

Returning to Pine and Gilmour's "Experience Economy" model, we can understand the LEGO store as a stage that enables and encourages customers to play. Where else on Fifth Avenue can you build, create and improvise? Play generates a tactile, memorable experience as well as reinforcing the otherworldliness of the LEGO universe. For children, the store is an immersive, absorbing experience within a familiar realm of filmic and game characters. For adults, it is a bounded space with permission to suspend daily behaviour and routines. And purchasing a box set on the first floor enables both to continue playing at home.

Huizinga's definition of play – particularly the opposition between serious and unserious activities – continues to haunt our understanding of play.[31] Yet the dichotomy is not always clear cut. A jazz trumpeter, for example, plays a melody on and around a beat, quotes other melodies and improvises freely in a serious musical performance. Such an example highlights Huizinga's "rationalist view according to which human activities relate, on the one hand, to dreams, gratuitousness, nobility, imagination, etc. and on the other to consciousness, utility, instinct, reality …".[32] With these loaded terms, "reality" serves as the primary means of understanding the world, while play is relegated to a secondary role. More than this, play guarantees the serious, rational norms of daily life.

Huizinga also separated play from profit, material interest and economic exchange. But play is never "free expenditure", as it consumes time, energy and materials. Play is never separate from such expenditure and "cannot therefore be isolated as an activity without consequences. Its integrity, its gratuitousness are only apparent, since the very freedom of the expenditure made in it is part of a circuit which reaches beyond the spatial and temporal limits of play."[33] In the LEGO store, play's gratuitousness and frivolity are only superficial. Play is not separate from economic activities but coextensive with them. Customers within the LEGO store can revel in its otherworldly narratives and playfulness, but LEGO is founded on plastic bricks and aims to sell ever more boxes of them.

Within the store, moments of "free play" still exist. The classic brick table I described at the beginning of this chapter invites the customer to play without a script, an endpoint or reference to any media narratives. Here, LEGO designed a place for customer improvisation, a space in which to indulge in the fundamental level of construction play. Yet this is the least popular in-store site. More spectacular sites are LEGO designed spaces for digital-physical hybrids such as the Brick Lab. These fluid play spaces, combined with the virtual worlds of Star Wars characters and Marvel superheroes comprise the LEGO universe: a twenty-first-century play space.

For children who have grown up in a digital era, play is characterized by both this fluidity between physical and virtual realms, and a fundamental remix aesthetic. Games study theorist Seth Giddings argues children today play differently from those of the past:

> Children's imaginative play has a powerful gravitational pull, dragging all manner of physical objects and symbolic material into the orbit of any particular game or event of play. As well as the interconnected playspaces of the virtual and actual, videogame characters and actions join other media images, everyday and familiar scenarios and stories and songs from the oral folklore of childhood itself. All of these are gathered together, broken up, reassembled and synthesized …[34]

Giddings' definition could almost be a description of the LEGO store. His final point about the method of play – gathering, breaking up and reassembling physical and virtual materials – equally applies to LEGO play. This practice is also known as *bricolage*.

Coined by French anthropologist Claude Lévi-Strauss, *bricolage* loosely translates to "do it yourself", an improvised practice using materials at hand.[35] In media studies, "bricolage" is often used interchangeably with "remix" or "mash-up" to describe how users combine separate media materials to create a new whole with a new meaning.[36] In cultural studies, bricolage describes "the remixing, reconstructing and re-using of separate artifacts, actions, ideas, signs, symbols and styles in order to create new insights or meanings".[37] This approach permeates a range of twenty-first-century digital practices – from memes to TikTok videos – in which people cut, copy, paste, edit and publish text and images.

Importantly, Lévi-Strauss argued that bricolage was an implicit, coherent system of communication between physical things and "magical" systems that "are capable of infinite extension because basic elements can be used in a variety of improvised combinations to generate new meanings with them".[38] So too LEGO's flexible system allows for improvised combinations, mixing bricks from different sets to create new castles, spaceships, creatures or cities that bear no relation to original box sets. This is also a useful way to understand the LEGO store's juxtaposition of scales, characters and narratives, too, with the system containing both physical and narrative components. Yet Levi-Strauss also claimed that bricolage had a limited repertoire: societies combine and recombine cultural elements, symbols and ideas into recurring structures or patterns: bricolage reinforces cultural norms.

In this sense, bricolage should not be conflated with unlimited creativity: play is limited to the materials at hand. For LEGO, this means keeping play within the bounds of the LEGO universe and the rules of its borrowed fictional worlds. Darth Vader fights with a lightsaber, not Thor's hammer, and he is always an "evil" character. The LEGO store reinforces the limits of play as well as the limits of the LEGO style (as per the Apple store and the Apple style): the aesthetic style of bricks and minifigures are strictly circumscribed. Finally, in the LEGO universe, play, imagination and creativity are colourful, bright and glossy, never dirty, messy or dark.

More generally, the late twentieth-century shift to cultural postmodernism reconceived common sense ideas about play. Postmodern culture, as a challenge to the rational, utilitarian ideals of modernism, refocused play as a central activity, with a renewed interest in bricolage, remixing and pastiche. Fredric Jameson, for example, described postmodern culture in terms of its aesthetic recycling: "the imitation of a peculiar or unique, idiosyncratic style, the wearing of a linguistic mask, speech in a dead language".[39] Jameson characterized postmodern culture as one abounding with references and quotations.

He described Star Wars, for example, as "a complex object in which on some first level children and adolescents can take the adventures straight, while the adult public is able to gratify a deeper and more properly nostalgic desire to return to that older period and to live its strange old aesthetic artifacts through once again".[40] When I saw *Star Wars* in 1979, I saw a science fiction film set in a galaxy far far away, inhabited by aliens and spaceship pilots. When my father saw it, he saw a film that recycled the cowboys, swashbuckling pirates and Second World War fighter battles of his childhood. This double-coding – and cross-generational appeal – is fundamental to LEGO's ongoing success.

LEGO's "fluid play", despite its cross-over into the virtual realm, is inextricably linked to physical toys. While toys are ancient, their modern mass-produced versions developed from the broader development of consumer culture from the mid-nineteenth century when children were recognized as a separate market. Toys were initially associated with middle-class domestic life, indoor spaces and safe play. Early wooden and metal toys – such as Ole's original duck-pull toy – linked children's creativity and imagination. But they also reinforced gender distinctions and aspirations to model the adult world. For Roland Barthes, writing in the 1950s, "… toys *literally* prefigure the world of adult functions".[41]

Intrinsically, the toy is cueing for an inner world of play, a parallel world that exists only through play. Dolls, toy cars and construction sets foster the creation of an intrinsic, object-centric context that emanates from the toy itself. In this way,

> A toy is both a cultural object that performs a function in the ecology of play and a device created to perform that function. Toys are defined by their cultural and technical dimensions: the toy as expression and the toy as a thing.[42]

Toys excel when they are ambiguous, open for numerous possibilities and interpretations with which children (or adults) can construct stories, scenarios or worlds.

LEGO's narrative shift in the 1970s arose with a new concept of play and the role of toys within play:

> Rather than offering wholesome imagery of children engaged in quiet play, company designers now presented the toys *themselves* as the actors and agents of playtime; packaging and catalogs showed buildings, vehicles, and minifigures in tableaux of frozen action.[43]

This accelerated with LEGO's licensing of Star Wars and other media franchises in the early twenty-first century. LEGO's shift from a construction system to integrated cross-marketing with films, video games and associated merchandizing ultimately proved profitable. Did the shift from an open construction system of bricks without a script to a "mediatized" set with an instruction manual and existing narrative ultimately limit children's imaginations? Not according to LEGO.

For LEGO, twenty-first-century play occurs across physical and virtual boundaries, combining physical brick play with digital gaming and screen-time consumption in a concept it refers to as "Fluid Play":

> Play has been reimagined as a dynamic, overlapping, frictionless experience that brings the real world, imaginary play and digital experiences together as one.

> In uniting these play worlds across time and space, children today are mastering the art of finding new moments and forms of play. In this report, we call this "fluid play".[44]

Integrating the physical and digital was one of LEGO's goals for decades. Their work with researchers from the MIT Media Lab, for example, resulted in the launch of Technics in 1982 and Mindstorms in 1998. The first focused on building robotic toys, the latter on fictional world building. Both also associate LEGO play with education, particularly STEM learning.[45]

Unlike Huizinga, LEGO play actively encourages transgressions, the store epitomizing LEGO's method of remixing historical and contemporary scenes, fictional and real, and digital and physical. Going off-script, remixing and reuse are fundamental in this play mode:

> Play is also an activity in tension between creation and destruction. Play is always dangerous, dabbling with risks, creating and destroying, and keeping a careful balance between both. Play is between the rational pleasures of order and creation and the sweeping euphoria of destruction and rebirth, between the Apollonian and the Dionysiac.[46]

LEGO's version of play exemplifies this tension – the desire to create and then destroy, a passion for order and a passion for subverting order. LEGO play allows children to be disruptive – or destructive – but within the boundaries circumscribed by the LEGO universe.

LEGO play has several other distinctive characteristics. LEGO is associated with quiet, safe indoor play (year-round, not weather-dependent). LEGO play is also ideally suited to individual play as it does not require a group (as in a sport or board game). Historically, play

> has been a collective activity. But in modern societies, which require massive amounts of individualized symbolic skill from their members, habituating children to solitary preoccupations has been a primary function of toys.[47]

This solitary aspect of LEGO play is reinforced in the store's multiple sets that target specific ages, interests and genders. For a family or a group of friends, one box is never enough as LEGO caters to individual identities and desires.

For LEGO, creativity is tied to assembling and reassembling existing materials (plastic blocks or pop cultural narratives). Their embedded symbols can be remixed, recontextualized and reused within the LEGO universe. In this way, LEGO is a quintessential postmodern play form that "privileges bricolage as a hybrid experience of mediated material and virtual, analog and digital, object and system".[48] The experience of the LEGO store reflects this mode of fluid play – a space in which Captain America, Thor, a 1960s subway attendant, the Statue of Liberty and an oversized Big Apple can seamlessly coexist.

For adults, now a significant market, the LEGO store contains abundant boxes that enable them to participate in the twenty-first-century version of play. Not only the complex and technical sets such as Technics or the Millennium Falcon, but boxes designed to provoke nostalgia – from a classic Porsche 911 to a model of the *Friends* television series apartment – LEGO offers adults the chance to rebuild childhood memories in brick form. This return to childhood is part of a broader twenty-first-century "rejuvenile" trend, particularly among males, whereby adults collect and play with LEGO toys and watch LEGO films.[49] Imagine Johan Huizinga's surprised look – shock combined with horror – if he could see adults buying LEGO sets for themselves.

The LEGO store highlights the collectable aspect of LEGO box sets. One of Godtfred's founding principles when developing the LEGO system in the 1960s was "extra sets available".[50] In-store, LEGO has organized sets into lines comprised of numbered products, each set carefully catalogued and documented to appeal to the archival instinct of collectors. Additionally, limited-edition sets and minifigures, some available only in certain LEGO stores, highlight scarcity and rarity. These encourage store visits as some limited-edition sets run out soon after their release.

A final aspect of play worth commenting on is its "unserious" or "frivolous" nature. LEGO films and video games are *playful*. They abound with irreverent quips and slapstick scenes. There's something funny about a short, squat minifigure Darth Vadar. Unusual dimensions make evil less threatening, perhaps even cute. The LEGO store's juxtaposition of popular icons and comic book heroes is likewise humorous, playful and not intended to be taken too seriously. But, if we suspend our disbelief for a moment, what is LEGO selling here? The short answer is plastic.

A 2014 Greenpeace campaign drew attention to LEGO's long collaboration with Shell. This partnership began in the 1960s when Shell petrol stations sold LEGO toys, including LEGO-designed Shell petrol station sets, trucks and racing cars.[51] The Greenpeace campaign focused on Shell's drilling in the Arctic and, while it ended LEGO's Shell-branded sets, few critics connect LEGO and environmental issues. Some have drawn attention to LEGO's focus on private automobiles and cars as central to their City playsets as promoting unsustainable futures.[52] With the rise in sustainable consciousness, LEGO have recently – reluctantly – started to address its environmental impact in terms of its production and distribution chains. But not in terms of its raw materials.

LEGO have used the same type of plastic for its bricks since 1963. Though each individual brick is tiny, the scale of LEGO's brick production is staggering. The company produces billions of plastic bricks every year. Consider the energy required to pump the petroleum distillates, synthesize these into ABS and mould the resulting plastic into a brick. ABS is not only a flexible material, but an extremely durable one. In 2020, scientists analysed LEGO bricks collected from an English beach to try to estimate how long a LEGO brick would take to disintegrate in the ocean. Their conclusion – "we estimate residence times in the marine environment on the order of hundreds of years" – with an upper limit of 1,300 years.[53]

Although LEGO regularly publicize its intention to design bricks from alternative plastics or plant-based materials, the results account for only a tiny fraction of their production.[54] Promotional campaigns typically generate goodwill but little in material success, such as an experiment to make bricks from recycled plastic bottles which was shelved in 2023.[55] ABS is still used in 80 per cent of LEGO bricks. The material's durability, strength and stability, the very qualities that make it an ideal toy-making material, also make it an unsustainable one. I guess few customers of the LEGO store reflect on such issues, as its immersive space encourages participation in a playful, fun and creative experience.

Finally, a playful coda. In 2021, LEGO launched LEGO store sets, known as "LEGO LEGO stores". Available in limited editions for the opening of select stores, these sets are designed so customers can build their own LEGO store at home. LEGO's signature playfulness is doubled as customers are offered a miniature stage set of the stage set they're standing in. In the end, the LEGO LEGO store sets also highlight the churn – LEGO consistently makes sales on new products (typically over half of sales in any given year). The abundance of new box sets, the ability to choose your own bricks, and the possibilities to construct and play with physical toys and narratives all generate more sales.

Chapter 4
Lifestyle Assemblage: IKEA

A giant blue box emblazoned with yellow, blocky letters looms in my car's front windscreen. As I drive into the IKEA parking lot, I'm greeted by a sign, "Hej! It's great to see you", and below that, an explanation: "Hej is how we say hello in Swedish." The Swedish flag flutters above the sign. Inside the door, a smiling staff member greets me (in English, though her blue and yellow t-shirt says "Hej!") and offers me a large yellow bag. Determined not to buy anything, I politely decline and step onto the escalator that takes me up into the store. I'm also determined to get through the store quickly. I will fail on both determinations.

At the top of the escalator, I'm enclosed within a series of room sets, as if I've stumbled into a movie studio. "Hey, you look great in this room!" a wall sign says. I see no staff and few customers as the store has only just opened. I sit on a lounge chair, put my feet up and look great. I consider my new room: framed pictures on the wall, a TV cabinet and a skeletal hanging lamp, each with a prominent price tag (Figure 19). From this angle, I can see through the window. Silver and orange pipes run across the ceiling, reminding me that I'm not in a lounge room but a giant warehouse.

Arrows on the floor lead me on a winding path through more lounge rooms, bedrooms and home studies. In couples or families, fellow customers stop in a set, distractedly open a cupboard or finger a fabric as they discuss dimensions and options. Open sections follow each room set collection. These display chairs or sofas in an assortment of colours, forms, and materials. The choice is overwhelming. Large yellow signs with "Great Products for Less than $10" above bins full of bargains remind me of the low prices.

As in a casino, this part of the IKEA store contains no windows. I lose track of time in an interior world of fantasy home sets. There's a "Skip the Line and Save Time" station with IKEA's famous tiny pencils, pads and instructions on how to use the IKEA app, which can be downloaded from a QR code projected onto the floor (Figure 20). I stop at a bench with a computer to design a cupboard. A simple programme lets me to add or subtract components, change finishes and position my final assemblage in a virtual room on screen.

I step inside the bedroom of "Kim and James from Brunswick" and a sign explains how an IKEA consultant "solved their home furnishing problems, bringing their dreams to life". The young couple left a tray with a coffee maker

Figure 19 IKEA Richmond, Melbourne, a view of the ceiling. Author photo.

Figure 20 IKEA Richmond, Melbourne, QR code. Author photo.

Figure 21 IKEA Richmond, Melbourne, everyday activities. Author photo.

and cups on the bed, all with prominent price tags. I walk through the kitchen of "Nathan and Jo, the home baking heroes", sit down at the kitchen table of "Shirley, the storage superstar" and watch a video of Shirley explaining how an IKEA consultant helped organize her kitchen. Such lifestyle imagery recurs with a series of photos displaying everyday activities – cooking, making coffee – with the tools to do these activities waiting on shelves below (Figure 21).

Among the room sets filled with blonde timber and muted fabrics, one stands out: "Let Nature In". Below these words sit three plastic plants. Is this a metaphor? Large green signs highlighting IKEA's sustainability appear repeatedly throughout the store. Ironically, in one section, signs that reassure me of IKEA's commitment to "sustainable solutions for everyday life" and "responsibly sourced wood", appear beside a display of plastic flowers (Figure 22).

Though I spoke to no staff on my journey, I had many interactions. I read signs that offered me decorating tips, as well as personal addresses such as "build a combination that fits exactly your needs", and reminders of IKEA's low prices. Three signs featured designer profiles with short explanations of their inspiration for a particular chair or table. Of the three designer profiles I read, two were Swedish. Strangely, the third profile, for Friso Wiersma, contained no biographical notes so I Google him. He's a Dutch designer based in Amsterdam.

By the time I reach the children's furniture, I'm dazed, overwhelmed and over-stimulated. I push on through and arrive – thankfully – at the cafeteria-style "Swedish Restaurant". I pick up a tray with the word "Hej" on it, and take a cinnamon bun and a coffee cup, pay, then fill my cup at the self-service station. I sit down on an IKEA chair at an IKEA table and look around. A large poster

Figure 22 IKEA Richmond, Melbourne, Responsibly Sourced Wood. Author photo.

Figure 23 IKEA Richmond, Melbourne, abundant choice. Author photo.

on one wall, an aerial photograph of Stockholm, reinforces the Swedish-ness. Customers eat meatballs with mashed potatoes and broccoli. When I'm done, I return the tray to a conveyor belt that disappears into the wall. Energized, I descend into the Marketplace. Here, I'm faced with towers of containers, piles of plates, lines of glasses, cutlery and kitchen implements: an abundance of irresistible items (Figure 23).

Finally, I reach the Warehouse. It's a huge space with towering rows of metal shelving filled with cardboard flat packs. In front of one row sits a display of IKEA's famous Pöang bentwood chair, three assembled chairs with throw rugs draped over each one (Figure 24). Below it sits a stack of cardboard boxes – unassembled Pöangs – ready to put on a trolley. The check-outs are mostly self-service so customers can scan the flat packs themselves. A small store

Figure 24 IKEA Richmond, Melbourne, Pöang chairs in the Warehouse. Author photo.

outside the checkout sells Swedish-themed food and I buy meatballs – made in Australia – a powdered gravy sachet – made in Hungary – and a jar of lingonberry sauce – at last, something made in Sweden.

IKEA is a giant global corporation with many facets, but two aspects – refined over the past six decades – are central to IKEA's retail experience. First, the imaging of domestic life. "Lifestyle" describes how IKEA encapsulates the domestic realm through room sets, products, photos and videos. Second, "assemblage" describes how customers actively participate in the IKEA experience, from interaction in the store, self-service and self-assembling furniture to ongoing digital engagement. But before addressing these two, a brief history will outline its origins and help explain IKEA's insistent Swedish-ness.

A Short History of IKEA

Ingvar Kamprad founded IKEA in the southern Swedish province of Småland in 1943. He composed the name from his name's first two letters (I and K), plus Elmtaryd, his family's farm, and Agunnaryd, a nearby village. This intimate bond between founder, place and company not only defined IKEA's early development but also established myths still used in the company's branding today. A teenaged Kamprad began by importing small products – fountain pens from England, cigarette lighters from Switzerland and ballpoint pens from Hungary – at wholesale prices and sold them locally and by mail order.[1] His 1950 mail order catalogue featured neckties, razors, pens, pipes and bags, as well as furniture.[2]

While furniture had mail-order potential, Kamprad understood that, unlike pens or lighters, customers wanted to physically interact with furniture: it represented not only a larger investment but also a more personal and intimate expression of themselves. So, in 1953, he designed his first furniture exhibition in the Småland village of Älmhult. According to Kamprad, this was the prototype for the IKEA model: "first and foremost, use a catalogue to tempt people to come to an exhibition, which today is our store".[3] Yet he also appreciated that most of his customers needed to travel to rural Älmhult, so sold them coffee and buns as part of the shopping experience. This was the roots of today's "Swedish Restaurant".

Buoyed by his initial success, Kamprad opened the first purpose-built IKEA store in Älmhult in 1958. Designed by Swedish architect Claes Knutson, the store was a white, boxy, concrete building that stood four floors high. Inside, Kamprad displayed furniture in home-like tableaux. Customers, tempted by the catalogue's modest prices, would drive to the store, lounge on a sofa in a living room set and envisage it in their home. An IKEA restaurant, generous parking facilities and a nearby hotel helped shift the perception of furniture shopping from a necessary (and potentially stressful) activity to a pleasurable one. Kamprad even promoted the store as a family-friendly, tourist destination.

The earliest IKEA range comprised inexpensive chairs, sofas, tables, bookcases, lamps and cupboards. An often-repeated myth that IKEA invented furniture for self-assembly is untrue. Stockholm's premier department store, Nordiska Kompaniet (the Nordic Company, or NK), had developed a line of "knock-down" furniture as early as 1943.[4] But IKEA certainly popularized the practice in the late 1950s. Flat-packed furniture made shipping easier, reduced transit damage and lowered prices. Although Kamprad hired designers in the mid-1950s, including Gillis Lundgren and Danish architect Erik Wørts (who had helped design the "knock-down" furniture at NK), IKEA's furniture was neither innovative nor original. Whether he sold copies of popular Nordic pieces or locally made originals was irrelevant – affordability was Kamprad's focus.

In fact, Kamprad's low prices provoked the Swedish furniture trade organization to lead a supplier boycott against IKEA. Kamprad worked around this, initially sourcing furniture from outside Sweden then producing furniture in Poland (from 1961), at almost half the cost of Swedish production.[5] Swedish-designed, Polish-made furniture, constructed from Polish timber proved a successful strategy and the start of a long-standing relationship. Today, Poland is the second-biggest producer of IKEA furniture (after China) and Polish forests account for 28 per cent of IKEA's timber.[6]

In 1965, Kamprad opened a huge store south of Stockholm, also designed by Knutson. This store, a curved structure inspired by Frank Lloyd Wright's Guggenheim Museum, blurred the boundaries between a furniture showroom and a museum. As at Älmhult, customers encountered a series of living sets containing mass-produced furniture and household objects elevated to art. Art they could interact with. Surrounded by parking, the store proved popular immediately and its 1970 incarnation included a children's playground, another key element in later stores. The store's success coincided with the Swedish government's "Million Programme" (1965–75), a project to build a million affordable dwellings. Affordable dwellings required affordable furniture.

IKEA's 1960s product range comprised a limited aesthetic adopted (or in many cases copied) from traditional and modern Nordic models but manufactured using cheaper methods and materials. The mail-order catalogue remained an essential component and means to tempt customers to visit the store. By visualizing ideal domestic scenes with photographs and text, the IKEA catalogue was both a marketing tool and an inspiration for customers wanting to modernize their lives.[7] In the 1960s, IKEA distributed over two million copies per year. Although IKEA no longer prints a catalogue (the last version was in 2021), at its peak in 2016, it distributed over 200 million copies in thirty-two languages.[8]

Although growth was one of Kamprad's driving forces, IKEA's retail expansion began modestly. He opened stores in Oslo and Copenhagen in the 1960s, Switzerland in 1973 and Germany in 1974. In his 1976 manifesto, *A Testament of a Furniture Dealer*, he wrote:

> We know that we can be a beneficial influence on practically all markets. We know that in the future we will be able to make a valuable contribution to the process of democratisation outside our own homeland too. We know that larger production runs give us new advantages on our home ground, as well as more markets to spread our risks over. That is why it is our duty to expand.[9]

Continuing this evangelical fervour, Kamprad penned IKEA's mission statement, repeated on all corporate communications today: "to create a better everyday life for the many".[10]

Anxious to present himself as one of "the many", Kamprad's media image – "down-to-earth, modest and charmingly unassuming … unbelievably thrifty, jovial, friendly and folksy" – became inseparable from IKEA's.[11] IKEA's furniture was likewise unpretentious and modest, while Kamprad's famed thriftiness (he swapped his Porsche for an old Volvo) could be interpreted by customers as a commitment to keep costs low. Kamprad used this media image and human weaknesses (he claimed to be both dyslexic and alcoholic) as a "smoke screen" to deflect attention from IKEA's business practices.[12]

As IKEA expanded both within and beyond Europe in the 1980s, Kamprad developed a system to ensure all new stores were centrally designed according to standard rules. From that time until today, every new store "is meticulously planned by Inter IKEA which is also responsible for training management and staff, as well as ensuring that the store adheres to the concept which requires following all sorts of regulations and guidelines for running an IKEA store".[13] IKEA became the McDonald's of furniture retail, with a standard store design and product range. From Stockholm to Sydney, customers could buy the same Billy bookshelf and Pöang chair in a similar store for a relatively low price.

Globalization brought further standardization. IKEA's logo, originally with an accent on the "e" (to make it appear French), was redesigned in 1984 in today's familiar blue and yellow.[14] Around this time, IKEA began painting the exterior of stores blue and yellow and standardizing the restaurant and meals (including the famous meatballs) and the product naming system.[15] As it became a global retail empire, Swedish-ness became another smoke screen: IKEA stood for good (that is, Scandinavian) design, egalitarianism and progressive social and political ideals (like Sweden itself).

But as a company, IKEA was no longer Swedish. Kamprad moved IKEA's base to Copenhagen in 1974 and his family to Switzerland two years later, both to avoid paying Swedish taxes. In 1982, Kamprad and his lawyers moved IKEA's headquarters to the Netherlands and designed a network of trusts and shell companies based in Liechtenstein, Luxembourg, Switzerland, the Netherlands, Antilles and Curacao. This complex, opaque corporate structure served both to avoid taxes in IKEA's growing territories and to conceal Kamprad's personal wealth and autocratic control over the IKEA empire.[16]

So close were Kamprad and IKEA intertwined that, upon publication of a 2011 book by Swedish journalist Elisabeth Åsbrink in which she detailed not only his Nazi affiliations but his ongoing admiration for Swedish fascist leader Per Engdahl, the company acted:

> It took a month for Ikea to respond, and when it did it was by way of a $51 million donation to the United Nations High Commissioner on Refugees, the single-largest donation in the agency's history.[17]

Kamprad's image remains central to IKEA's brand. Quotes by Kamprad pepper the website and interviews by senior management even today. The IKEA Museum in Älmhult, the company's history and website repeat myths of Kamprad's Småland origins and struggles "to create a better everyday life for the many people". In this way, customers naturally translate abstract values such as frugality, modesty and practicality into cabinets, sofas and bookcases.

For IKEA, "democratization" would increasingly be associated not with the right to vote or egalitarianism but with consumerism. Kamprad's mission of democratization, first stated in his 1976 manifesto, recurs again and again. Launched in 1995, for example, IKEA's "democratic design" collection comprised supposedly well-designed products that reinforced a long-standing idea in Swedish design – affordability. IKEA's "democratic design" is encapsulated by objects that balance five elements: "function, form, quality, sustainability and low price".[18] Despite the "democratic" rhetoric, IKEA remains a paternal, capitalist enterprise: "democratic" does not refer to an egalitarian management structure (Swedish men have always maintained control of IKEA) nor sharing the wealth with "the many people".

IKEA continued its spectacular global growth into the twenty-first century. The company opened over 150 stores between 2000 and 2009, more than in the previous fifty years, and became the largest furniture retailer in the world. *IKEA: The Book* (2010) and the conversion of the original Älmhult store into a museum in 2016 reinforced IKEA mythologies, while the website and social media posts continue to reproduce Kamprad lore.[19] Although the founder died in 2018, his three sons continue his legacy in leadership roles.[20] The association between IKEA and Sweden remains a reciprocal one: the company reinforces stereotypes of the nation and vice-versa.[21] And Kamprad's "duty to expand" continues to drive IKEA, with its first South American outpost opening in Santiago in 2022.

Lifestyle

In Kamprad's manifesto, he declared that our "product range is our identity" and its coherent aesthetic – both then and today – served to differentiate IKEA from other retail stores.[22] But, though customers encounter a seemingly large range of furniture in-store, each item is categorized within a matrix of only four "styles": Traditional, Scandinavian, Modern and Popular. Products within each style are then divided into four price levels: high, medium, low and BTI (breathtaking item). For the customer, the limited range makes it easier "to mix and match from a coordinated selection when planning a home, than from a selection that has grown at random".[23] IKEA's designers coordinate colours, forms and finishes across the styles so that the entire range works together. In-store, a customer thus encounters what appears to be a large selection of products, but all fall within a limited aesthetic.

Customers associate this aesthetic – IKEA's style – with Sweden. There are two intertwined parts to this: Swedish design and Swedish culture. Unlike Target or Walmart, IKEA is associated with Swedish "design" and scholars have identified many connections between IKEA's borrowings from Swedish or broadly Nordic design cultures.[24] While such accounts are compelling historically, they do little to explain why young urban professionals in Shanghai or Santiago are drawn to IKEA today. If the general customer still automatically connects Swedish, Scandinavian, Nordic and "good" design, this may be due less to widespread design consciousness and more due to IKEA's powerful marketing.

Many Swedish designers worked for IKEA, particularly in the early years. Gillis Lundgren, for example, who designed the Billy bookcase in 1978, was one of Kamprad's first and most long-standing employees. But IKEA also utilized global design expertise from very early on. Japanese designer Noboru Nakamura, for example, designed IKEA's best-selling Pöang chair, launched in 1976 (Figure 24), while Dutch designer Monika Mulder designed the iconic Vållö watering can in 2002.[25] IKEA's "Swedish design", rather than designed by Swedish designers, is distilled into characteristics that have little to do with the designers, the nation or its culture. Customers understand Swedish design as modest, useful, functional products without fussy decoration or ornament.

Yet Swedish branding within the IKEA store is insistent and consistent. The store's repetition of the Swedish flag and its colours, the Swedish-themed food, the Nordic (not just Swedish) names for the furniture, the poster of Stockholm, and the repetition of "Hej" all serve to reinforce IKEA's Swedish-ness.[26] Customers do not encounter neutral furniture but objects covered with a cultural veneer, making the store "a living archive in which values and traits identified as distinctively Swedish are communicated to consumers worldwide".[27] But what are these Swedish values? Beyond "good" design, customers also associate Sweden with political, social and moral values.

According to IKEA, "Folkhemmet, the 'people's home' of the Swedish welfare state is here, and IKEA is furnishing it."[28] Formulated by Swedish Prime Minister Per Albin Hansson in the 1930s, "Folkhemmet" was the vision of a democratic, egalitarian society founded on a close connection between a benevolent state and its people. On the one hand, this represented a liberation from traditional institutions such as church and family, but on the other, a standardization of lifestyles and paternal control of people's lives.[29] By reiterating this idea, IKEA reinforce Swedish-ness as a social and political symbol. IKEA stores continue to reproduce an ideal nation, "perpetuating Sweden's international image as a model democracy".[30]

Sweden's Social Democratic welfare state, aka the "Swedish model", involved a large public sector, high taxes and state provision for housing, education and medical services. But this Swedish model – whether it achieved the Folkhemmet vision or not – was built in the 1950s and 1960s. While IKEA benefited from the large, government-funded public housing programmes, by the time IKEA globalized in the 1980s and 1990s, Swedish politics had changed. Certainly, by the twenty-first century, the Swedish model of the welfare state and progressive democracy was well and truly historical.[31] Yet for IKEA, Swedish exceptionalism – real or fictional – is still a useful brand for a global company devoted to "democratic design" for "the many people".

Importantly, repeating its claims to Swedish-ness erases IKEA's global nature. In-store, a customer receives no information about a Dutch-based corporation, with production facilities in Poland and China that use raw materials drawn from Eastern Europe or Asia. Although the product design team remains in Älmhult, Sweden, other design teams are spread all over the world. Suppliers, contractors, distributors, "these workers' labor is erased from the Showroom floor and from IKEA's organized and progressive archival narrative of ingenious Swedish labor, inscribed via Nordic names".[32] Swedish-ness functions as a smoke screen to distract attention from IKEA's global complexity.

Despite its Swedish-ness, IKEA's style matrix and product range are neutral enough to appeal widely. In-store, customers will find few references to local culture, aesthetics or lifestyles. IKEA's marketing, however, does consider regional or national differences. In the retail stores, over 90 per cent of the sets are determined centrally, thus "protecting the 'Swedishness' of the brand but allowing for a minimal amount of tweaking to suit the local market".[33] Within the room sets and the product range, whatever trace of Swedish-ness remains, European and American customers now understand IKEA as conventional, familiar and modern. Critics have pointed out IKEA's homogenizing effect in interior furnishings across the world.[34] And they are, but with some regional differences.

IKEA in China is an interesting case in this respect. IKEA opened their first stores in Shanghai and Beijing in 1998 and the brand's Chinese popularity grew over the next decade, culminating in the Shanghai Pudong IKEA store in 2011, the world's second largest at that time. Despite a fraction of regional allowances, the range of the Pudong store was the same as in European or American stores, sixty room stages, where a "combination of European design, 'do-it-yourself' (DIY) style, and friendly price has attracted many young professionals and families in trend-setting fashion-leading cities like Shanghai".[35] Yet IKEA in China does not have quite the same connotations as in Europe.

IKEA's Chinese expansion over the first two decades of the twenty-first century related to changing Chinese ideas of consumption, ownership and aspirations to a global, cosmopolitan lifestyle (rather than one associated specifically with Sweden). Using the same furniture range, designers in IKEA's Chinese stores adjusted room sets for typical Chinese apartment sizes and spatial configurations.

They added rooms such as a balcony (often used as a living or storage space), as well as Chinese kitchenware – chopsticks, steamers, and a large range of bowls. Chinese customers had different attitudes towards self-assembly and DIY service culture and the "big box" concept of buying all home furnishings in a single store was also new. Finally, IKEA's low prices in Europe were not so low in China, so the furniture appealed to urban professionals (China's "many people" could not afford IKEA).[36]

Overall, IKEA's product range remains the same with the same four styles across the globe. One of the problems of such a holistic aesthetic is that there is little room left for family heirlooms, decorative objects, thrift shop purchases or antiques – these produce both an aesthetic and moral clash:

> Ikea objects ... only travel in aggressive packs, bent on the total domination of what-ever space they happen upon — and they are generally successful in this venture. Their claims of Scandinavian sensibleness with a touch of fun, of pure functionality, effectively mock the raison d'être of any other decorative object, even the most distinguished.[37]

Here, IKEA fits well with contemporary minimalism and, in design, continues a long history of attacks on ornamentation, decoration and extravagance going back to Adolf Loos' "Ornament and Crime". Simplicity, modesty and practicality – IKEA's aesthetic values – slide easily into moral ones.

As we saw in Chapter 1, recent anxiety around over-consumption, highlighted in the 2010s "Minimalist" trend, finds a parallel in IKEA's simple furniture and thrifty messages. Both target "a kind of enlightened simplicity, a moral message combined with a particularly austere visual style".[38] But the problem of over-consumption is also solved through IKEA's extensive storage solutions. As in the IKEA store, every item within the contemporary home should have its proper place, "a deliberate strategy of normalization of the idea of order and correct organization as fundamental values for an efficient, safe and pleasant domestic life".[39] Ordering is a central anxiety of IKEA's middle-class customers.

Despite its limited aesthetic styles, the IKEA showroom offers a wide range of choices that aim to appeal to my identity and needs. In a society of flexible, adaptable and instantly transformable identities, IKEA offers different veneers, fabric covers, textiles, and the ability to mix and match between ranges. This empowers the customer to feel – if not a designer – at least some creativity in curating their home. Here, the customer's bricolage practice at IKEA parallels that at the LEGO store. But the emphasis is never on singular pieces of furniture but a lifestyle: "IKEA design redefines home space, away from established fixed activities, toward a larger set of social activities which are instantiated and enhanced by the set design."[40]

The IKEA showroom's museum-like quality is curated,

with consistency and coherence, to prompt imaginative immersion and to build up meaning. The spectator's gaze is more like that of a visitor than a buyer at first, as the experience is crafted to capture the attention and interest in understanding and being inspired by possible ways of contemporary furnishing. Moving from one diorama to the other, the product itself is not the protagonist. Rather, the showcase of opportunities to inhabit and the inspirational value they convey is.[41]

Less a repository of functional objects for the home, the IKEA showroom is more an immersive domestic theatre. IKEA kitchens, for example, shifted from practice places to a "lifestyle kitchen" around 2000, moving "away from a functional space to one in which is about social interactions and creativity".[42] Kitchens become entertaining, socializing spaces for friends and family in IKEA's lifestyle imaginary. An IKEA kitchen is represented – in-store and online – as a space of leisure, friendship and family interactions, rather than a space of cooking, cleaning and arguing about whose turn it is to do the dishes.

In the late twentieth century, a customer's first encounter with IKEA lifestyles would have been the catalogue. Now, in the post-catalogue era, IKEA's website and social media feeds fulfil this function. Both feature videos and photographs of families engaged in "everyday rituals" – Sunday morning pancakes (with recipes), communal baking and impromptu dance routines with friends. Reminders of the low prices tempt customers with the idea that IKEA sells the props they need to achieve these desirable scenarios.

In 2023, IKEA appointed photographer Annie Leibovitz as its first "Artist in Residence". The company announced that for the IKEA *Life at Home Report* "she will travel around the world, photographing people in their homes in seven different countries: Japan, the United States, Germany, Italy, India, Sweden, and England. She will create a series of 25 portraits that illuminate the nuances of 'life at home', creating a powerful photographic document inspired by the Life at Home Report."[43] The latter, IKEA's annual research report, began in 2014 as a way for IKEA to better understand customer needs. Leibovitz's ability to expose the intimacy of her subjects and their inner lives will focus equally on their homes.

The Consequences of Lifestyle

One aspect of IKEA's lifestyle emphasis worth scrutinizing is its relation to sustainability. Kamprad, obsessed only with achieving the lowest prices for labour, production, distribution and raw materials, had no time for "tree huggers". Yet IKEA maintained a "Teflon" corporate reputation according to one former employee, partially by using thousands of suppliers and subcontractors, but also through donations and ongoing projects with NGOs such as Greenpeace and WWF. He described these as a "shield of bought and muzzled NGOs and a handful of others equally-bought charity projects that IKEA can wheel out if a media tornado is on the horizon".[44] These include projects such as a rainforest regeneration programme in Indonesia, which clearly fits with a company that uses so much timber.

In smoke-screen style, IKEA highlight projects it wants customers to see – from "responsibly sourced wood" to forest regeneration projects and solar panels on store roofs – and avoids mentioning its insatiable appetite for timber and plastics. In terms of sustainability, IKEA is "a significant agent of a twofold subtle cultural commitment to the *removal* and *negation* of key elements in the political consciousness of the many".[45] Specifically, its use of global labour disparities and the exploitation of natural resources. An IKEA customer has no possibility of collective action to change production or consumption practices, only to buy more and cheaper furniture. IKEA's churn of new products is evidence of this. While IKEA produces over ten thousand products overall, it introduces over two thousand *new* products every year.[46]

IKEA's opaque corporate structure and global supply chains also serve as a sustainability smoke screen. Despite this, news of its material consumption appears in the media occasionally. With the demise of Soviet regimes in Eastern Europe after 1989, the forests of Poland, Russia and Romania represented a gold mine for IKEA. The Carpathian Mountains, which run through these countries, remain home to over half of Europe's old-growth forests. In 2015, IKEA began buying forests in Romania, purchasing so much land that it became "Romania's largest private landowner".[47] Still, illegal logging, threats and violence towards environmental activists remain at arm's length from IKEA. Although a customer cannot trace the exact lineage of any given piece of IKEA furniture, old-growth Romanian forests are ground down into particle board for Billy bookshelves. Prior to the 2022 Russian invasion, IKEA also devoured forests in the Ukrainian Carpathian Mountains, Belarus and Siberia.[48]

IKEA's obsession with low costs has led some critics to refer to their furniture as "fast furniture" designed for short-term use and disposal. Particle board and veneers are not durable materials designed to last a lifetime but designed for a mobile customer who will move many times and modernize their lifestyle regularly. As with Apple's products, IKEA furniture is not designed with repair or recycling in mind. The resin that holds together particleboard, plastic laminates and connections make repair and recycling too complex and too costly. This is by design. IKEA's churn of new products encourages customers to continually upgrade, resulting in furniture conceived as a throwaway commodity.

While precise furniture recycling figures for IKEA furniture are difficult to find, an United States EPA report from 2018 on durable goods recycling stated that 80 per cent of household goods ended up in landfill.[49] The Covid-19 pandemic boosted furniture and home-ware sales and the affordability of IKEA furniture –

at least in certain markets – lent it the feel of disposability.[50] Finally, even the most efficient process and supply chains cannot account for the distances IKEA furniture covers – my Billy bookshelf began in a Romanian forest, was prepared in a Polish factory and shipped in a flatpack to Australia via ships and trucks: every step increased its carbon footprint.

Assemblage

Assemblage is the other key component to the IKEA experience. Customer participation – physical and digital – keeps customers engaged and helps establish a long-term relationship with the company. This occurs on several levels. Physically, customers serve themselves in-store, choosing within the home sets, finding their own flat packs in the warehouse and taking it home. Psychologically, customers develop emotional connections – from frustration to satisfaction to accomplishment – by assembling their IKEA products. Digitally, social media, advertising and the IKEA app further encourage engagement and co-creation.

By simply picking up a big blue and yellow bag at the store's entrance, you are participating. You have an empty bag to fill. Undisturbed by hard-selling staff, you wander freely through the room sets. Yet IKEA's designers have composed a series of psychological and emotional interactions. A former manager described how he, "spent hours, days, discussing whether … a sofa in the compact by the entrance should meet the flow of customers at an angle of 45 or 60 degrees".[51] Anticipating every view and touch, IKEA presents you with finished room sets to inhabit followed by open areas that contain their full range of colours, surfaces and price points. You feel inspired by stylish ensembles and then empowered by choice.

The store's layout is a journey. No stretch of the grey path is more than 15 metres (50 feet) without a bend. Each bend guides your vision onto strategically placed bins filled with the latest "hot item". IKEA store designers map "hot" and "cold" areas, matching best-selling items with hot spots. This seduction is detailed and well-developed, as "IKEA has consistently followed the basic principles about hot and cold areas, about bins, compacts and room sets in their stores for many years".[52] Two interactions on the journey stand out. First, the constant reminder of low prices, which leads customers to think everything in store is cheap. Second, the repeated signs such as, "Hey, you look great in this room", that hail each customer personally.

Over decades, customers have been trained to grab a bag and fill it, grab a trolley at the end, get their own flat pack and assemble the furniture themselves. Reflecting on the newly rebuilt Stockholm store in the early 1970s, Kamprad noted:

Self-service, numerous and efficient checkouts in the exit area, and a decrease in order sales provide a formidable boost to profitability and turnover. The customer took over what was perhaps the weightiest element in all furniture sales: delivery and unpacking.[53]

Refined over the decades since then, Kamprad's self-service model now includes self-checkouts. Self-service not only reduces staff costs but, importantly, invests customers more in the shopping experience. That is, you feel empowered by choice then determined to take and make your own furniture.

Even though the IKEA experience is personal for each customer, it is also social. IKEA stores are rarely empty. While I sat on a couch, lay on a bed or let my imagination drift in a room set, I also witnessed others doing these activities. In this sense, the showroom

> ... provides an interactive space for the consultation, browsing, and occasional keen awareness of other domestic arrangements, other people, other couples, and families. Instead of a presentation of how one would really like to be, the warehouse experience reiterates collective domestic endeavor, through which one must negotiate a unique presence.[54]

In what appears to be a warehouse full of almost unlimited choices, customers pick and choose from IKEA's limited aesthetic styles, creating a sense of order not only for themselves but a sense of social belonging. An IKEA showroom is also a means to train customers in patterns of domestic behaviour. Who doesn't want to drink coffee in bed like "Kim and James from Brunswick" and organize their chaotic kitchen like "Shirley, the storage superstar"?

Assembling furniture at home contributes to the IKEA experience. For some customers, this can be a frustrating struggle with tiny screws and Allen keys, but a finished piece typically evokes satisfaction or achievement. Although IKEA furniture lacks the emotional attachment that accrues over time (such as family heirlooms or antiques), it offers instant attachment.[55] Researchers refer to the "IKEA Effect" to describe the "the increased valuation people have for self-assembled products compared to objectively similar products which they did not assemble".[56] For customers, the participatory experience of co-creating furniture involves an investment of time and labour into an otherwise neutral chair or bookshelf.

For a generation who grew up without skills in making and repairing things (as their parents or grandparents did), a chance to build something is compelling. Even though assembling IKEA furniture is an easy physical, spatial and conceptual challenge, it does represent a rare chance to make something useful, particularly for customers whose work and leisure time is spent interacting with digital screens. But, for those customers too frustrated by the assembly experience or too time-poor, IKEA can organize someone to assemble it for you. In 2017, IKEA even bought the online "handyman" service TaskRabbit, as building IKEA furniture was a particularly popular job request on the platform.[57]

Assembling and arranging furniture also contributes to a sense of customer involvement, achievement and control over their living spaces. Importantly, IKEA products shift the customer's position from that of a passive recipient of mass-produced goods to an active producer. The physical time and effort required and the tactile engagement with every piece of particleboard and every screw, helps engender a sense of ownership and affection. But, while transforming a cardboard box filled with particleboard and screws into a bookshelf may engender positive feelings in me, for visitors to my home, it is just another bookshelf.

Self-assembly also contributes to the idea that my labour helps offset the cost. That is, my labour is contributing to making this product cheaper. In design terms, this has been described as a "prosumer", whereby the designer cedes some productive power to the consumer and "veers toward mere flattery, companies convincing individuals that their manual labor is worth something in an effort to sell products".[58] The customer's physical engagement with the product produces not only a feeling of mastery and control but an opportunity to exert a little manual labour in a digital world devoted to seamless efficiency.

From the store's entrance to assembling products at home, customers play an active role in the IKEA experience. Self-service extends to choosing for myself (rather than taking advice from salespersons), pencils and paper for noting down dimensions, picking up boxes, transporting them home and deciphering the instructions to create the final product. At every point, the customer actively participates. And within the final part of this process, IKEA has trained their customers in putting together furniture with an Allen key or a screwdriver. This is what marketers refer to as the "co-creation" of value, whereby customers actively contribute to their experience.[59]

But if the IKEA experience is designed as a collaborative one between the customer and IKEA, it includes a tacit suspension of disbelief. If the customer's project is to assemble a piece of modern furniture infused with Swedish style, any designer ideals are dispelled when assembly begins:

> IKEA customers are under no illusion that the slabs of compressed sawdust and glue they schlep home and put together themselves is bespoke Scandinavian furniture, or otherwise unique in any way. In the spirit of true fetishistic disavowal, they know perfectly well, yet this knowledge does nothing to quell their desire.[60]

This is an interesting phenomenon. Although customers know these are cheap materials (particleboard covered in plastic veneer) and know their construction is shaky, they actively participate in creating something that *looks* modern and stylish.

While self-service and self-assembly are an essential part of the IKEA experience, even before customers get to the store, they have probably encountered IKEA online. Digital participation is another part of the IKEA experience. In the past, the IKEA catalogue was the main means of spreading the word, but this was gradually replaced by digital marketing in the 2010s. After 2021, the final year of the catalogue, IKEA's marketing channels include not only its website, but also social media, digital advertising and the IKEA app. More than simply aids to reinforce the messages of the physical store, IKEA use digital platforms to interact with customers and potential customers.

Pinterest, for example, proved a perfect social media platform for IKEA. People use the site as a kind of digital scrapbook to post inspiring photographs. Here, IKEA's room sets fit with the latest aspirational hairstyles, fashion and wedding photos. But IKEA's strategy involves interaction as well as advertising. For example, I did a chatbot quiz, "Travel A.I. Gent", on Pinterest, which involved a cartoon character who posed questions about my favourite holiday destination and activities. At the end of the quiz, I got a Pinterest board of related product recommendations, such as beach-themed IKEA furniture.[61] If I cannot afford a vacation, perhaps I can afford to redecorate – a "renocation"?

On Instagram, also primarily visual, IKEA's feed features clickable photographs of room sets that link to products and prices. But IKEA's images and videos do not focus primarily on single products but events, celebrations or occasions. These occur within domestic spaces, with titles such as "Holiday Hosting Guide: Extra seating for guests", or "Quick IKEA tips for a perfect holiday bash". This way, customers are encouraged to see IKEA furniture as essential props to create memorable social experiences. IKEA's constantly changing content aligns with current seasons, holidays or events – and thus needs to be national or regional rather than global. IKEA also encourages customers to take photos of their IKEA furniture and share it, engaging in an ongoing conversation about their home.

In 2017, IKEA (in collaboration with Apple) launched its Place smartphone app, an augmented reality (AR) app that allows customers to virtually "place" IKEA furniture in their homes. Users can superimpose 3D renderings of IKEA furniture onto photos of their home. IKEA's catalogue of photo-realistic renderings includes over two thousand products. Users scan a room of their homes, browse IKEA products then place one in their virtual room. At the time it was launched, the Place app replicated the experience of the popular AR game Pokémon Go (launched in 2016) – so, for a generation used to playing such games, AR makes shopping fun.[62]

Since then, IKEA has updated the Place app and added more sophisticated AR apps, most recently, IKEA Studio. Using this app, customers can take a picture of their room and digitally erase their own furniture and replace it with an IKEA piece. But such apps have never quite lived up to the hype. Some studies have shown, for example, that "the AR condition outperforms the web condition regarding the effects on immersion and enjoyment". That is, AR apps rate highly among customers for novelty and fun, but poorly for information (cost, materials and specifications).[63]

During the pandemic, IKEA shifted online by offering click and collect services, video consultations and live streams on Instagram. IKEA's latest app aims to offer customers relief from the anxiety of choice by using an algorithm:

> This software enables users to photograph an interior, place IKEA furniture to scale in the framed digital reality and receive furnishing advice from an algorithm. The app aims to bridge the so-called "imagination gap" by "delegating" decisions from the prospective user to the algorithm.[64]

Such digital interactions aim to further personalize furniture choices and create specific ensembles – composed of IKEA furniture – for individual homes.

In 2021, IKEA launched an AI chatbot called "Billie" that began taking half of its customer calls. Anxious to allay the idea that this was replacing human workers with robots, IKEA announced they retrained 8,500 workers to work as "interior design advisors". Post-pandemic, this remote interior decoration advice (via video) suggests that IKEA's virtual sales channels are growing.[65] This constitutes another aspect of co-creation that was repeated in the store I visited at the beginning (remember "Shirley, the storage superstar"?): IKEA offers consultation services which promise personalized co-constructed plans and purchases.

If following the instructions to assemble a piece of IKEA furniture involves the customer in a kind of co-design process, some customers take this further by designing "hybrid" IKEA pieces or monstrous products that combine IKEA pieces with found objects. This practice, known as "IKEA hacking", parallels that of LEGO users who build and share their own "off-script", remixed creations. Spread by chatrooms and blogs, a subculture devoted to IKEA "hacking" grew in the 2000s. One of the most popular sites documenting this activity, IKEAhackers.net, started in 2006 by Jules Yap, began as a forum for hackers to post pictures, videos and instructions.

For some time, IKEA tolerated such hacking websites, but in 2014 the company began lawsuits, including one against Yap's site. After bad publicity among IKEA fans, the company reversed course to allow "hacking" sites. From IKEA's perspective, hackers still buy IKEA furniture. While some portray hacking as subversive and linked to a broader contemporary crafting culture, a better description of IKEA hacking is "a kind of material fan fiction, augmenting, distorting, and often talking back to the original text".[66] As with LEGO, IKEA's standardization – consistent measurements, screw types, ready-made holes and the same materials – makes mixing and matching possible.

These two aspects of IKEA – lifestyle and assemblage – combine to create a compelling retail experience, refined by IKEA over the past six decades. Global in scope, the IKEA store offers an ideal domestic lifestyle. Despite the Swedish branding, the material components are global, the long supply chains difficult to trace and the company's complex and opaque structure remain distanced from customers in-store. In design terms, the flexibility of the IKEA system (like LEGO's) was a significant design innovation, particularly in its ability to allow customers to mix and match many pieces within a coherent aesthetic. But in the twenty-first century, IKEA have extended their active participation to include digital offerings that integrate virtual IKEA with the physical store.

Chapter 5
Performance and Innovation: Nike

Fifth Avenue's reputation as New York's hub of discrete, elite stores – think Tiffany, Saks and Bergdorf Goodman – is largely gone. Today, LEGO, Zara and Banana Republic attract a very different clientele. These new brands have, for the most part, fitted new stores within Fifth Avenue's early twentieth-century streetscape. Nike's House of Innovation stands out. Opened in 2018, the six-storey building features a gridded façade comprised of dark, "carved and slumped" glass, patterned with parallel lines (Figure 25).[1] These lines and the sliced angle of the entrance repeat the angle of the prominent white "swoosh" logo on Fifth Avenue. On the street level, a digital screen envelops pedestrians with Nike ads and slogans.

As I step in, I'm hit with a sensory barrage: loud hip-hop, fast-changing images on digital screens, Nike logos and the latest slogan, "Feel Your All" scroll along digital LED strips (Figure 26). Videos feature women doing yoga poses, kickboxing and stretching in their Nike Zenvy leggings made from "Infinalock™ fabric". The leggings appear on mannequins, on silver racks highlighted by fluorescent tubes, and stretched out like a hide so I can feel the "buttery softness". Prominent iPads invite me to scan a QR code to get further information on sizes, colours and styles and download the Nike App (Figure 27). The security guard tells me that this opening space changes regularly depending on the season, sporting events or new product launches. This week, opposite the leggings, there's a heat-sensing installation with a tenuous link to the new fabric. Children jump around in it, interacting with their colourful shadows.

After trying to take it all in, I ride the elevator to Level 5, "Nike By You". At the top, I'm greeted by a wall slogan: "Choose, design, create – come make it your own". It's calmer up here. On this floor, customers can customize their new Nike shirt or sneakers by choosing a transfer or sew-on badge from a glass case. Behind the case, staff wait in a white, tiled, lab-like space with a row of machines to apply these additions while you wait (Figure 28). The transfers and badges are both Nike and New York-related – "Just Do It" on a classic New York paper coffee cup, for example, "Nike" on a pizza slice, or various combinations of "NYC" and the swoosh. Staff mill around, offering customers design advice.

Figure 25 Nike's House of Innovation, New York, exterior. Author photo.

I walk downstairs to Level 4, the Sneakerlab. The heart of the store, this level contains the largest range of seasonal Nike shoes in the world. Single shoes are displayed within a white modular box system. On plastic pedestals or thin metallic ones, they appear to be floating on air (Figure 29). Diagrams beside some shoes detail their features and materials. "Nike Air Zoom Tempo Next %" reads one, "the next generation of fast". Subtle, black and white graphics in the background seem to be archival photos of athletes in action. I ask a staff member – an "athlete" in Nike terminology – if they are famous. He shrugs.

Level 3, the Men's Store, is noticeably dimmer. Its low, black ceilings and dark stone floor suggest a "man cave". Neon strips and spotlights highlight the main clothing sections: basketball, workout and streetwear. Mannequins stand in active poses on colourful stands that echo the heat-sensing installation on Level

Performance and Innovation: Nike

Figure 26 Nike's House of Innovation, New York, new leggings display. Author photo.

1. It's an open space with racks of clothes hanging from the ceiling on black belts with white swooshes. The displays change every month or so, an athlete tells me, as new products appear or the seasons change. "Feel Your All" is stencilled onto the floor, alongside tape with the words "House of Innovation NYC000". There are QR codes everywhere.

In contrast, the Women's Store on Level 2 has high, white ceilings and pale floor tiles. The space is lighter and brighter, and features mainly workout and streetwear. Strangely, there's no basketball wear here, even though Nike is a sponsor of the WNBA, nor soccer wear, even though Nike is a sponsor of the National Women's Soccer League. As in the Men's Store, mannequins stand in active poses on colourful stands and large hanging posters feature images of women twisting in yoga poses or frozen mid-stride. A glass case displays a

Figure 27 Nike's House of Innovation, New York, digital interaction. Author photo.

Nike-Apple collaboration: Apple Watches with a swoosh and "Just Do It" band, a QR code and the slogan "Let's Run Together" (Figure 30).

Finally, the basement level contains Nike's children's collection. This level is a lot smaller than the previous ones, with smaller mannequins arranged in active poses like future athletes. As I walk back up the stairs and out on the first level, I realize what's missing: celebrities. I expected to see images of current Nike-sponsored sports stars such as Lebron James, Naomi Osaka or Cristiano Ronaldo. Or photos of older stars such as Tiger Woods or Serena Williams. At the very least, I expected to see Michael Jordan somewhere. Celebrity athletes aren't the focus. I'm a little puzzled. What is Nike's House of Innovation about?

New York's "House of Innovation 000" replaced Nike's previous Fifth Avenue flagship store, Niketown, and similar stores opened in Shanghai (House of

Figure 28 Nike's House of Innovation, New York, Nike By You. Author photo.

Innovation 001, 2018) and Paris (House of Innovation 002, 2020). While these showcase the latest Nike retail concepts, Nike also operates over a thousand other stores worldwide, many of which have been upgraded to incorporate aspects of the new flagship style. To understand Nike's latest retail strategy, it's worth returning briefly to the rise of Nike from its humble Oregon beginnings in the 1960s. This story parallels some of the corporate narratives of previous chapters, but it is worth sketching out to understand how Nike's House of Innovation continues and disrupts this legacy.

Figure 29 Nike's House of Innovation, New York, the Sneakerlab. Author photo.

Figure 30 Nike's House of Innovation, New York, Nike and Apple Watch display. Author photo.

Performance

Nike began as Blue Ribbon Sports, a 1964 collaboration between Phil Knight, a business graduate and former runner, and University of Oregon track coach, Bill Bowerman.[2] Knight began importing Onitsuka Tiger shoes (known today as Asics) from Japan and sold them to runners at track meets. He believed that Japanese-made shoes, with their lower labour costs, could undercut the biggest-selling athletics shoes at that time, German-made Adidas. It was a specialized market. In the mid-1960s, few people were interested in track, even fewer in middle- and long-distance track, and recreational running was almost non-existent.[3]

Bowerman not only coached Olympic-level distance runners but also customized their shoes. Relentless in his pursuit of improving their performance, he added inner soles and arch supports, or inserted foam heels into their shoes.[4] Now with a factory to work with, Bowerman "convinced Tiger to start trying nylon uppers in their training flats, and technology now made a sandwich of a smooth nylon woven against the skin, a layer of foam, then a coarser, more durable nylon exterior".[5] Such experiments culminated in the Cortez running shoe, launched in 1968 to coincide with the Mexico City Olympics.[6]

In 1972, Blue Ribbon Sports began producing its own shoes in Japan and Knight broke the relationship with Onitsuka. He commissioned a design student, Carolyn Davidson, to design a logo for their new brand, Nike. She intended the "swoosh" to suggest the dynamism of a runner. Meanwhile, Bowerman, in pursuit of better tread for his runner's shoes, famously poured urethane into a waffle iron. This technique, refined and patented in 1972, improved traction.[7] But for Knight, Nike's "waffle shoe" combined performance and aesthetics:

> It didn't just feel different, or fit different—it looked different. Radically so. Bright red upper, fat white swoosh—it was a revolution in aesthetics. Its look was drawing hundreds of thousands of new customers into the Nike fold, and its performance was sealing their loyalty.[8]

At the same time, Blue Ribbon Sports sponsored their first athlete, a middle-distance record-holder named Steve Prefontaine. Trained by Bowerman, Prefontaine was charismatic and enthusiastic about the new brand.[9] Knight described watching Prefontaine win a race:

> I'd never witnessed anything quite like that race. And yet I didn't just witness it. I took part in it. Days later I felt sore in my hams and quads. This, I decided, this is what sports are, what they can do ... When sports are at their best, the spirit of the fan merges with the spirit of the athlete, and in that convergence, in that transference, is the oneness that the mystics talk about.[10]

Though Prefontaine died in a car accident in 1974, this "convergence" between fans and star athletes would become central to Nike's identity over the next four decades. In 1980 – coincidentally in the same week as Apple – Knight floated the company on the stock market.

Nike's initial success was in running shoes but their mainstream breakthrough came when they signed basketball rookie Michael Jordan in 1984. Nike designed him a shoe, the Air Jordan, that gained instant attention as it broke an NBA restriction on shoes. The initial marketing hype, "Banned by the NBA", gave the shoes a rebellious reputation.[11] More importantly, Jordan's on-court success made him a household name. As Jordan dominated basketball, the "Jumpman" logo sealed an inseparable relationship between Nike and basketball. Every year, Nike produced new Air Jordan shoes, accompanied by a new slogan that stressed Jordan's athletic ability and competitive spirit.[12] Even though Jordan retired in 2003, his Jumpman brand and Air Jordans remain best-sellers today.[13]

Jordan's team, the Chicago Bulls, won six NBA championships and dominated the 1990s. Journalists canonized Jordan as "the greatest player ever". His – and Nike's – rise also coincided with that of the NBA as a global brand. Styled for television, the NBA during the Jordan era became known for high-speed intensity and dramatic, close finishes. Relentless marketing of the NBA, Jordan and Nike all reinforced one another, and helped fuel the sport's incredible growth: by 2000, NBA games were broadcast in over two hundred countries. If contemporary sports provided "transcendence from the banality and suffering of everyday life",[14] Jordan was basketball's first deity – a player who could "fly", defying gravity with his hang time and balletic leaps.

For both Nike and the NBA, Jordan proved a positive role model. "As a black superstar", wrote one critic, "he presents the fantasy that anyone can make it in the society of competition and status, that one can climb the class ladder and overcome the limitations of race and class".[15] Jordan carefully avoided comments on political, social or racial issues, including the police beating of Rodney King in 1992 and resulting riots. Unlike previous generations of African American athletes – Jackie Robinson and Muhammed Ali, for example – off-court, Jordan represented only boundless wealth, acquired through his salary, Nike sponsorship, advertisements and endorsements.

Professional sports such as the NBA became the epitome of an unregulated and privatized free market in which only the strongest thrive:

> Elite athletes ... literally come to embody the competitiveness, determination, responsibility, and rationality underpinning neoliberalism's base individualism, as they are lauded for reaping their just rewards in the form of success on the playing field, and (oftentimes) bounteous wealth off it.[16]

Jordan's success, perpetuated by Nike advertisements, shifted the public perception of basketball from a team sport to one emphasizing individualism. Not renowned as a great team-mate, instead, he embodied, "hyper-masculine excess where self-destructive and self-harming practices are normalized if not celebrated, the verbal and sometimes physical abuse of others is ignored if not excused".[17] Even team-mates are obstacles to overcome in the relentless pursuit of high performance. Sport, no longer simply a healthy pastime or fun activity with friends, became a winner-take-all battle, a legacy that continues today.[18]

Distinctive advertisements and slogans were an essential part of Nike's popular rise. Seattle advertising agency, Wieden+Kennedy, which began with a Nike account in 1982, helped construct and maintain myths around Jordan, with a constellation of advertisements around air, flight and transcendence. Perhaps most famously, their 1988 campaign "Just Do It", hailed each customer to leap into action and achieve whatever it is we have been avoiding. The tagline reiterates the idea of consumers simply doing whatever they desire, emphasizing individual performance. Teamwork rarely appears in Nike advertisements.

Although Jordan remained Nike's most famous star, its sponsorship expanded in the 1990s and 2000s to include collections and marketing campaigns for other athletes in other sports. Stars such as tennis players Serena Williams and Maria Sharapova, golfer Tiger Woods and Jordon's heir, basketballer LeBron James, all signed multi-million-dollar Nike deals. Nike carefully constructed an image for James, who joined the NBA in 2003 just as Jordan retired. Since then, James has been portrayed as a "Messianic figure" via consistent Christian references and repetition of nicknames such as "King James" and the "Chosen One".[19]

But Nike's impact went beyond sports. The Air Max sneaker, for example, designed by Tinker Hatfield in 1987, became a fashion icon. The shoe featured a transparent section in the sole to highlight the idea of "running on air". Subsequent models became associated with various subcultures. Amsterdam's Gabber hardcore dance culture adopted the Air Max BW, for example, the Air Max 90 took off in England's rave scene, and youths in Paris and Marseille renamed the 1998 Air Max Plus "Le Requin" (the Shark). In all cases, Nike athletic shoes were adopted by counter-cultural, working-class or underground scenes.[20] There were plenty of styles to choose from: in 1989, Nike designed over three hundred models and nine hundred styles of shoes; by 1996, this increased to around 1,200 different models.[21]

Yet shoes were not Nike's only products. Diane Katz, Nike's first design consultant for apparel, designed Nike's first popular item of clothing, the Windrunner training jacket in 1978. Using water-resistant ski fabrics, the jacket was specifically designed for off-season running in rainy Oregon. Katz went on to design apparel for Michael Jordan's signature collection, including the red and black Air Jordan "flight suit", made from aviation flight suit fabric. Many of Nike's apparel innovations in the 1980s and 1990s used nylon or polyester, new materials that gradually replaced cotton in high-performance sportswear.

Buoyed by success, Nike opened their first flagship store, Niketown, in Portland in 1990, followed by Chicago (1992), New York (1996) and London (1999). Part-sports museum, part-shrine to celebrity athletes, Nike's store designers focused on sports stars. The Chicago store, for example, featured extensive Jordan memorabilia in glass cases:

> … the store incorporated features of contests and festivals in its images and dramatic narratives of unconventional, underdog triumphs, and in the festive nature of the process through the site, with consumers cast in the roles of explorers and tourists in search of clothing, souvenirs and meanings. It was linked to athletic contests, such as the Olympics and Super Bowl, through depictions of athletic stars and their accomplishments.[22]

A plaster sculpture of Michael Jordan hung suspended three feet above the floor. The Chicago Niketown also featured museum-style glass cases containing his signature shoes as well as signed singlets and shorts.[23]

New York's Niketown was a five-storey brick building with a large arched glass façade that resembled an old school gymnasium. It featured a basketball half-court, a huge screen reeling Nike athlete videos and shoes, or sporting memorabilia displayed in glass cases. Niketown featured prominent images of basketballers, tennis players, runners, baseball and football stars. By 2000, Nike had sixteen Niketown flagship stores: twelve in the United States, two in Europe, one in Canada and one in Australia. With themed environments such as Planet Hollywood or the Hard Rock Café, Niketown stores focused on Nike's celebrity athletes, competition and high-performance.

In the first two decades of the twenty-first century, Nike built upon its reputation to become the dominant global brand for sneakers and sporting apparel. Beyond American sports, Nike moved into soccer with sponsorship deals with the Brazilian national team, the FIFA World Cup and English Premier League team, Manchester United. They continued to dominate American sports, particularly the NBA and NFL, with official supplier deals in 2012 and 2015 that meant all players wore a swoosh on their uniforms. Nike also became a major sponsor for women's sports, particularly basketball and football. For the 2023 FIFA Women's World Cup, Nike launched the Phantom Luna boot specially designed for women.

In 2017, in response to the Black Lives Matter movement, several NFL players knelt while the national anthem played before the game. Nike sponsored the most high-profile of these, Colin Kaepernick, quarterback for the San Francisco 49ers. Although Kaepernick's contract was not renewed for the following season (and he could not get another), Nike continued to support him. For the thirtieth anniversary of "Just Do It" in 2018, Wieden+Kennedy created the "Dream Crazy" campaign. "Believe in something", said Kaepernick in the advertisement, "even if it means sacrificing everything". The campaign did not feature Kaepernick kneeling and avoided any imagery associated with BLM.[24] Instead, the video told success stories of individual athletes – LeBron James, Serena Williams, wheelchair basketball player Megan Blunk and boxer Zeina Nassar – all individuals "dreaming crazy" to overcome all obstacles.

Given the political nature of Kaepernick's protest – then-president Donald Trump was the most prominent critic – Nike's campaign was bound to be controversial. Some fans posted videos online of themselves destroying their Nike shoes and clothing. But overall, the Dream Crazy campaign was successful for Nike, resulting in a 5 per cent share price increase, which added $6 billion to Nike's market value.[25] This "carefully calculated risk" campaign "targeted to the most appropriate audiences: Gen Z, Millennials, and Gen X generations of consumers who want companies to have a viewpoint and to take a stand on important issues in society".[26] Although the campaign seems to signal a shift from the Michael Jordan era, Nike carefully avoided any reference to systemic racism, structural economic disparity or social injustice to focus on individuals fighting against all odds to perform their best.

Besides being the world's largest sportswear brand, by the 2010s, Nike had also become one of its biggest fashion brands. The company's apparel collections had moved beyond sports to become everyday wear, while collaborations with leading fashion designers such as Virgil Abloh, Riccardo Tisci and Rei Kawakubo blurred the line between high fashion and sportswear.[27] But this is not surprising. Abloh, for example, grew up in Chicago surrounded by Michael Jordan apparel. He even sent his first sneaker designs to Nike at age fifteen. Riccardo Tisci, chief designer at Burberry, wears Air Force 1 sneakers almost every day. Today, Nike designs clothing that stretches across elite sportswear, casual wear and high fashion.

High-Performance Materials

A central component of the Nike in-store experience is interaction with high-performance materials. The initial display of leggings focused on Nike's "Infinalock" fabric, while the Sneakerlab featured references to high-tech materials. From its beginnings with Bowerman's experimentation with nylon and foam, material innovation has remained central to Nike's brand. The customer in-store makes the connection between such high-performance materials and their own possible self-improvements. If I want to run faster, more efficiently or with more stamina, Nike's high-tech shoes and clothing will improve my performance.

Today, a single Nike sneaker contains dozens of components produced in factories in up to five different countries. The company's global logistics systems source materials from various places but the final assembly of shoes in factories has been an issue of some media and consumer interest over the years. Although Nike's shoes are mass-produced, they require human labour to assemble, glue and stitch the pieces together. Sewing machines can sew flat forms but a complex, three-dimensional form such as a sneaker involves bending fabrics and stitching up to fifty pieces together – a labour-intensive job done by hand in production-line factories. From the beginning, Nike took advantage of cheap Japanese labour, and then switched to South Korea and Indonesia in the 1980s when Japanese labour costs rose.

Exactly who made the dazzling shoes that appeared in Nike stores and advertisements became an object of scrutiny by activists following strikes at Nike's Korean factories in the 1990s.[28] Then a *Life* magazine article in 1996 featured Pakistani children making Nike soccer balls for six cents an hour.[29] Criticism of Nike's "sweatshop" labour practices included documentaries by Michael Moore, *The Big One* (1997), and Jim Keady, *Behind the Swoosh* (2001), and Naomi Klein's classic book, *No Logo* (2001).[30] As activists highlighted appalling factory conditions in Korea, Pakistan, Indonesia and Vietnam, Knight became one of the richest men the United States and Nike a billion-dollar company.

By the twenty-first century, Nike's labour practices and outsourcing escaped such scrutiny. Partially, Nike better regulates its outsourcing via a code of conduct and better monitoring. But it also shifted production to China and Vietnam, countries that are harder for journalists to monitor due to restrictions on the press, labour organizing and human rights groups. Despite this, in 2020, reports emerged that members of the Uighur minority produce Nike shoes and apparel in forced labour factories in China's Xinjiang province.[31] Nike seems to be continuing its long history of pursuing low-cost labour in countries with loose labour and environmental regulations. But such issues are far from New York's House of Innovation.

The Sneakerlab erases not only the labour and material conditions of the workers who assemble its shoes, but the materials of the shoes themselves. Displayed against a white background, shoes appear as futuristic sculptures. The only text highlights the shoe's innovative new materials. Yet even these are mysterious. The text accompanying the "Air Zoom Tempo Next %" for example, noted its "ZoomX foam" in the forefoot and its "Flyknit" upper. In the clothing section, references to "Dri-FIT" and "Forward" likewise provide little clue as to specific materials. For the customer, it is difficult to peel away the pseudo-scientific neologisms and find out what these shoes and clothes are made of.

This is by design. Nike sneakers are composed of polyester, rubber, EVA foam, cotton, synthetic leather and leather. Both polyester and EVA foam are made from petroleum, while Nike uses synthetic rubber or composite materials composed of natural and synthetic elements. The uppers are typically plastic fibre threads woven together, the foam a composite and the rubber also a composite of natural and synthetic materials. In short, almost every part of a Nike shoe contains plastic.[32] And petroleum-based materials have a large carbon footprint because of the energy required to make them.

Despite releasing some information about supply chains, Nike provides few details about where these materials originate. Nike's 2023 Manufacturing Map included 490 factories located in thirty-six countries that employ over one million workers. Of these, 22 per cent of factories are in China and 24 per cent in Vietnam, with 31 per cent of materials coming from China and 26 per cent from Vietnam. In total, China and Vietnam make up 48 per cent of factories and 57 per cent of materials, although actual production numbers in each are probably higher.[33] Most Nike footwear and apparel is produced in Chinese and Vietnamese factories. The only other certainty is that these factories employ mainly women.

Environmental impact is also difficult to assess. Nike's relentless pursuit of performance has resulted in new materials and new material combinations. In the 1990s, Nike was at the forefront of using polyester in sports and activewear. Nike's Dri-FIT material, for example, is a "high performance" fabric, lightweight and designed to allow air to circulate around the body and allow sweat and heat to escape. FIT stands for Functional Innovative Technology, and this fabric replaced traditional cotton training clothes. Nike introduced it in athlete uniforms for the 1996 Olympics, Nike stores in the early 2000s and the company has since expanded its range to shorts, shirts, hoodies, hats and gloves. Dri-FIT is a polyester-based fabric.[34] Polyester is typically combined with natural fibres such as cotton, but "blends are very difficult if not impossible to recycle".[35]

Nike's response is to use more recycled plastics in their shoes and apparel. The Zenvy leggings, featuring "Instasoft" fabric, are made from "at least 50% recycled nylon" from carpets or fishing nets.[36] Another example is Nike's Flyknit shoes, composed of recycled plastic bottles with "at least 20% recycled materials". It is worth noting that Flyknit shoes retail for twice the price of standard Nike sneakers. In both examples, plastic is an ideal material – lightweight, elastic and durable – but involves a considerable environmental hazard in its creation, use and disposal. Even recycled plastic causes problems.

Microplastic pollution is the latest concern for plastic-based clothing and shoes. While there is some public knowledge about larger plastic items that degrade (such as bottles) to create microplastics, microfibre shedding is less well-known. This occurs both in the production of polyester fabrics (in the factory) and when users wash them (at home). Microfibres can even shed from polyester clothing worn in the rain.[37] Nike agrees that its polyester products shed microplastics. To mitigate this, the company publicizes its membership of the Microfibre Consortium, an organization of apparel brands dedicated to researching microfibres. With no reported progress since 2018, the Consortium appears to be a greenwashing initiative.[38]

At the end of their life cycle, Nike's high-performance shoes are difficult, if not impossible, to recycle. One recent European report suggests 90 per cent of all sneakers end up in landfills, while a US report suggests 95 per cent, or 300 million pairs annually, end up in landfills.[39] In response, Nike promotes their Reuse-A-Shoe programme, to recycle old sneakers, and Nike Grind, whereby used sneakers are recycled into playground surfaces. The Reuse programme is limited to a single hub in Europe and one in the United States. Thus, "… the benefits provided from the recycling of shoes are questionable due to the GHG emissions of increased transportation".[40] Regardless, such schemes recycle only a tiny fraction of Nike shoes and apparel. The rest ends up in landfill.

Performance trumps all at Nike's innovation lab in Beaverton, Oregon. Here, Nike employs

> over 40 researchers in areas such as biomechanics, physiology, engineering, physics and kinesiology. In their quest to develop innovative materials, physiologist researchers use a life-sized sweat mannequin called Hal to test clothing performance. Hal simulates human performance on a treadmill and has 139 ports that simulate sweating while simultaneously providing thermoregulation information to researchers.[41]

This emphasis on scientific research and new technologies to achieve even greater performance erases all other aspects of Nike's shoes and clothing. Yet if performance remains a key goal – and the House of Innovation contained constant reminders of Nike's high-tech, material innovations – my initial question remains: what happened to the embodiment of peak performance, Nike's celebrity athletes?

Innovation: Digital Nike

Although celebrity athletes remain crucial to Nike's branding, promotion and advertising, their retail strategy has shifted over the past two decades. Nike designed their new House of Innovation flagship stores as spaces for customers to see, touch and try on shoes and clothing. Yet the stores are equally designed to encourage and enable digital interactions with the Nike website and apps. Nike's self-conscious promotion of innovation – from high-performance fabrics to futuristic shoes – has been around for decades. But Nike's digital strategy is more recent, and it is worth briefly tracing its roots to better understand the House of Innovation.

Nike's digital presence began with a website in 1998 that featured images of athletes, inspirational slogans and some of their footwear range. The company then launched sport-specific websites such as NikeFootball.com. But Nike's digital strategy increased exponentially in the mid-2000s. In an early digital promotion, "the Art of Speed" in 2004, Nike commissioned filmmakers to create short videos specifically for online viewing. Nike created one of the first branded YouTube channels in 2005, and separate Facebook pages for every major sport it sponsored athletes in. These proved popular, so that "by 2012 Nike had garnered more than 10 million fans for the main page, 13 million fans for Nike Football, and 4.5 million for Nike Basketball".[42]

For the 2006 FIFA World Cup, in collaboration with Google, Nike created Joga.com, a social network-like site. The site – launched the same year Facebook became public and long before Instagram existed – allowed soccer fans to upload videos of themselves playing while other fans could comment on and rate their performance. Its user-generated content garnered over a million participants.[43] For the same World Cup, Nike created an additional website for fans to interact with professional players. Both platforms provided fans with the sense that they were participating (in some small way) in the World Cup.

Nike also launched the Nike+ platform in 2006. This website offered members access to running resources and soon expanded to soccer, golf and other sports. Within a decade, the platform boasted "close to 30 million users across 190 countries".[44] At the same time, Nike released a collaboration with Apple, the Nike+iPod, that allowed runners to log and monitor their activities via iTunes and the Nike+ website. For members, the platform provided a personal running experience to access data such as time, distance, calories burned and pace.[45] The Nike+ platform was a good example of co-creation, establishing an ongoing, interactive relationship between a customer and Nike.

Users could create graphs and diagrams to visualize their progress and share them with friends. Running enthusiasts could also access expert advice on training methods.[46] Such interactions also provided Nike with a wealth of data, including what distances people run, where, who they run with and their running conditions. As with Amazon, Nike uses customer interactions to better market to individuals or specific communities by better understanding local conditions, needs and desires. Buoyed by the engagement in these platforms, Nike invested in further digitization. In fact, "between 2009 and 2012, the company cut traditional media expenditures by 40 percent, and allocated more than eight hundred million dollars to digital and social marketing – more than any other U.S.-based advertiser".[47]

Nike launched their wearable activity tracker, the FuelBand, in 2012. The FuelBand was Nike's response to the popular Fitbit, released two years earlier. Although Nike's version lasted only two years, Nike returned to wearables – and to the Apple collaboration – with the recent Apple Watch and Nike+. Featured in the House of Innovation, the Apple Watch plus Nike Sports Bands are the material components of a digital experience. This experience aims to motivate and challenge individuals, as well as provide information such as weather alerts, pace, distance, heart rate, and social aspects such as shared summaries and competitions.

In the 2010s, wearable devices such as the Fitbit or Fuelband aligned with a broad interest in the "quantified self".[48] Nike's role in promoting the monitoring, measuring and recording of bodily movements was so central that one of the original *Wired* articles in 2009 that popularized "the quantified self" focused on Nike. In it, the quantified self was explained via "the experiences of people who were using what was then a new technology: Nike+, the wearable sensor device and associated platform for monitoring physical activity".[49] According to this idea, a runner – at least a *serious* runner – can no longer simply lace up shoes and run around the park. Now, a runner requires personal analytics to constantly monitor and improve performance. New digital technologies such as Nike's platforms and apps shape a concept of exercise and the body that highlights order, control and regulation.

For Nike, digitized personal information can be translated into data for product development and personalized selling. An individual's data can be cross-referenced with others to develop local profiles for retail stores, advertising or promotional campaigns. For Nike, such data can be cross-referenced with data obtained via their apps or paid for from other companies so as to build profiles of spending habits, location or social media activity, "expanding the reach of the surveillance to which we willingly subject ourselves, eroding the private space in our lives …".[50] Although Nike can access and use a potentially huge amount of data, users can only access a fraction of their own data, and even this is presented via proprietary algorithms.

The design of such platforms, while appearing universal and neutral, also reflects the interests of the primary demographic – white, able-bodied males of the Global North – that is, its aims are culturally, socially and politically specific. Researcher Katherine Hepworth argues:

> Central to neoliberal manifestations of biopower is the dispersed regulation of bodies, which encourage individual self-regulation of the internal processes of body and mind. In neoliberal manifestations of biopower, notions of agency, personal responsibility, and self-esteem are emphasized to such an extent that systemic, structural, and personal conditions are all but ignored.[51]

But the Nike app not only connects people, it also incorporates health, medical care and sports. For example, the Nike + Run Club app provides runners with music, GPS position, calorie calculations, mileage, time, community links and

Performance and Innovation: Nike

more. The app enables runners to access data such as time, pace and maps to share with friends. Yet this continual interaction with Nike occurs within a closed ecosystem:

> The NikePlus platform did not allow users to enter performance and activity data manually; only Nike devices could transfer such data. This put one major requirement on NikePlus users: in order to participate, they had to synchronize relevant devices with the platform. That meant that users had to buy Nike's shoes or devices. Put differently, users had to pay up front to be able to meet strangers or interact with friends.[52]

Beyond the quantified self, Nike was also connecting customers to other Nike customers. In this way, amateur sports became a social experience, mediated by Nike's digital platforms.

For some, Nike's gamified apps have transformed their sports experience. The Nike+ app, for example, can transform running, a potentially solitary, boring activity, into a fun, interactive one. Sociologist Jennifer R. Whitson, for example, described her experience using Nike's running app:

> This process exemplifies what the digital does to play: the lovely sound of simulated coins clinking, or bars levelling-up, or an encouraging simulated voice, provides the feedback and support I crave, bringing me into this relation with myself and the machine, and persuading me to stay. These sounds, colours, badges, etc. let me know that the system is listening to me, that it is reading me, that its sensors are working. This feedback feels good. It works to mask the pain of my wheezing lungs and staggering feet.[53]

She also noted that sharing data via the app made the solitary activity of running seem communal. This way, a Nike customer interacts not only with an automated system, but with other members of Nike's running community.

The Nike app makes use of emotional interaction and gamification within a controlled ecosystem (comprising Apple Watch, Nike app and its software). Gamification is an essential tool to encourage, motivate and keep customers using the app. In this way, participation and co-creation are crucial.[54] Aside from statistics, the app creates narratives. Competitions, points, rewards and tables visualize an individual's progress and performance. Additionally, the community aspect enables users to share success with others, post achievements and encourage others. Nike platforms transform running into a kind of "gamified service" mediated by Nike.

Ironically, running does not require any of this. In his book, co-founder of Nike Bill Bowerman wrote that jogging is free and "requires no special skills or equipment".[55] Yet, five decades later, Nike has transformed this simple activity "into a gamified social sport that offers users an enormous amount of data about their personal achievements, which enables them to become better at running and thus in a healthier lifestyle".[56] A free activity that once required no specialized equipment now requires high-performance shoes, clothing and digital wearables.

Launched in 2010, Nike Run Club (NRC) (originally Nike + Running app) is Nike's latest and most popular running app. It allows users to monitor and record their runs and to share and compare accomplishments with other users. Besides gathering customers' information and connecting them, NRC's enticing features include immediate as well as daily (or weekly) feedback, ranking on leaderboards to encourage a social aspect as well as trophies and badges to sustain engagement. It also includes runs coordinated with soundtracks integrated with music from Apple Music or Spotify playlists, to motivate and engage users.

Beyond individual interactions, Nike's digital strategy directly affected its retail experience. In 2017, CEO Mark Parker announced a new digital strategy, the "Consumer Direct Offense", aimed at increasing ecommerce and direct-to-customer sales. This included an experiment to sell Nike products on Amazon marketplaces. From 2017 to 2019, customers could buy official Nike products on Amazon. But Nike found that Amazon's algorithms consistently put competitors above Nike products and Amazon continued to sell copies and counterfeits.[57] Fortuitously, in November 2019, only a few months before the Covid-19 pandemic, Nike quit Amazon to concentrate on their own direct sales.

The pandemic, with its associated lockdowns and more online shopping, worked in favour of Nike's direct-to-consumer strategy. Immediately following the pandemic, "Nike's online sales spiked by 75% to just under $2 [billion] … Nike relied on direct-to-consumer sales for 30% of its revenues – a target it had not expected to reach until 2023."[58] Additionally, Nike reduced their retail partners by 30 per cent and closed many accounts (including long-time supportive independent stores) to concentrate sales in Nike stores.[59] In 2017, Nike sold its products to thirty thousand retailers but since then has reduced this to about forty partner chains who must put Nike products in their own section.

Interestingly, Nike's latest CEO, John Donahoe, has no background in shoes or apparel. A former CEO of ServiceNow and eBay, he joined Nike in 2020 to further accelerate the company's digital transformation. In an interview with the *Wall Street Journal*, Donahoe described his strategy as trying

> to see things through the eyes of the consumer. When you're buying something, you aren't thinking digital or physical. You're thinking, I want to get what I want, where I want it, how I want it. Increasingly, that's a blended digital and physical experience. I believe that experience is the future. The winning companies of the future will bring immersive, blended, digital and physical experiences.[60]

Here, flagship stores such as the House of Innovation perform important functions not only as shrines to the brand but as places to entice customers further into Nike's digital ecosystem.

Using the Nike app, customers to the House of Innovation can checkout instantly and scan QR codes in-store for more information on items (such as colours and variations). Of course, the more you use the app, the more customized information it retains, such as your shoe size, favourite colours or materials, to further personalize the retail experience. Before entering the store, customers can build a virtual try-on list in the app and have products ready at the change room, or reserve items online. All such initiatives further link Nike's digital with its in-store experience.

As part of its digital strategy, Nike bought four data science and analytics firms between 2018 and 2020. These included a computer vision company, an AI customer data analytics company and a predictive analytic company.[61] Such companies aim to both further personalize the customer's experience and better aggregate and analyse the vast quantity of data generated within Nike's digital ecosystem. As with Amazon, Nike are building digital systems to collect more detailed data about customers to create increasingly intimate relationships with each individual.

In another recent move into the digital realm, Nike signed Chinese esports star Jian Zihao, known as Uzi, a professional League of Legends player. Beginning in 2019, Nike's sponsorship included a Chinese advertisement and promotional campaign. But, due to diabetes and arm pain, Uzi retired less than a year into the sponsorship deal. In response, Nike helped Uzi regain physical fitness and stage a comeback, with Nike able to leverage a connection between esports and fitness.[62] Nike also sponsors other well-known esports players, as well as the T1 tournament in South Korea. In all of these, Nike also aims to connect gaming with physical training, connecting the digital and the physical.[63]

Another recent Nike digital initiative, "dotSWOOSH", comprises a platform for customers to buy unique, virtual shoes and apparel. Launched in 2022, the platform began with an edition of twenty thousand NFTs (though Nike carefully avoids the term). One limited edition virtual shoe, "Cryptokicks", designed by Japanese artist Takashi Murakami, sold for $134,000.[64] The promise – yet unfulfilled – is that customers will eventually be able to "wear" their virtual sneakers in games such as *Grand Theft Auto* or *Fortnite*. This initiative began at the end of 2021 when Nike bought RTFKT, a virtual sneaker company already selling NFTs. Although the NFT phase was short-lived, Nike's long-term interest is in developing a market in trading, displaying and co-collaborating on virtual shoes and apparel.

Nike also runs over three hundred social media profiles across Instagram, Facebook, Twitter, YouTube, TikTok, Pinterest and LinkedIn. These combine to reach a wide variety of audiences – so that Nike Basketball, Nike Football, Nike

Running or Nike Women appeal to different market segments. Nike also runs social media accounts for specific locations, such as Nike London or Nike Seoul. Its social media marketing revolves around sport and its associated values and Nike accounts abound in short slogans and emotionally driven narratives – individuals overcoming obstacles to achieve greatness or extreme perseverance to achieve personal goals. Despite sponsoring numerous sports teams, Nike's social media feeds overwhelmingly spotlight individuals.

In-store, Nike's digital experience is also set to further expand. The Shanghai House of Innovation 001, for example, caters to a membership-based Nike experience, including exclusive sneakers and access for app users. It also contains more digital screens and real-time information. One commentator described the store's entrance as:

> the hard-to-miss, floor-to-ceiling screen panels spread across the store, shoppers can directly observe their own health data through their WeChat mini-program when they exercise at the Centre Court – the entrance to the store.[65]

Nike's most recent flagship store, the Paris House of Innovation, features even more digital interaction, including "the Kids Pod, which offers interactive gaming experiences to encourage movement, a bra fitting service based on machine learning and advanced algorithms, and a suite of Nike App Services …".[66]

Nike's other concept stores, designed to be even more digitally interactive, are known as Nike Rise. First opened in 2021, Rise stores in Guangzhou and Seoul feature digital interactions specific to their location and local customers. The Seoul store, for example, features a three-storey atrium with a digital screen that displays local weather conditions and feeds about sports events in Seoul. Here, Nike highlights both localization and personalization, with the underlying strategy to connect customers with the local store through physical and social activities:

> One area of the store, dubbed the "huddle", allows shoppers to sign up for local events, including wellness discussions with experts, local runs or even workouts within the store itself. It also features a grab-and-go section with an assortment of nutrition and hydration products for pre- or post-workout snacking. A "broadcast booth" in the area allows the retailer to hold virtual training sessions and events in addition to in-person ones.[67]

Nike Rise stores also feature more experiential activities for customers such as workshops, personal training, wellness and style advice consultants. While this represents a turn towards localization in Nike's retail stores, customers access most of these services via Nike apps.

Finally, I can return to answer my initial question about celebrity athletes in the House of Innovation. With Nike's digital marketing, whatever your favourite sport, you are already aware of star athletes from scrolling social media or watching them on television. By 2017, Nike had the largest social media traffic (primarily Instagram and Facebook) of any company, and remains the most popular brand on Instagram. Nike-sponsored stars such as Cristiano Rolando are among the most popular individuals on social media.[68] Nike no longer needs to focus their stores on athletes. By integrating customers into its digital ecosystem, Nike can appeal to a basketball or a football fan, a runner or a yoga enthusiast. As the centre of the Nike House of Innovation experience, the customer has replaced Michael Jordan.

Chapter 6
A Sensual Respite: Aesop

As I weave through the crowds on a busy weekday, I catch a glimpse of Aesop's modest sign – a single black word in sans-serif font – before losing it in the background. It sits on a uniform row of glass-fronted stores on a narrow street in central Melbourne. Once home to the local garment industry, Flinders Lane is now filled with cafés, bars, restaurants and boutiques. It's central to Melbourne's image as a global capital of coffee and culture. As a key pedestrian thoroughfare, Flinders Lane is criss-crossed by other alleyways and arcades, and bustling with lunchtime office workers, shoppers and tourists.

The only aspect of the Aesop store that stands out from the Lane is three brown handwash dispensers that sit on a rack attached to the door handle. A passing pedestrian pauses to try one. She squirts some onto a cupped hand, rubs her palms together then lifts them to her nose. On the front window, the Aesop wordmark from the sign is repeated in white alongside a text that reads, "A place to dwell in". Below that is another line: "Evocative aromas for restorative spaces". The dim interior looks empty but enticing (Figure 31). It looks *calm*.

I step in and immediately sense a change. A woody, citrusy scent. Soft music. A calm ambience that contrasts the clashing sounds and smells of the Lane outside. An undulating form of compressed cardboard covers the right-hand wall and ceiling, forming an organic, cave-like interior (Figure 32). Spotlights accentuate its curves and hollows. On the opposite wall, plain bottles and aluminium tubes stand in tight, repeated rows on short shelves. The colour palette – warm beige and browns – highlights the soothing atmosphere.

An assistant welcomes me in. Strangely for a store that sells body products – hand washes, facial cleansers, scrubs and shampoos – there are no mirrors. Nor glossy photos of models or celebrities. In fact, the Aesop store is relatively empty. A few dozen products with identical labels, a sculptural wall and a central sink. Unlike in a mainstream cosmetic store such as Sephora, there are no bright, primary colours or shiny, reflective surfaces. Raw and matt, the cardboard, recycled from industrial packaging, reveals its internal layers. These are stacked upon other layers. It's an unusual texture. I fight a desire to reach out and touch it.

After a brief conversation, the assistant rubs a lotion onto the back of my hand, invites me to smell it, then washes it off my hand at the sink. Talk focuses

Figure 31 Aesop store, Flinders Lane, Melbourne, entrance. Author photo.

on my skin. Is it dry, oily, or somewhere in between? What kind of daily cleansing rituals do I employ? Local and seasonal conditions, such as Melbourne's dry summer, also arise. The aim of skincare, I'm told, is to rebalance and maintain the skin's equilibrium, and there's a hydrating lotion or a balancing gel for all types. The assistant mixes scientific terms, such as sebum (skin's natural oil), with natural ones, such as rosemary and tea tree. As we speak, the assistant offers me a cup of tea: peppermint, rosehip and liquorice root. I savour the herbal flavour and realize all five of my senses – sight, sound, smell, touch and taste – have been stimulated in this short visit.

I take my design and architecture students to this Aesop store. Few have been before. It's expensive. One student suggests that the layers of cardboard are like layers of skin. Another says honeycomb. Yet another says the interior

Figure 32 Aesop store, Flinders Lane, Melbourne, interior. Author photo.

is like being inside a womb. Metaphors abound but circle around the Aesop store as a calm place of nurture, an escape from the clamour of noise, emails, meetings, worries. One student, struggling to describe the mood evoked by the store said: "This isn't a shop, it's a vibe." Although not a very academic term, vibe – an ambience or emotional state perceived by the body – is an apt description. Yet the Aesop vibe is distinctive. It's a vibe I've felt before in numerous Aesop stores.

Like the Flinders Lane store, Aesop Chelsea in New York is a decade old. That's a long time to remain unchanged in retail design. It sits on Ninth Avenue in a strip of restaurants, cafés, laundries, pet shops and grocery stores. Small and narrow, copies of *The Paris Review* literary magazine hang from the store's ceiling (Figure 33). When it moved from Paris in 1973, I'm told, the magazine

Figure 33 Aesop store, Chelsea, New York, ceiling. Author photo.

based its headquarters nearby. Although the magazine is still going today, the walls are papered in handwritten and typed letters, black and white photos and receipts in a collage of *Paris Review* memorabilia. Neat rows of Aesop products, arranged in series on dark timber shelves, create patterns that stand out against the chaotic background.

An assistant offers me tea. I take the cup and read the quote by Franz Kafka running around its inside, below the rim: "Anyone who keeps the ability to see beauty never grows old." There are two antique sinks along one wall and a short shelf. I place my tea on the shelf next to a sculptural brass incense holder (Figure 34). Nearby candles also have inspirational quotes inside. In this Aesop store, I'm immersed in another facet of the Aesop experience: literature. On its website, Aesop notes how *The Paris Review*, like a moisturiser for the brain,

Figure 34 Aesop store, Chelsea, New York, teacup. Author photo.

"stimulates, enriches and nourishes enquiring minds".[1] Since 2013, Aesop has stocked new copies in select stores and collaborated on special events with the literary magazine.

As with the Flinders Lane store, the Chelsea Aesop store is a tranquil oasis. The experience is consistent – an immediate shift in bodily perceptions, a greeting, a cup of tea and a personal consultation, followed by application and washing off of formulations. But at the same time, these two interiors are composed of different materials, and the designers have utilized different lighting, colour schemes and spatial layouts. This difference has been a hallmark of Aesop's global expansion over the past two decades: distinctive stores attuned to their location yet consistent with the Aesop vibe.

Designing an Ethos

Amid claims about the "death" of bricks and mortar shopping, Aesop expanded from the first iteration of the Flinders Lane store in 2007 to over 230 stores around the world (as of 2024). It grew from a niche Australian brand to a $2 billion global one.[2] Central to Aesop's growth over this period were its stores that dotted fashionable neighbourhoods around the world like brand ambassadors. But to understand what makes an Aesop store distinctive, we need a brief overview of the company's history before returning to how it designs its interior experience. Despite a steady global expansion, Aesop stores have remained consistent with the brand's original ethos, with the products, branding and store interiors all working to reinforce it.

Aesop began as an idea in a Melbourne hairdressing salon in the mid-1980s. Dissatisfied with the artificial scents of haircare products at that time, its owner, Dennis Paphitis, thought natural ingredients, essential oils and plant-based extracts would not only smell better but might be healthier for his customers. With the aid of a chemist, he experimented with formulations that combined natural with synthetic ingredients. In 1987, Paphitis launched Aesop as a series of haircare and skincare products. He distributed these through Australian department stores, slowly gained a local clientele, then secured distribution in up-market department stores in the United States and Europe. By the end of the 1990s, Aesop was a niche brand with a small but loyal customer base.

Central to Paphitis' brand ethos was a certain design-consciousness, exemplified by Aesop's minimal packaging. Aesop's amber bottles resembled old-fashioned apothecary bottles. Their black and white labels with sans-serif typography contained only essential information (ingredients and use). The plain packaging suggested nothing inessential. No waste. But also, no promises of eternal youth or sex appeal. Paphitis was determined to avoid traditional strategies of the beauty industry. No models or celebrity endorsements. Instead, "cruelty-free" and "plant-based" highlighted the brand's ethical stance and, like the minimal design and packaging, gestured towards sustainability.

But by the late 1990s, such a stance was hardly new. In some ways, Aesop's brand ethos followed in the footsteps of The Body Shop. Founded by Anita Roddick in Brighton, England, in 1976, The Body Shop aimed to become "a model of Green conscience: all products are biodegradable and natural; animal testing is avoided; containers are basic and can be refilled; and packaging is minimal".[3] Even as it went global in the 1980s, The Body Shop eschewed traditional advertising, instead promoting their brand through interviews, launches, events and advocacy of environmental, fair trade and social justice issues.[4] But a 1994 exposé and ensuing press articles questioned the company's "natural" ingredients, ethical sourcing of ingredients and ultimately described their branding as "greenwashing".[5]

Among other brands, Lush Cosmetics took up The Body Shop's ethical skincare mantle. Liz Weir, Mark and Mo Constantine founded Lush in 1995 in Poole, England, and similarly centred their brand ethos on natural ingredients, cruelty-free products and "a marketing strategy strongly integrated around transparency, fair trade, human rights, and justice".[6] Lush also shunned models and celebrities. Instead, they partnered with non-profits and charities to support social and environmental causes. Marketing cosmetics around the absence of animal testing was also an attempt to attain an ethical high ground on what was (and remains) a complex issue.[7]

Both The Body Shop and Lush sold their products in distinctive yet uniform stores. The original Body Shop store design, by Brian Lowe Design, "featured a dark green modular system constructed in timber, and extensive use of dark green tones on both the facia and in the interior".[8] The Body Shop deployed this "green box" scheme into thousands of stores around the world in the 1980s and the 1990s. The product range, including body butters, facial scrubs and cosmetics, was arranged on timber shelves, with the forest-green logo repeated throughout the store. The Body Shop interiors were simple, self-consciously "inspired by nature" and uniform around the world.[9]

Lush stores also deployed a consistent aesthetic. Recycled timber joinery, wooden boxes and hessian sacks were filled with unwrapped, candy-coloured "bath bombs" and soaps. Lush stores emphasized their "fresh, handmade cosmetics" and natural products in displays that resembled a fruit market, and signs and labels that featured handwritten script. Lush presented and sold many of their products without packaging, and wrapped them for the customer in paper (not plastic) bags. Products with packaging featured simple, black and white labels and stickers with an illustration of the product's maker, emphasizing Lush's fair trade and labour credentials.

Through their store design, both The Body Shop and Lush aimed to promote a brand ethos centred on environmental sustainability, ethical and cruelty-free products. With such an emphasis, both skincare brands also tried to differentiate their stores from department store cosmetic counters or chains that carry hundreds of brands. Even today, the latter interiors tend to be glossy, shiny, brightly lit and covered in photographic posters of flawless faces. Customers there rarely find mention of "handmade", "vegan" or "cruelty-free" products, nor references to environmental, fair trade or social justice campaigns.

Meanwhile, Aesop remained a niche brand in the 1990s that sold its products in department stores and other retail outlets. According to CEO Michael O'Keeffe, around 2003, the company implemented a conscious shift from "product-centric to retail-centric".[10] Modest brown bottles with black and white labels, he recalled, got lost in a department store cosmetic section. Aesop's strategy was to create stores to complement the products.[11] Its first trial, a collaboration with architects Six Degrees in 2004, was a small, temporary store in a parking garage below the Prince Hotel in Melbourne's suburb of St Kilda. The walls and ceiling were painted white. On one side of the narrow space, shelves filled with amber bottles stood out against the background, while on the other sat a row of sinks. The modest space, lack of overt signage and minimal fittings resonated with Aesop's brand ethos.

Buoyed by this experiment, Aesop opened a store on Flinders Lane in 2007. It began as a temporary installation designed by March Studio.[12] Given a fortnight and a brief that stipulated the use of recycled cardboard, March Studio staff folded, cut and arranged boxes to function both aesthetically and as shelves. They displayed bottles and jars within the cardboard cubes in rhythmic patterns that suggested a 1960s Minimalist art installation. Along one wall, the designers left an exposed stack of cardboard sheets so customers could see the interior structure of the industrial-grade material. Recycled cardboard reinforced an affiliation with sustainability while the absence of artificial colours and materials reinforced Aesop's emphasis on natural ingredients.

Though originally intended as temporary, the cardboard installation remained until 2015 when Aesop's in-house design team redesigned the Flinders Lane store. This version is the one described in this chapter's opening. Led by Aesop's in-house architect Kian Ya, the design team continued the use of recycled cardboard and a similar visual language to the first iteration. But this time, the designers created an undulating, sculptural form from the recycled cardboard. They first modelled the form digitally, then laser-cut layers of cardboard and hand-finished them into seamless contours.[13] As with the original version, this store also contained no partitions separating customers and staff. Importantly, the Flinders Lane store now centred around an essential feature of all later stores: a sink.

As the company built more stores around the world, Aesop adopted a different approach to not only department stores but to The Body Shop and Lush. In a 2012 interview, founder Dennis Paphitis explained the strategy:

> Architecturally our criteria is always to try and work with what is already there and to weave ourselves into the core and fabric of the street, rather than to impose what we were doing. We didn't ever want a standard Aesop shade of orange or green that was plastered onto stores with a nasty logo over it, but instead to look at the streetscape and try to retain and redeem existing facades that are there, and work with a local and relevant vocabulary to contextualise what we do …[14]

Utilizing these strategies, Aesop engaged well-known local designers and architects such as Ilse Crawford (who designed the first London store in 2008),

Figure 35 Aesop store, Upper West Side, New York, exterior. Author photo.

Snøhetta (who designed the Oslo store in 2014) and Paulo Mendes da Rocha (who designed the first Sao Paulo store in 2015) to collaborate on stores. Aesop also collaborated with smaller studios such as Paris-based Ciguë, New York-based Tacklebox and Melbourne-based March Studios (who have designed eighteen stores to date). Aesop developed a website, "Taxonomy of Design: An Archive of Aesop Spaces", to showcase store designers and photos of each store's distinctive materials, fixtures and furniture.

Using recycled local materials, furniture or fixtures became a central feature of Aesop's stores. Minimal intervention to existing buildings became a means of integrating a new store into its local neighbourhood. In their 2017 Upper East Side store in New York, for example, Aesop's design team – in partnership with Tacklebox Architecture – retained the façade of a former dry-cleaner's store.

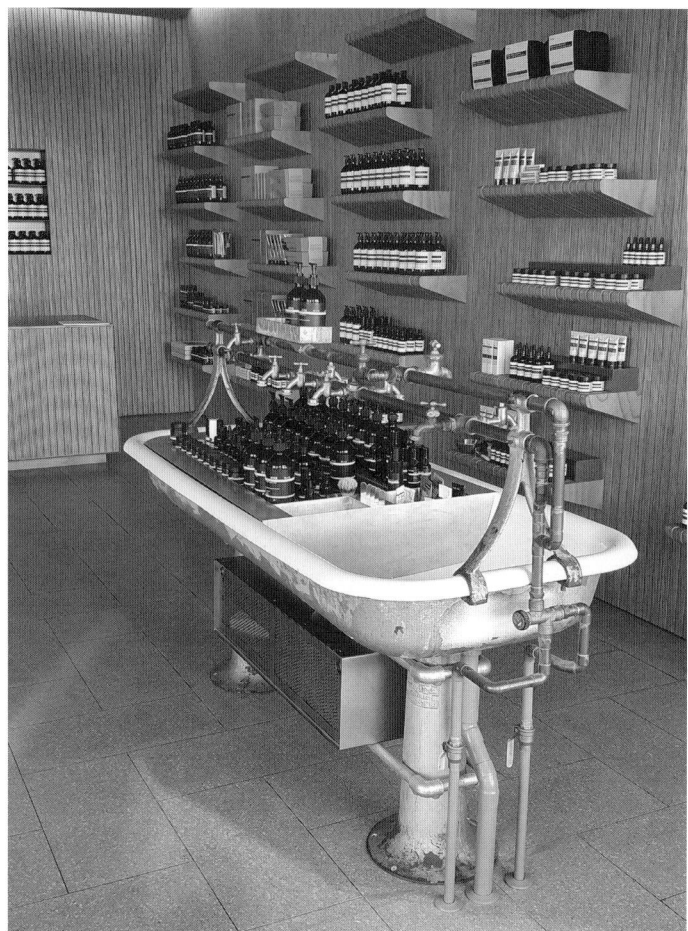

Figure 36 Aesop store, Upper West Side, New York, interior. Author photo.

Originally "Chanel French Cleaners", the owner took down the C and H from the sign in the 1960s to avoid a legal battle with the famous fashion house.[15] Instead of starting afresh, the Aesop team preserved the "Anel French Cleaners" signage and stainless-steel façade (Figure 35). Continuing the homage to the past, interior details included milled pine plywood walls and shelves curved to echo rows of clothes hangers (Figure 36). Aesop bottles line these shelves, while the other visual highlight is an antique sink that features a sculptural arrangement of old pipes and taps.

This juxtaposition of recycled objects and the reuse of old buildings is a design strategy consistent with Naomi Leff's classic flagship store for Ralph Lauren that opened in 1986. Situated in an old mansion on Manhattan's Upper East Side,

Leff's interiors for Lauren comprise a series of stage sets containing historical props – from antique polo mallets and saddles to crystal chandeliers and gold-framed portraits – within which to display Lauren's clothing and homeware collections.[16] The building, furniture and fixtures comprise a bricolage – carefully curated materials that resonate with the customer's fantasies, memories and sensory experiences. Framed by historical cues, such stores stage the new within the familiar.

Local references put each Aesop store in dialogue with its local surroundings and ensures that an Aesop store in New York differs from one in London or Tokyo. Paphitis once expressed his horror at the idea of Aesop developing into a "soul-less chain", instead describing the series of stores "as the equivalent of a weighty, gold charm bracelet on the tanned wrist of a glamorous, well-read European woman who has travelled and collected interesting experiences".[17] His characterization is telling. A cosmopolitan, educated and affluent woman is also an ideal Aesop customer. But, to take his metaphor literally, it is possible to imagine such a design-conscious customer visiting multiple Aesop stores on her travels, particularly given most are in fashionable neighbourhoods of global cities.[18]

Although Aesop stores respond to their individual locations, Aesop's in-house design team, including graphic designers, copywriters, videographers and photographers, maintain the brand's virtual coherence. The Aesop aesthetic, based on simplicity, muted colours and clean lines, remains consistent across their website and social media. Brooklyn-based Work&Co redesigned the website in 2017 to align with the brand's "look and feel":

> To create Aesop's e-commerce site, we distilled the essence of the company down to its core elements. Then we created a digital design system to match the overall brand look and feel. Layouts and typography are inspired by the iconic product packaging. Elegant motion design creates calm transitions that mirror a relaxing in-store experience.[19]

The website's imagery is consistent: a calm, muted colour palette with sharp contrasts and clean lines. No bright, primary colours or blurry edges. Product pages feature a photograph of a bottle or tube with simple information about the formula's "feel", aroma and ingredients. As well as a platform for ordering products, the website also provides a deeper experience, with a link to The Atheneum, a section that includes articles on skincare, design and literature.

Similarly, Aesop's social media feeds contain carefully curated photos and videos. Aesop's Instagram account appears more like an architecture or design magazine than a skincare company. Photos and short videos of Aesop stores, meticulously staged bottles and close-ups of raw ingredients feature prominently. Special events such as collaborations with chefs or musicians, temporary installations within stores (such as filling a store with autumn leaves or spring flowers) and photos of new stores appear seamlessly with product photos. Interspersed between the stores and products are book covers, art, and music videos (broadly "ambient" or "chill") commissioned by Aesop.

Within a hectic social media stream of news, gossip and toxic comments, Aesop's signature aesthetic stands out. Close-up photos and videos of herbal tea or flowers highlight natural connections while terms such as "nourishment" and "serenity" reinforce the store's ambience. Aesop's social media feeds also link to Spotify playlists that evoke a certain mood or theme. "Music for the Task at Hand", for example, features minimal or meditative music by artists such as Brian Eno. No hip-hop or bright pop, this is music to evoke a contemplative mood. Importantly, Aesop's social media feeds are less a sales pitch (prices are never mentioned) and more a repetition of the Aesop vibe – calm, cultured and sustainable.

Designing a Sensual Experience

In "Welcome to the Experience Economy", Joseph Pine and James Gilmore advised companies to "sensorialize", or design each product and detail to accentuate "the sensations created from its use".[20] This certainly correlates with the way Aesop design stores as sites for sensory engagement. For a skincare brand, such an approach seems logical. But Aesop goes further. Aesop's in-store engagement includes not only a customer's immediate, bodily sensations but also collective memories and cultural knowledge evoked by materials, fixtures and details. While location is an important factor that Aesop store designers consciously reference, their design also aims to immerse customers in a universal Aesop experience.

Of course, Aesop was not the first company to design immersive stores. As we saw in Chapter 1, Apple was a contemporary precursor and there are some parallels between the two worth drawing out. Although selling very different products – consumer electronics and skincare – both developed a similar visual language across products, packaging, digital promotions and branding. Both use carefully curated physical spaces to complement this language. In this shared design language, products, packaging and interiors are stripped of excess colour, decoration and ornament. Every detail is carefully considered for its aesthetic effect. Design-savvy customers understand this modernist aesthetic as "good design".

Apple's staged experience was intimately connected with its aesthetic, developed through devices such as the iPod, iPhone and iPad. Beyond simply a surface, Apple's approach to product design is celebrated as synonymous with "integrity, essence, deference, style and honesty".[21] This celebrated aesthetic extended across Apple's interface and web design, ensuring a coherent and consistent user experience. As the company expanded, Apple translated this minimal, refined design language into its clear, sober interiors. Like Aesop, Apple pursued the strategy of curating their own retail experience that could differentiate their products from competitors. Importantly, the open spaces, free of artificial surfaces, decoration or hidden surprises, also underline a moral dimension: integrity and honesty.

In both Apple and Aesop stores, minimalism serves to eliminate distractions and focus customers' attention on interaction with the products. Clear, simple signage and clean surfaces offer a calm and orderly respite for customers. The interiors of both contain little furniture and few fixtures. As with Apple stores, Aesop stores borrow from the language of the modern art gallery, channelling the customer's attention onto the few significant objects on display. Aesop staff, who are not only expected to be knowledgeable and passionate about the products, also adhere to rules such as a ban on takeaway coffee cups or personal objects in stores.[22] Eliminating distractions to focus on the customer's sensory experience is crucial.

Another parallel to the Aesop store is the fashion boutique. Interiors for high fashion brands "are often financially and sensually extravagant, short-lived and rely as much on publicity as on their own physical form for their effect".[23] Certainly the Aesop stores fit the "sensually extravagant" part of this definition and, like the fashion boutique, aesthetic qualities differentiate them from mass market stores. Starting in the 1990s, numerous collaborations between architects and fashion houses resulted in distinctive, extravagant interiors. Prada, for example, beginning with Rem Koolhaas and OMA's celebrated 2001 New York flagship store, forged a reputation for unique boutique interiors, while Louis Vuitton also worked with leading global architects to design distinctive flagship stores in the 2000s.[24]

Beyond architectural distinction, fashion boutiques have long offered customers a transformative experience that parallels the Aesop one. As Mark Pimlott notes about 1960s boutiques such as those of Mary Quant and Chanel: "Shoppers often left the shops wearing their purchases, as though their visit to the boutique was part of their own personal transformation."[25] Such boutiques and their transformative experiences set the scene for the twenty-first-century flagship stores of Prada or Louis Vuitton. But, with the rise of internet shopping, a physical store needed to promise more than simply the opportunity to buy something.

Although similar in some ways, the modest Aesop store offers customers a different experience to an architect-designed fashion boutique or an Apple store. The company's design programme is closer to a specific architectural tradition that emerged (or re-emerged) in the 1990s. This "phenomenological approach" to design, which involves a renewed interest in local context and sensual engagement, has its roots in the work of architects and theorists such as Christian Norberg-Schulz, Juhani Pallasmaa and Peter Zumthor. It comprised designers who opposed a modernist tradition that emphasized abstract form, scale and universal space but not the "experiential" aspects of architecture.[26]

From the 1970s, Norwegian architect and educator Norberg-Schulz popularized the idea of *genius loci*, the "character" or atmosphere of a place.[27] In contrast to post-war modernists who perceived architectural space as universal and anonymous, Norberg-Schulz argued that designers should engage with a site's specific topography, history and culture. Aesop store designers clearly begin with the *genius loci* of the local neighbourhood as a starting point for some stores, as in the example of the Upper East Side store. In other stores, designers use recycled local materials that evoke memories – timber or tiles from a recently demolished warehouse, for example, worn and marked by past use.

Yet other stores express their sense of place with new materials. The 2018 Century City Aesop store in Los Angeles, for example, is a circular-shaped space covered in pale blue tiles. The tiles curve over the edge of the sink and counter, reminding customers of California's outdoor pool culture. Brisbane's James Street store (another design by March Studio), opened in 2016, features a curved fibreglass shell that evokes surfboards or kayaks, connecting the store to the city's leisure activities. Or an Aesop store in Fukuoka, Japan, designed in collaboration with Japanese architects SIMPLICITY in 2015. Located near the city's Samurai district, the store's walls and counter are covered with oxidized iron and polished steel sinks, the raw metals suggestive of ancient craftsmanship.

Building upon Norberg-Schulz's critique of modernism's abstraction, architect and writer Juhani Pallasmaa responded to architecture's "hegemony of vision". Pallasmaa argued that "the inhumanity of contemporary architecture and cities can be understood as the consequence of the neglect of the body and the senses, and an imbalance in our sensory system".[28] Spaces of our technological world, he argued, engender feelings of detachment and alienation. To counter this, designers should situate the body (not only the eyes) as central to architectural experience. Beyond the traditional five Aristotelean senses (sight, sound, touch, smell, taste), scientists have added others such as balance, perception of hot and cold, pain, time and hunger, and architects have begun to take these more seriously too.[29]

Certainly, Aesop designers carefully consider sensory interaction when designing stores. Beyond the striking visual aspects and tactile quality of the materials, the first thing most customers notice when entering an Aesop store is the distinctive smell – citrus, cedar, lavender – some kind of herbal or botanical aroma. Different Aesop stores have different scents and change them according to local seasons, so it is hard to be precise about the exact qualities of the scent.[30] As well as being notoriously difficult to describe in words, smell typically goes unnoticed in design and architectural projects. Yet smells produce what Walter Benjamin described as "the inaccessible refuge of the *mémoire involontaire*", the involuntary memory often associated with intensely personal and intimate memories.[31]

Aesop is not the first brand to consciously design ambient scents to entice or entrance customers. Paul Poiret's fashion house, for example, developed a signature perfume in 1911, followed by Chanel, Worth, Schiaparelli and others in the 1920s. Most famously, Chanel sold her fragrances only in her boutiques, and smelling them was part of the retail experience:

> ... she atomized *No.5* in her fitting rooms, presenting it as an essential part of the Chanel dressing process. The sense of smell therefore became an integral aspect in the consumption experience, and was as important within the process of shopping for womenswear or accessories as it was in shopping for perfume itself.[32]

In this way, customers associated a scent such as Chanel's No.5 with both Chanel's clothing and a shared culture – in this case, membership of a fashionable elite.

In the first decade of the 2000s, some mass market retailers experimented with signature scents within stores.[33] Abercrombie & Fitch, for example, were famous for emitting their "Fierce" cologne into stores in the mid-2000s, while electronics retailer Samsung developed a signature fragrance called Intimate Blue, designed "to evoke Samsung's cobalt blue logo".[34] Sensory marketing companies aimed to fill retail spaces not only with distinctive colours, forms and materials, but also with distinctive scents. While this was a passing phase for most retailers, designing products with natural aromas was Paphitis's original inspiration and remains central to Aesop's in-store experience.

Smell can evoke powerful memories. "Odour memory", writes one theorist, "has an embodied presence".[35] This is sometimes referred to as the "Proust effect", named for his famous lines in *Remembrance of Things Past* where the narrator's childhood memories vividly return with a specific smell. But smells do not conjure up memories any better than other senses (consider music, for example). What smells do well is evoke a particular context, that is, smells trigger memories of an environment and its people.[36] Even so, there are no universal or consistent meanings to a particular smell. Aesop's designers can only create a set of consistent cues that customers associate with their fragrances. In both physical and psychological reactions to smells, we associate them with specific environments and interactions – in this case, the serene vibe of an Aesop store.

Aesop's website contains a handy guide to identifying smells according to four categories: fresh (citrus, herbs), floral (jasmine, rose), woody (cedar, spices) and opulent (patchouli, sandalwood). Their aromatic formulations typically combine these categories to create a blend. Not only are the smells distinctive, but to make them truly memorable, Aesop aims to associate them with a specific place. As opposed to the cosmetic counters of a department store or stores that sell many brands, the Aesop store is a controlled place within which customers can categorize and remember odours.[37] As a concentrated sensory experience, the Aesop store also contrasts the city outside. Importantly, the customer can take some of this memorable experience home in the form of a scented lotion, cream, exfoliant or shampoo.

Touch is another essential part of the Aesop sensory experience. Importantly, the in-store experience includes staff applying creams, hydrators, oils and serums onto a customer's hands and washing them off. Aesop staff are trained to wash a customer's hands – a particularly intimate interaction – and advise on skin treatments. Engaging a customer's sense of touch is important for a skincare brand, and such intimacy generates trust. In a digital world comprised of automated and impersonal interactions, an intimate ritual like this is rare.

While this aspect of touch is obvious, in a more subtle way, the materials of an Aesop interior are also designed to engage our tactile senses. This desire to run your fingers over a worn stone basin or trace the grain of aged timber is a compelling part of the Aesop experience. Here, the Aesop store opposes Apple's cool, smooth surfaces and hard materials. An Aesop store, in contrast, is a carefully curated textural environment in which touch, smell and taste are engaged as emotional and intimate senses. Unlike Apple's emphasis on new – anonymous, universal – materials, Aesop's self-conscious inclusion of worn materials, recycled fixtures and sinks prompt an engagement with a neighbourhood and its history.

More recently, theorists have discussed this sensory approach in terms of "atmosphere".[38] For architect Peter Zumthor, for example, atmosphere is something we perceive "through our emotional sensibility".[39] He writes of the immediate, spontaneous response to a building or a space, and how this holistic perception affects our body akin to listening to music. Atmosphere is a term that attempts to encapsulate that elusive resonance of an interior, "perceived by the felt-body in a given space, but never fully attributable to the objectual set of that space".[40] Juhani Pallasmaa argues that our experience of architecture is not only multisensory, "but it also involves judgments beyond the five Aristotelian senses, such as the sense of orientation, gravity, balance, stability, motion, duration, continuity, scale and illumination".[41] This embodied experience, perceived in a diffuse and peripheral manner "fuses perception, memory, and imagination".[42]

An Aesop interior encapsulates this holistic, embodied experience. In contrast to alienating and anonymous "non-places", airport terminals and shopping malls, for example, filled with artificial surfaces and "non-human mediation",[43] an Aesop store offers customers a personal, sensory and intimate experience. Yet customers are not alone in this experience, but part of a perceived community. As General Manager Suzanne Santos puts it:

I'm always reluctant to categorise our customers – they really are such a diverse range of people – yet I do believe there's a shared consciousness amongst them, there's a belief in the ability to make change through their cosmetic purchases.[44]

If sensory impressions are subjective and personal, this shared consciousness suggests something universal. Aesop's tranquil, minimal interiors offer customers a respite from noise, distractions and the speed of the city: a moment of sensual indulgence and self-care. This, combined with their carefully curated collection of products evoke a shared experience.

Self-Care and Sustainability

Aesop's sensory experience aligns to two popular, contemporary discourses: wellness and sustainability. The first centres on self-care, the second on planetary care. In the first, customers understand skincare as a means of individual transformation, related to practices such as meditation, mindfulness, yoga, health spas and nutrition regimes. Such techniques aim at improving our bodies, minds and emotional states. But Aesop customers also care about the planet. Aesop's emphasis on sustainability serves to alleviate that sneaking suspicion that wealthy lifestyles of the Global North are a primary contributor to climate change. The rhetorical strategy of an Aesop store offers customers transformative cures for mind, body, soul and the planet.

In a later reflection on the "experience economy", Pine and Gilmore argue that corporations should aim to produce increasingly customized experiences, or "creating more and more value for individuals by getting closer and closer to what each individual truly wants and needs, culminating in the individual-changing offerings of transformations".[45] Transformative experiences are defined by other critics as *meaningful* experiences.[46] Here, Aesop's interiors offer a transformative individual experience, as General Manager Santos explained in a 2013 interview:

> To be able to give a person an opportunity to understand Aesop through demonstration, whether the person actually wants to put it on their face, or if they just want the pleasure of it on their hands, is vitally important to us. We invite the individual to become involved. It beckons you to be part of it. Companies generally try to force their own culture onto you, but we'd rather invite you to immerse yourself in it.[47]

An Aesop store is a calm cocoon for an individual to immerse themselves in with staff who attend to their individual needs. But more than this, a customer also feels like a participant, a co-creator of their own transformation.

If we take the idea of a sensory experience seriously, interiors – "ambient environments delimited by the aura of affect and subjectivity" – can be transformative.[48] This seems particularly acute when considering an Aesop store. We inhale its scents, touch its surfaces, consume its visual language and interact with its materials and products *before* we can rationally reflect on the experience. But how does such an interior transform us? Philosopher and psychoanalyst Teresa Brennan suggests that affective environments can, "if only for an instant, alter the biochemistry and neurology of the subject. The 'atmosphere' or the environment literally gets into the individual."[49] In this way, the sensory experience of an Aesop store has a transformative effect our bodies and our minds.

Rather than the mirror of a cosmetics counter, an Aesop experience centres on the sink. A customer's face and body are not called into question by photographs of models' unattainable beauty or mirrored surfaces to make them feel inadequate. It contains no screens or cameras monitoring their every move. Instead, authenticity is reinforced by "natural" aromas, herbal teas, "raw" materials, minimal packaging and clean, open spaces. The sink functions as a kind of central altar around which the hand-washing ritual occurs. It is not too much of a stretch to see a spiritual dimension to this experience:

> In religious rites, the altar serves as a physical surface upon which devotional practices are prepared and performed, whereas in rhetorical performances of piety the altar is a metaphorical locus of devotion, an organizing point toward which the pious person directs their attention.[50]

Rather than a distant deity, the Aesop experience is devoted to the customer. The emphasis on clean and pure design reinforces the association between Aesop's products and purity – recall the Instagram feed with its clear, sharp images, clean lines, simple colours and minimal typography – to reinforce an honest, uncluttered, authentic lifestyle.

This is a realm of wellness, a lifestyle model that "promises each of us repair, autonomy, purification, respite, and optimal functioning, and it also provides us a script for becoming better versions of ourselves".[51] Aesop is a hair, body, skincare and fragrance brand but, more than each of these individual products, it offers the customer a promise of transformation. As an early manifesto stated, "We advocate the use of our formulations as part of a balanced life that includes a healthy diet, sensible exercise, a moderate intake of red wine, and a regular dose of stimulating literature."[52] Nourishing skin care treatments accompany nourishment for the mind.

In another recent interview, Santos again emphasized the ritual nature of the Aesop experience:

We host our customers in calm, warm, comforting spaces that look, feel and smell good—each store is a restorative haven of visual harmony where they can sit and have some tea if they wish, and explore formulations with us. We have a meaningful conversation to understand their concerns, skin type, environment, and preferred textures, then demonstrate each product at the sink so customers may experience how it feels on their skin.[53]

Such ritual and conversational aspects of the Aesop store situate it in direct contrast to the Amazon Go model of automated retail: impersonal, functional and efficient. In a society increasingly defined by automation and anonymous transactions, an Aesop store offers customers a tactile, caring experience that combines bodily ritual and personal interaction.

The rhetoric of care evoked by the Aesop experience is heightened in busy urban contexts where bodies are increasingly pushed to their limits. From office workers' long hours to gig workers' constant hours, contemporary work cultures demand bodies that are commodities to be consumed by work. The results are exhausted bodies consumed by stress, anxiety and fatigue. In this context, a few minutes of luxurious self-care in an Aesop store make sense, particularly if it comes with the promise of repair and renewal.[54] In this respect, a visit to Aesop parallels wellness rituals such as attending yoga or meditation classes, spa treatments or other rituals designed to mitigate burnout, stress and over-work. Restoration and calm are reinforced with every Aesop interaction – from the stores to the products to the social media feeds – all are designed to rebalance, nourish and rejuvenate customers' bodies and minds.

Aesop capitalize on the connection between wellness and luxury. A key part of its promotion strategy, for example, has been partnership with up-scale hotels and restaurants, especially to have their signature handwash, the Resurrection Aromatique Hand Wash, stocked in the bathrooms. Composed of Mandarin Rind, Rosemary Leaf and Cedar, the citrusy, woody aroma is distinctive enough to trigger memories and to associate Aesop with a specific place. These are carefully chosen places and businesses, designed to complement the brand, such as the Gramercy Park Hotel, New York, which has stocked Aesop shampoos and hand soaps since 2014.[55] The emphasis is on luxury places that exude a similar vibe.

Along with luxury, Paphitis forged a reputation for Aesop by using high culture, particularly literature. An intellectual emphasis was a distinctive foil within a cosmetics industry renowned for superficial images of models and celebrities. From Aesop's inception, Paphitis used literature and storytelling as part of his marketing campaigns. The brand is named after Aesop, the ancient Greek writer whose fables functioned to instruct correct behaviour or convey moral lessons. With Aesop as a key motif, the brand immediately carried connotations of ancient Greek wisdom but without asking customers to think too hard.[56]

This attachment to literary and ancient Greek culture continued. A section of the 2021 Aesop website titled "The Athenaeum", for example, featured short articles such as "Anti-Oxidants in Skincare" alongside the more intellectual "View from Above: a Stoic practice for daily perspective", an article that concludes with a quote from Roman Stoic and Emperor, Marcus Aurelius.[57] Prior to its recent redesign, the Aesop website was sprinkled with inspirational quotes from famous writers. Quotes also appeared on the walls of the stores, as well as cups and candles. Walt Whitman and Virginia Woolf, philosophers Baruch Spinoza and Walter Benjamin, composers Frederic Chopin and Felix Mendelssohn were all represented by one-line aphorisms – bite-sized intellectual snacks for a busy, information-saturated customer.[58]

More recently, the Queer Library initiative in select stores in Australia, the United States, United Kingdom, Canada and Taiwan continue the literary theme. In 2022, for example, to coincide with Pride Week, Aesop stores in Sydney and Melbourne were emptied of products and filled with books by Queer authors. These were offered to customers for free (one per customer), and Aesop repeated the initiative in 2023 and expanded it to include BIPOC authors. In this way, Aesop positioned itself not simply in relationship to literature but to alternative narratives, asking its customers "Consider your bookshelf: who is – and isn't – on it?"[59] In 2022, Aesop stores in Singapore and Shanghai featured a similar Women's Library for International Women's Day.[60]

The ongoing relationship and collaborations with writers and literary organizations includes a Future Fables podcast, launched in 2022 in collaboration with the Literary Hub website. Promoted as "bedtime fables for adults", these are described by Aesop as best "paired with an aromatic candle and cup of freshly brewed tea (or else something a little stronger), these stories are catalysts for conversation, contemplation and moments of quietude".[61] The short podcasts – seven to eight minutes – offer intellectual stimulation, designed to complement the smells and tastes familiar to customers of an Aesop store.

But Aesop's rhetoric of care extends beyond self-care. Sustainability is continually reinforced throughout the Aesop store experience – the plain, no-waste packaging, the raw or recycled materials in-store and the emphasis on natural, plant-based ingredients. Yet the material realities of an expanding global corporation differs from this reassuring rhetoric. In a 2020 interview with CEO Michael O'Keeffe, for example, the interviewer asked what keeps him up at night. O'Keeffe replied:

> Over the last 12 months plastics have almost become a four-letter word. Probably 60 per cent of my packaging is in plastics. According to analysis, glass actually has a larger carbon footprint than plastics, but it is seen in a different light. Part of it is balancing our PR with real, underlying sustainability

objectives. Ideally, we'd be ahead of public sentiment, where it's moving and what customers expect. Sometimes we're a little bit behind and need to catch up.[62]

Perhaps this is no surprise. The rhetoric of sustainability rarely stands up to the reality of a growing corporation with complex global supply chains, manufacturing and product sourcing. Here, the Body Shop's "greenwashing" exposé is a telling lesson for Aesop customers. As is its subsequent fate.

Despite originally positioning The Body Shop as an alternative to major cosmetics brands, Anita Roddick sold the company to L'Oréal in 2006. In 2017, L'Oréal sold it to Brazilian cosmetics giant, Natura. Natura began in 1969 "to create and sell products and services that promote the harmonious relationship of the individual with oneself, with other and with nature".[63] It capitalized on an interest in natural ingredients from the Amazon rainforests and built a well-known brand across South America. In 2012, Natura bought a majority stake in Aesop, then took over the company in 2016.[64] The Body Shop and Aesop were thus part of the same multinational, but briefly. In 2023, L'Oréal purchased Aesop. Despite its Melbourne origins, Aesop is now part of a global cosmetics giant based in Paris.

My analysis above focused on Aesop's signature or flagship stores in global cities. But the company has also designed "watered down" versions for malls and less-glamorous locations. A larger, new format store on London's Regent Street with four treatment rooms for consultations suggests another shift to more obviously tourist locations rather than the trendy neighbourhoods formerly favoured by Aesop.[65] Part of the appeal of Aesop in the 2010s was the "word-of-mouth" or "in the know" appeal of hip locations. The brand's literary aspirations have also dissipated over the past decade and there is now an Aesop counter within my local department store. Aesop is in danger of committing that cardinal sin of luxury brands: becoming ubiquitous.

Chapter 7
Acceleration and Materiality: Zara

After marvelling at Porto's blue-and-white tiled São Bento station, I walked up a twisting street to Rua Santa Catarina. I stopped to admire the curling patterns of the street's rough-cut cobbles, its shops and apartments tiled or painted aqua, terracotta or pale yellow. People sat outside cafés drinking espressos and eating *pastéis de nata*, Portugal's famed custard tarts. Though tempted to join them, I'd come to visit Zara's first store outside of Spain. Opened in 1988, it launched the brand's global expansion. I was here to experience the store's latest incarnation, a 2022 renovation of the historic façade, expansion and refurbishment of the interiors and the integration of new technological innovations.[1]

Zara occupies a three-storey, nineteenth-century building. In contrast to its neighbours, the façade is discreet: grey masonry, white paint and thin, cast-iron black balconies. Each element highlights the rectilinear, formal façade. Zara's flagship store does not attract passers-by with bright signs, digital screens or technicolour window displays (like Benetton opposite), only a wall of windows onto the street with a logo quietly above them. In the context of Rua Santa Catarina, the Zara store appears otherworldly. Visible through the windows, the opening ensemble comprises three mannequins sitting, standing on and standing beside a twisted white sculpture (Figure 37). Like those minimalist steel sculptures that inhabit corporate plazas, the sculpture stands simply as an abstract form to pose with.

Inside, I'm struck by the luxurious emptiness that recalls the minimal interiors of 1990s fashion boutiques. The walls, ceiling and floor are off-white. Thin, black hanging racks occupy the centre of the large, open space, while low shelving and racks punctuated by large mirrors run along each wall (Figure 38). The lighting is subtle: both uplighting and downlighting illuminate the walls, while fluorescent tubes highlight the escalators. Pop music plays quietly. Thin trees in pots pose at the edges of the space. The few mannequins – white figures in humanoid form – are as simple as possible. A single digital screen displays images of models wearing the clothes in front of the screen. Otherwise, the store features no posters or photographs of models. No promotional signage. No distractions from the clothes.

Figure 37 Zara store, Porto, exterior. Author photo.

Figure 38 Zara store, Porto, the luxury of space. Author photo.

The store's three levels, accessible by escalators on one side or an elevator on the other, begin with Women's wear on Level 1, Women's and Children's wear on Level 2, and Men's and Sports' wear on Level 3. Such spatial division is indicative of the primary market – Zara's customers skew female.[2] Level 1's clothing is targeted towards younger women – these are fashionable, unusual, statement garments. Each rack holds six to a dozen pieces. This week, a used look is on-trend. Pre-distressed jeans, pre-stretched tops, threadbare sweaters with runs, frayed hems and readymade holes (Figure 39). Though new, some pieces look like they are already at the end of their life. One or two outings and they will disintegrate.

I head upstairs, past the white canvas bags with black Zara logos that sit by the escalators. As at IKEA, the bags are waiting for me to fill them. Beyond the on-trend "show pieces", I encounter more conventional shirts, trousers and coats, presented in ready-made ensembles with bags, shoes and other accessories beside them (Figure 40). Shoes below trousers, shirts matched with hats. There's a mix-and-match approach too, that suggests I can combine these with clothing nearby that has similar materials, colours or patterns. There's such a wide variety it's difficult to identify a distinctive Zara style.

Neatly stacked shirts and trousers sit on minimal timber tables that remind me of Apple's tables. But, as I look more carefully, I notice that some are timber while others have a faux-stone veneer, as if they were marble (Figure 41). But

Figure 39 Zara store, Porto, distressed fashion. Author photo.

Figure 40 Zara store, Porto, mix and match ensembles. Author photo.

Figure 41 Zara store, Porto, stone veneer tables. Author photo.

who examines the props that closely? The store's design is consistent across the Women's and Men's sections, the only significantly different display is "Zara Athleticz", an all-silver section at the back of the Men's level. Even here, the display furniture is unobtrusive. Behind it stand similarly minimal change rooms: white cubicles with plain, brown curtains that contain only a mirror and a few pegs.

Rather than at the exit, Zara payment sections are at the rear of each level. On one side is a regular checkout, on the other, an "Automatic Payment Points" where customers can scan their purchases at a machine on a silver shelf (Figure 42). Simply pick up new garments, scan the labels and tap a card or phone. This way, there is no waiting in line and no need to engage with the store's staff. To answer questions, every garment has a label with a QR code which connects customers to the Zara website where they can find further information on materials, sizes and colours.

Figure 42 Zara store, Porto, self-checkout station. Author photo.

I understand the self-service, the latest on-trend clothing and even the mix and match fashion for a digital generation accustomed to cut and paste. On racks or thin pseudo-mannequins, the clothes appear flat enough to drag and drop across a screen. It's the store's neutrality and calm atmosphere that I find strange. It corresponds to traditional expressions of luxury – the empty space, minimal details and sober décor. But, given Zara's reputation as a "fast fashion" brand, the store seems modest, serene and – I have to say it – slow. This contrast of ever-increasing speed with the static store and its clothes makes Zara an intriguing case study.

A Short History of Zara

Zara's origins lie in the small town of A Coruña in the north-western Spanish province of Galicia.[3] In the 1950s, Galicia was a relatively poor province with an economy based on shipbuilding, canning, fishing and farming. With no textile industry or history of garment manufacturing, it was an unlikely place to launch a fashion empire. Yet here, Zara's founder Amancio Ortega built one of the world's largest fashion brands. At thirteen, he dropped out of school to join his brother Antonio and sister Josefina to work in a clothing store. In post-war Spain, clothes stores were small, family-run businesses that offered a modest range at modest prices, and the store he worked in sold clothes made mainly in Catalonia.

In 1963, Amancio pitched an idea to the shop owner to sell dressing gowns, which he said he and his brother and their wives could make at home for a lower price and similar quality to their usual suppliers. When this proved successful, the brothers and their wives quit their jobs to devote themselves to their new clothes-making business, with Amancio assuming the managing role. By the mid-1960s, their small workshop expanded to an industrial factory on the outskirts of A Coruña. Here, they designed and manufactured clothes – particularly women's clothes – and sold them to Spanish wholesalers, and, by the early 1970s, to wholesalers in France, Germany, Belgium and Lebanon. But Amancio Ortega believed a direct connection between production and customers would prove more profitable.

Ortega opened his first – and short-lived – bazaar-type retail store called Sprint in 1972.[4] More successfully, Ortega opened the first Zara store in A Coruña in 1975, opposite the city's most popular department store. The original store was described as "spacious and set up like a bazaar: it sells not only clothing produced by Ortega's plants and those of other manufacturers, but also records, books, gifts and an assortment of items".[5] But the store soon dispensed with this wide range to stock only clothes designed and produced by Ortega's factories. Zara sold clothes for middle-class women, clothes that looked like high-end fashion but cost considerably less.

Over the next decade, Ortega opened dozens of Zara stores all over Spain. After years of dictatorship and relative economic hardship – Francisco Franco died in 1975 – the late 1970s and 1980s were a period of growth and consumerism. Zara rode this wave and Ortega restructured the company as Inditex (Industria de Diseño Textil) in 1985 to integrate the factories and stores. By this time "Inditex had forty-one stores, $86 million in annual sales, 1,100 employees, and seven manufacturing subsidiaries".[6] In 1988, Zara opened their first store outside Spain in Porto – the one described in this chapter's opening – followed by stores in Paris (1989) and New York (1990).

Zara's first logo was a simple one that resembled a cardboard label with a tie, drawn in black with white lettering, capital letters "ZARA" and below, in white serif, "Tiendas de Moda" ("fashion stores"). In the mid-1980s, Zara used a simpler, single wordmark: black capital letters on white. It has changed little since then. A stretched-out version appeared in 2011, then a compressed version where the letters overlap in a 2019 redesign by Baron & Baron. The wordmark remains compact, concise and readable at a glance, while the serif lettering looks elegant and classic, like that of luxury brands such as Dior or Louis Vuitton.

Like IKEA, Zara established their own supply chains, built their own factories and used a network of workshops around Galicia to make their clothes. By eliminating intermediaries between factory and customer and copying the latest trends, they offered middle-class women "high fashion" for a modest price. In this sense, Ortega's mission to "democratize fashion" was remarkably like Kamprad's for furniture – neither mass market nor high fashion, but products that appeared to be elite and fashionable but at lower prices. The two companies' expansion in Europe, then globally, in the 1990s and 2000s also followed a similar pattern. But fashion had opportunities that furniture did not.

In the 1980s and 1990s, the fashion industry was still organized around seasonal collections, with fashion houses typically spending six months or more to design, prepare, produce and distribute clothing to stores. Some collections sold out immediately while others left companies with remaindered stock. Zara's strategy was to disrupt this seasonal cycle by continually updating stock in stores yet limiting volume to ensure that each style would sell out. Rather than retain clothes for a season, Zara's cycled through styles every fortnight. For customers, a visit to a Zara store reinforced a new temporal regime – buy now as these clothes will be gone next time you visit.

Zara's constant churn of styles was founded not on originality but on a culture of imitation. Zara designers copy, mimicking luxury fashion brands, street styles and anything in-between that is currently on-trend. This practice has inevitably led to accusations of copyright infringement and court cases involving both major fashion brands and independent artists, designers and illustrators.[7] Such cases are notoriously hard to convict, with one legal scholar concluding that "fast fashion companies exploit the lack of protections and consequences, as a main component of their business model".[8] However, one 2018 Italian court case found Zara had infringed the copyright of Italian brands Diesel and Marni over jeans and sandals.[9] But, like IKEA, designing original, distinctive products was never Zara's aim.

Another distinction was Zara's lack of traditional advertising and marketing. In fashion, the 1980s and 1990s was the era of celebrity supermodels and controversial campaigns such as Benetton's "United Colors" or Calvin Klein's underwear advertisements. Supermodels commanded huge fees for endorsing a brand. Rather than risk association with a particular model or message, Zara persisted without advertising, famous models or celebrities. Word of mouth had helped spread the Zara message: fashionable clothes at low prices. Ultimately, Zara used the stores and their contents as its primary marketing tool.

Ortega constantly refined the design of Zara stores and remained intimately involved in every aspect of store design.[10] Even with hundreds of stores around Spain and Europe, Zara stores were designed to a consistent template. First, each was situated in a central city location with high visibility and foot traffic. Second, large display windows and spacious, light-filled interiors remained free of clutter. Third, every store was clearly divided into zones for females, males and children; and finally, stores were designed with little storage space so that the entire stock was displayed on the floor.[11]

In customer service, Ortega also sought to differentiate Zara from other clothing stores. Early innovations included extending the opening hours and a loyalty card for regular customers. Other services provided by Zara stores were quick alterations to the garments, almost unrestricted return and exchange, and staff could search for items that had run out in-store among other nearby Zara stores. Finally, staff left customers free to browse rather than hassle them for sales.

Zara's shop windows became particularly significant. Ortega hired Jordi Bernadó, a designer with set design experience, to design Zara's displays. He developed

> a kind of theatrical, almost cinematographic, scene rather than a conventional display window ... with predominant colours which suggested or emulated the chromatic trends of the clothing on display inside. The models, mannequins, were not locked in static postures but were in movement. They were not standing, staring forward, as was normal in shops and large stores but were seated or in postures which suggested group scenarios, at home, at a party, or strolling through the street of some city.[12]

To parallel the fast-changing collections, Zara redesigned their window displays every two or three weeks, and store layouts frequently. Store design proved so important that Oretga established a "1,500-square-meter pilot store ... in

A Coruña, where all new store layouts were designed and tested before being rolled out around the world".[13] This life-sized, fully equipped model store in Inditex headquarters is still used today to test new spatial arrangements, display windows and interior ideas.

In the 1990s, as Zara expanded globally, it refined its stores, including details such as lighting carefully designed to focus customers' attention on the clothing.[14] Overall, the interiors paralleled a broader, minimalist trend among fashion boutiques, associated with Japanese brands such as Issey Miyake, Yohji Yamamoto and Comme des Garçons and American brands such as Calvin Klein and Donna Karan. Zara adopted this minimal aesthetic – white, open spaces, unadorned surfaces and minimal furnishing or fixtures to distract customers – as did Apple (see Chapter 1). Ironically, customers typically associate minimalism in fashion boutiques with timelessness.

Ironically, as what Zara became known for was their "fast-fashion" model that could reproduce designer fashion quickly at a modest cost. As Zara launched its first store in New York in 1990, the *New York Times* used the term "fast fashion" to describe the store's mission. In this article, fashion reporter Anne-Marie Schiro quoted the head of Zara's United States operation: "'Every week, there's a new shipment from Spain … The stock in the store changes every three weeks. The latest trend is what we're after. It takes 15 days between a new idea and getting it into stores.'"[15] This timeframe – just over two weeks – from conception to customer gave Zara an advantage over high-end fashion boutiques. Even rivals like Swedish-based H&M took twice as long.

This quick turnaround was central to Zara's success. Fast fashion was predicated on speed. Since Zara's original market was restricted to Spain, distances were short, so Ortega was able to manufacture and ship clothes quickly to stores.[16] As the company grew and its stores spread across Europe, Zara expanded production to Portugal, Morocco and Turkey, countries with low labour costs but close enough to keep distances short and ensure the fastest possible time between design, manufacture and distribution. While other brands rushed to outsource to cheap labour in Asia, Zara kept most of their production close to Spain and developed sophisticated logistics and distribution systems to ensure fast delivery to stores.

Zara's first step was speeding up the design process. By the 1990s, fashion was a global industry and customers saw runway fashion from Paris, Milan, New York or London almost instantly in magazines. Zara's design process began not with a single designer's original idea, but with an understanding of what the customer wanted and at what price. To do this, their creative teams

> worked from information provided by store managers who reported daily what was selling. Sales staff, who had been trained to elicit customer comments regarding their tastes and preferences, also provided timely information. The

design teams also made use of style bloggers, trend watchers and staff who gathered design ideas from college campuses, concerts, clubs, bars, restaurants and other public gatherings.[17]

In A Coruña, a central team known as "commercials", comprised of designers and product managers, communicated between the stores and product development:

> They traveled extensively, observing what residents were wearing and talking at length with store managers to find out what kinds of clothes were selling. Even more importantly, they also tried to learn what kinds of clothes would sell if Zara made them. Store product managers communicated what they had seen and heard to the design teams, helping them keep abreast of fast-changing trends and demands.[18]

The next part of the equation was clothing production. Here, Zara adopted the Japanese "just-in-time" production processes, first developed by Toyota for car manufacturing. Also known as "lean manufacturing", this method involves producing only the amount of clothing needed at the time stores require stock. This way, Zara maximized efficiency, ensuring less waste and faster production times.

Logistics was another key to Zara's speed. In the 1990s, Zara shipped most of their clothes around Europe by road or rail. As the company expanded globally in the twenty-first century, it increasingly used not only fleets of lorries across Europe but 747 cargo planes. Zara's original logistics and distribution centre in Arteixo moved to Zaragoza, a more central location that proved better for lorry drivers around Spain and into France. But more importantly, Zaragoza had an airport that could better serve Zara's global distribution. Such was Zara's growth, that by 2018, Zaragaro became the second biggest cargo hub in Spain.[19]

As well as Zara's global growth, Inditex purchased another six brands. These are Pull & Bear (1991) for young, casual wear, Massimo Dutti (1991) for more luxurious fashion, Bershka (1998) for teenagers, Stradivarius (1999) for young women, Oysho (2001) for activewear and Zara Home (2003) for homewares. This portfolio of brands used the Zara production, logistics and distribution networks so that by 2005, Zara became the biggest fashion retailer in Europe, overtaking H&M, and by 2008, the biggest in the world, overtaking the US-based Gap.[20]

Most recently, Zara's 2022 Annual Report reported a net profit of 4.1 billion euros across the seven brands, more than 5,800 stores (of these, 1,885 are Zara stores) and almost 165,000 staff, mostly young women who work in the stores.[21] A team of over 700 designers work at Zara to produce over 20,000 new products annually. Almost half of the resulting 450 million garments are made in either Spain or nearby countries – Portugal, Morocco, Turkey – and the remainder in Asia. The most fashionable, on-trend garments are produced in factories and workshops close to Spain (to ensure fast delivery times) while longer-term staples such as t-shirts are produced in Bangladesh, China or Vietnam.

Although the current CEO is Armancio's daughter, Marta Ortega Pérez, Armancio retains a majority share of director voting rights. Yet Pérez has introduced changes to the Zara model recently, including celebrity and designer collaborators including Charlotte Gainsbourg, model Kaia Gerber and designer Narciso Rodriguez.[22] Other recent collaborations include a project with Vincent Van Duysen to design furnishings for Zara Home and a 2022 advertising campaign that featured supermodel Kate Moss. And, while Zara was slow to adopt to digital retail, its digital offerings have increased in recent years, particularly with its social media "Ambassador" programme. Yet, despite Zara's online sales and marketing shifts, the Zara store remains as a crucial site in which customers experience the brand's juxtaposition of ever-increasing speed and static clothes.

Acceleration

"The elite initiates a fashion and, when the mass imitates it in an effort to obliterate the external distinctions of class", wrote sociologist George Simmel in 1957, "abandons it for a newer mode – a process that quickens with the increase of wealth".[23] Although this process sped up in the decades following Simmel's article, fast fashion accelerated it to an almost instantaneous cycle. But, contrary to Simmel's analysis, the elite are no longer the sole drivers of this process. In our digitally mediated culture, the accelerated rate of change occurs in a feedback loop between celebrities, social media, high fashion, fast fashion and consumers. In such a complex fashion realm, one aspect stands out: the speed of change.

The Zara store is a good place to unravel a popular image in which new technologies have sped up various aspects of daily life and made us busier than ever.[24] Here, the Zara store stands as a neutral stage where we can experience the abstract idea that the "acceleration of processes and events is a fundamental principle of modern society".[25] While a logical perspective would suggest that technological progress should lead to a deceleration, for most people in the Global North, daily life, activities and processes have sped up over the past two decades. The internet, then smartphones, meant many daily activities became enmeshed in digital systems premised on great efficiency and convenience: faster is better. Strangely, the experience of the Zara store is not a fast-paced experience but a calm and sober one. Perhaps, like an Apple or Aesop store, a Zara store represents a serene space for customers who live fast-paced lives.

Yet a Zara store's neutral appearance is also crucial. Unlike established fashion houses – Gucci, Yves Saint Laurent or Chanel, for example – a customer in a Zara store sees no prominent logos, brand marks, monograms or distinctive patterns. In the 1980s and 1990s, fashion brands displayed ever more prominent names and logos on their clothing and accessories. But fast fashion shifted expectations from identification with a specific brand to one centred around the customer. That is, everyone recognizes a Chanel bag due to its prominent interlinked "CC" and signature padded fabric, but a bag bought in Zara appears anonymous. It may be similar in form, materials and colour to the latest Chanel bag, but it is not visibly branded. It's *your* designer bag.

Importantly, a Zara store's accelerated sense of time effects a customer's identity. Since the 1970s, traditional, fixed social positions and identities defined by family, profession or other means, have made way for fluid notions of identity. The varied explanations of "postmodern" identity

> converge in the thesis of a liquefaction of stable personal identity in favor of more open, experimental, and often also fragmentary self-projects. Even in its late modern form, individualization means the increase of possible choices and contingencies with respect to the shaping of one's biography, where this increase primarily involves freer combinability and easier revisability of the building blocks of identity.[26]

Revisable identity is central to understanding the appeal of the Zara store. With a wide range of clothes on display at relatively low prices, the customer is invited to co-design their identity. Sociologist Zygmunt Bauman argues that our contemporary, "all-encompassing culture demands that you acquire the ability to change your identity (or at least its public manifestation) as often, as fast and as efficiently as you change your shirt or your socks".[27] Zara's range of mix-and-match garments and accessories invites the customer to become a bricoleur, using these "building blocks" to construct, edit and revise their identity.

Within Zara's fast fashion model, new styles swiftly supersede the old. For its followers, the idea of "multiple selves in evolution" is central.[28] Permanence, solidity or rootedness are expunged from their lives. Instead, they embrace social identity as fluid or malleable. As opposed to the twentieth-century sense of a stable identity, twenty-first-century identities are fleeting, and the constant churn of fashion devalues the idea of deep, lasting identities or relationships. In a world in which self-projects directed towards stability appear anachronistic, forms of identity based on flexibility and change are systematically favoured.

The Zara store is a neutral container without overt branding, symbols or signs, and without posters or photographs or screens of famous models or celebrities. Instead, Zara positions the customer at the centre of its fashion world. These fashionable clothes are a chance for you to edit and revise your identity (although chances are this identity is one already mediated by social media and celebrities). Unlike previous "lifestyle brands" which relied on heritage, personality, a particular style or aesthetic, Zara remains neutral, with simply a wide range of choice. No longer bound by traditional expectations of class, status, gender, age, culture, identity needs to be continually edited, revised, reasserted and reinforced.

Zara's relative affordability – among the middle classes of the Global North – means identities can be tried out and quickly discarded. In this way, its fast fashion is a response to the fluid nature of identity construction, as well as encouraging its continuation. The store's "constant refreshing of clothing supplies caters precisely to individuals who increasingly need to update their appearance to appropriately 'brand' or package their self".[29] If the continual creation of a lifestyle requires a series of choices, the Zara store offers a wide range. It is particularly suited to customers whose ongoing performance is part of their self-brand: social media influencers, for example, need a constantly updated wardrobe to keep their feeds fresh.

Not only do fast fashion consumers celebrate the fluidity of identity, expressed through different garments over time, but some purchase different garments for different social contexts. One study found that:

> Rather than consistency across contexts, fashion assemblages can be based on an individual's definition of the situation – differing, for example, between not only attending a concert and visiting with friends, but between types of concerts and groups of friends.[30]

While previously a stable self was seen as authentic, now a constantly changing, performative self is. For the performative self, "being 'marked' in the same dress, even on different occasions", is unacceptable.[31]

If postmodern identity arose in the 1980s and 1990s, social media accelerated its revisable and editable sense of identity. Instagram, launched in 2010, proved a perfect platform for this through its immediacy and appearance of spontaneity and authenticity. Fashion was no longer defined by glossy fashion magazines and glamorous models, but "ordinary" people suddenly could become fashion icons. At least that was the perception. Influencers carefully curate and stage posts and reels, crop and manipulate photographs via filters and Photoshop, then compose each image into coherent series or narratives. The phenomenon of personal imagery merging with brand imagery overlapped as fashion brands quickly populated Instagram.[32]

More recently, TikTok has become even more influential than Instagram for a "fashion-forward", younger generation. The platform is associated with even greater acceleration in the form of micro-trends and viral moments. In 2022, for example, Zara's pink satin dress, which sold for $60, appeared on TikTok with the viral hashtag, #ZaraPinkDress, and quickly generated millions of views.[33]

Of course, the trend lasted only a couple of weeks, the dress sold out and TikTok and Zara moved on. For such audiences, a performed life on social media requires the latest costumes and props: the Zara store is like a wardrobe full of them.

Interestingly, like the Zara store, the Zara website is self-consciously neutral and surprisingly calm. The site features predominantly black text on a white background. This gives it an elegant, sober appearance. It is populated by simple, clear photographs and short videos of anonymous models, typically with minimal props and in indistinguishable – rather than glamorous or exotic – locations. Most often, models appear against plain backgrounds, so the clothes stand out. As in the Zara store, the primary focus of the website is the clothes. It is free from distractions, including aspirational lifestyles, scenarios or locations that customers typically encounter on other fashion brands' websites.

Perhaps unexpectedly, Zara's social media feeds are "passive", in that they simply present the latest clothes in a similarly minimal way. Zara's feeds do not host competitions, polls or surveys. In this sense, they are not interactive. Instead, Zara uses digital platforms as an ongoing, changing catalogue of clothes with a strong focus on visual content. But this has not stopped the brand's imagery from being taken up and disseminated by young consumers. On Instagram, Zara is one of the most popular global brands.[34] Social media feeds act as fashion catalogues of the latest offerings presented in simple, neutral photographs and videos that focus on clothes.

The parallel between Zara's fast-changing fashion and the need to constantly update an Instagram or TikTok feed with new content is clear. Exemplified by the acronym FOMO, popularized in the 2010s to describe the anxiety of being left behind, customers know they need to have the latest styles now. Influencers (or would-be influencers) eager to grow their followers require a dynamic stream of new looks but cannot pay high-fashion prices. It is also worth noting here that, despite claims of the democratization of fashion with social media (from twentieth-century glossy magazines and runway shows), the fast fashion industry still reinforces traditional ideals and expectations of feminine beauty.[35]

The acceleration of fast fashion over the past few decades has led to a shift in the "time horizon" for customers. A recent survey suggested:

> The distinctive, recurrent factor is the time horizon that people attribute to fast fashion: it is something temporary that is not expected to last long. This aspect of a short lifespan is a matter of style in the case of young people (they do not expect a fast fashion garment to be "trendy"), while for adults, it is associated with the casualness with which one might buy a product without much thought.[36]

This also represents a shift away from fashion as functional clothing towards an experience: an in-store moment of trying on and walking out with an on-trend item for a single event or social media post. Customers of Zara's in-store experience are centred in a wardrobe filled with clothes and prominent mirrors:

> Consumers feel that they play the starring role in fast fashion: from the act of making a purchase without being under pressure, to the possibility of permitting oneself more license for self-gratification, to the reduction of the risk of remorse after making a purchase because one has purchased something superfluous.[37]

It is worth returning to the worn-looking clothing I encountered in the Porto store (see Figure 39). Consider the sweater with runs or jeans with holes or a skirt with frayed edges. This is new clothing designed to look old. Speed and nowness come to the foreground: no one will wear clothing long enough – years, in this case – for it to acquire such an aged look. But you can buy it right now. It may fall apart after wearing and washing it a few times but customers expect that. In Zara, fashion's planned obsolescence is accelerated to the point where customers

> … accept the short lifespan of things and their preordained demise with equanimity; sometimes with only thinly disguised relish. The most capable and quick-witted adepts of the consumerist art know how to rejoice in the getting rid of things that have passed their use-by (read: enjoy-by) date.[38]

The speed of fast fashion initiated a shift from conspicuous to constant consumption.[39] Even luxury fashion brands finally responded in the 2010s. Brands such as Burberry, Tom Ford, Moschino and Versace adopted an "'instant runway-to-shop" approach in which "a customer could buy a look as soon as it appeared on the runway, rather than having to wait six months for it to appear in the shops. This strategy effectively mimicked fast fashion as it dramatically reduced the time between the fashion show and the in-store availability of the new collection."[40] In this way, fast fashion brands such as Zara changed the production and distribution processes across the clothing industry by shifting customer expectations.

But acceleration may also prove to be Zara's downfall, as new, online-only fashion retailers accelerate processes even more. Although fast fashion brands such as Zara, H&M and Uniqlo expanded their market share "during the 2008 global financial crisis; now this new cohort of companies – known as ultra-fast fashion" are claiming a larger slice of the market.[41] During the Covid-19 pandemic, fast fashion brands such as Zara had the burden of physical store closures, excess staff and inventories.[42] Meanwhile, online-only brands such as

Shein and Boohoo, also known as "ultrafast fashion", operate without bricks and mortar stores. And they offer an even greater range of new styles, released daily, at low prices.

Finally, acceleration also reflects the contemporary precarity of work and the instability – or perceived instability – of oneself, culture or society. In this context, the Zara store represents a constant, physical presence. Within the stability of a Zara store, a mundane form of consumption such as buying inexpensive, fashionable clothes has become expressive, playful and fun. For customers, it is a frictionless fashion experience, designed to smooth away all effects of materiality, energy expenditure and effort. In this moment, customers do not ask where these clothes came from or where they will go. But it is worth pausing Zara's perpetual motion machine to rewind and fast forward: to consider the past and future of its products.

Materiality

The Zara store embodies a central paradox of fashion – and of modern life – a place where our "permanent state of becoming" confronts material reality.[43] Unlike the constantly accelerating instant of fashion, physical materials have both a past and a future. Although the Zara experience is designed to be seamless, it is worth picking at the seams to understand the materiality encountered by the customer, clothes made from fabrics and fibres that even an ever-accelerating digital modernity cannot erase. This section considers the clothes themselves, final touchpoints of complex supply chains that start in fields and factories and end in landfills.

Like IKEA, Zara offers customers designer products at an affordable price. This is a difficult position to counter. Who wants to argue for a return to expensive, exclusive clothing and home furnishings, available only to a wealthy elite? Zara, like IKEA, can claim to simply respond to what customers want: affordable fashion. Framed by desire and cost, all other aspects of production and consumption disappear. And desire and cost are what both the Zara store and IKEA warehouse present: a range of desirable products with modest price tags. But, of course, these products are made somewhere.

On the morning of 24 April 2013, an eight-storey building housing five garment factories collapsed in Dhaka, Bangladesh, killing over 1,100 people and injuring over 2,000 more. Workers in these factories produced clothes for Zara, Benetton, Primark, Walmart and other global brands. The collapse of the Rana Plaza building brought the issue of labour exploitation into the spotlight of the mainstream global media.[44] Heavy machinery of the garment factories made the building unstable, and, despite warnings, factory owners kept production running. While the Rana Plaza tragedy led to promises of reform and policy changes, a decade later, poor conditions and low pay have not changed for Bangladeshi workers.[45]

Maintaining low prices for the customer requires Zara to find the lowest possible labour costs. Despite mechanization of some aspects of clothing manufacture, assembling garments still requires considerable human labour, particularly sewing, a job typically done by women in poor countries. While Zara do roughly half of this in Spain and Portugal, the remainder is in countries such as Turkey, Morocco, Bangladesh, Myanmar and China. In 2017, another scandal reached the media when workers from a Turkish factory inserted labels into Zara clothes stating: "I made this item you are going to buy, but I didn't get paid for it".[46] Such reports, that stretch back over a decade – including "slave labour" conditions of Brazilian workers in 2011 and Bolivian workers in 2013 – have had little impact on the brand's reputation and "no impact on their revenues".[47]

A 2020 brand profile by the Clean Clothes Campaign reported that Zara is not transparent about its supply chain and only two-thirds of its factory workers are paid a living wage (a figure determined by Zara).[48] The most recent media attention, on Zara's sourcing of cotton garments from China's Xinjiang region, focused on the forced labour camps of the province's Uighur minority people.[49] A 2021 French court case accused Zara, Uniqlo, Skechers and French conglomerate SMCP of "crimes against humanity" for their support of human rights abuse in Xinjiang.[50] Both cotton production and garment production profited from human rights crimes in the region. Prosecutors dropped the case in 2023 as the French court lacks "jurisdiction to prosecute the facts contained in the complaint".[51] Chinese government restrictions on media and human rights groups make following up such cases impossible.

A global supply chain such as Zara's is both difficult to regulate and difficult to trace. It starts with textile production. Most of Zara's clothing is comprised of cotton and polyester. Cotton requires large amounts of water and pesticides, bleaches and dyes, all of which produce toxic runoffs. When it comes to fashion, sustainability is best considered in degrees – from less to more sustainable – as all textile production creates a significant environmental footprint. As one scholar put it:

> … there is no such thing as not harming the environment when it comes to textile production. There is always going to be significant harm, because current technologies cannot mitigate the pollution from the farming of cotton and other natural fibers to their ginning, bleaching, mercerizing, spinning, and weaving, and eventually dyeing the final fabric.[52]

Dyeing creates environmental hazards, as untreated wastewater from dyes is discharged into local water systems, releasing toxicants that impact the health of nearby residents as well as the environment.[53] Meanwhile, polyester, made from petroleum, is worse. As are polyester blends. These "inexpensive but high-quality fabrics that enable the diffusion of fashion to the masses create more toxic chemical pollution per item than any other industrial product".[54]

Exactly where Zara's production processes take place and under what conditions is difficult to identify as Inditex contract over 1,700 suppliers and 3,200 factories who complete spinning, weaving and raw material processes.[55] Tracing where any given Zara shirt is made is extremely difficult. But one thing is certain, Zara need to keep costs low and low costs mean social and environmental consequences somewhere. A recent environmental study concluded that, in "the two decades since the fast fashion business model became the norm for big name fashion brands, increased demand for large amounts of inexpensive clothing has resulted in environmental and social degradation along each step of the supply chain".[56]

On the other side of the Zara experience, what happens after these clothes leave the store? Zara's model encourages customers to consider clothes as disposable. The number of times clothing is worn has declined in the last fifteen years, and since 2000, fast fashion brands have doubled their volume of clothing produced.[57] In the United States, the biggest clothing market in the world, consumers dispose of more than 15 billion kg (34 billion pounds) of textiles or more than 45 kg (100 pounds) per person annually, with higher income people generating substantially more than their share.[58] Two-thirds of this ends up in landfills, while 15 per cent is "recycled". Recycled means bales of clothes exported to African countries such as Ghana, where it is known as "*obroni wawu*, or dead White people's clothes". Here, some clothing is reused but most ends up in landfill.

In 2017, with a great deal of publicity, Zara launched an in-store recycling programme. Strangely, I found no evidence of this in the Porto store.[59] It works as follows. Zara collect and deliver unwanted clothing to local organizations who sort and donate the usable clothes. Zara do not publish statistics on the results of this programme. Recycling clothing is time consuming, labour intensive and costly. Buttons and zippers need to be removed, while any dyes, solvents or blended materials used in designing the clothes create further obstacles to reuse. One scholar estimated that "less than 1% of used clothing is actually remade into new garments".[60] Of course, while this is not solely a Zara problem, the company's fast fashion model has exacerbated it.

Research studies suggest that young consumers, even those with strong sustainable practices, do not associate clothing with sustainability. "The bulk of the data suggest that young people separate fashion from sustainability", stated one typical research paper, while they "definitely support the idea of sustainability, but do not apply such ethics when it comes to sustainable fashion".[61] Particularly young, fashion-conscious consumers have little interest in sustainability or ethics when it comes to clothing.[62] Researchers use the terms "attitude-behaviour gap" or the "Fashion Paradox" to describe the gap between a concern for sustainability and purchasing behaviour.[63] Even those who consider the environmental and social impact of their consumption practices do not do so when it comes to clothing.

In 2015, Zara's launched its much-promoted Join Life sustainable collection. The collection uses "at least 50%" recycled wool, Tencel (a blend of natural and artificial fibres) and organic cotton. But, as stated above, even organic cotton has significant environmental impact, while any clothing comprising a mix of synthetic and natural fibres is too difficult to recycle. Most of Zara's Join Life range is manufactured in Bangladesh and Morocco, where environmental and labour conditions are difficult for a regular customer to assess.[64] In 2023, Zara reported that Join Life comprises half of their range and therefore it will no longer promote it.

Although the idea of sustainable fashion gained some attention in the 1990s, few consumers had any knowledge about how textiles are made, recycled or disposed of.[65] Critiques of the environmental and labour impact of fast fashion began in the 2000s as the model spread. In a well-known article advocating "slow fashion", for example, Kate Fletcher argued:

> Fast fashion isn't really about speed, but greed: selling more, making more money. Time is just one factor of production, along with labour, capital and natural resources that get juggled and squeezed in the pursuit of maximum profits. But fast is not free. Short lead times and cheap clothes are only made possible by exploitation of labour and natural resources.[66]

The call for "slow fashion" followed similar calls for slow food (as a counter to fast food) and involved examining fashion's entire ecosystem and advocating for a more sustainable model.[67] But, as a counter to fast fashion, slow fashion has – so far at least – had little impact on the mass market in the United States and Europe.

Immersed in a digital culture of constant newness and impulse buying, where speed and cost are the main priorities, the Zara store stands as a physical embodiment of fast yet affordable fashion. Both a stage for performing identities and a serene container that maintains the aura of clothing, the Zara store centres the retail experience on the customer. As such, its clothes' place of origin, materials, conditions of production and environmental impact are irrelevant. Interestingly, unlike IKEA, which constantly promotes its Swedish-ness, Zara have never promoted its Spanish-ness. After all, everyone knows fashion comes from Milan, Paris or New York, not A Coruña. Instead of Spanish-ness, a Zara store appears placeless: its stores and clothes are consistent across the globe.

By remaining geographically neutral, Zara can remain focused on individual customers, no matter their geographical location, cultural background, class or other traditional identity associations. The store functions as a neutral container to accentuate the "geographical dissociation" in which customers do not ask what the clothes are made from, where the clothes come from, who makes them or how they are made.[68] Zara make no visible claims about sustainability or labour conditions in store, although customers can find reassuring statements about these on the company's website.

The Covid-19 crisis forced Zara to strengthen its online ordering and service options such as in-store pick-ups. In the post-pandemic retail environment, Zara's new digital strategy included over $1 billion investment in digital capabilities and an "additional $2 billion in stores so as to improve the integration between the online and the offline environments for faster delivery and real-time product tracking".[69] But the threat from Chinese "ultra-fast" fashion brands is that they do not have to adhere to European or American regulations with regards to labour rights and environmental laws, and are largely free from media scrutiny. With post-pandemic customers even more accustomed to online shopping for their clothes, such brands offer lower prices and wider ranges. But, at the same time, trying on clothes in a Zara store and walking out with them immediately may still trump waiting for a delivery.

Chapter 8
A Korean Dystopia: Gentle Monster

Below Singapore's Marina Bay Sands Hotel – three skyscrapers connected by a boat-shaped bridge on top – sits a luxury shopping mall, also called Marina Bay Sands. I'd already visited its Apple and Zara stores, as well as a dozen other predictable chains so I wasn't expecting anything too innovative or interesting. But here, in an otherwise bland shopping mall was a giant, winking horse's eye on a spinning screen in a store window (Figure 43). As it slowly spun, the screen's image changed to a broken satellite dish for five seconds, then back to the horse's eye. Glowing in white over the store's entrance was its name: GENTLE MONSTER.

Weird. I'm in. Directly behind the spinning screen, kinetic sculptures sit on a ground of black soil and scattered volcanic stones (Figure 44). One undulates like a giant worm while the other makes a sweeping motion in the dirt. These strange creatures are covered with some type of organic fibres, like sisal or hemp. Yet the vibe is futuristic, as if these are alien life-forms struggling to survive on an inhospitable planet. This initial scene is so intriguing that I forget for a moment that I'm in a store.

Behind the alien creatures is a section of the store that contains rows of glasses on sleek, silver shelves. These are mostly sunglasses with smooth curves and moulded frames. Some have a small metal detail on the outside of each arm, a unique, if subtle, identifier. Others have "Gentle Monster" printed on the arm. Each different style – "My Ma" or "Lang" – has its name printed on the inside of an arm. Nothing on the shelves differentiates male from female glasses. There's a single digital screen with images of models. But looking at glasses is less interesting than exploring the rest of the store.

I ask a staff member about the store's design, and he points to a nearby wall. Etched onto a metallic surface is an explanatory text titled "The Data Addicts". The store, it reads,

> … tells the story of people becoming overprotective of themselves and obsessed with little information to survive in an excruciatingly harsh environment. The only source of information are a few large, high-tech

antennas that provides signals which they must analyse and use for their survival. However, the only real antenna on earth that can deliver information is in fact broken and abandoned somewhere people cannot see. All the information they've relied on is a lie. This is also a metaphor of modern people who are obsessed and overwhelmed by the invalid information they receive daily.

A shelf of glasses sits below this story (Figure 45).

Past the wall text, another section of the store contains the "antenna", a skeletal satellite dish – the same one on the spinning screen at the front – its weathered wire frame sits beside clumps of black-tipped white crystals (Figure 46). These crystals, made from some kind of soft material, grow on broken stone slabs.

Figure 43 Gentle Monster, Singapore, exterior. Author photo.

A Korean Dystopia: Gentle Monster

Figure 44 Gentle Monster, Singapore, kinetic sculpture. Author photo.

Like surrealist Meret Oppenheim's fur-lined teacup or Claes Oldenberg's soft sculptures, there's a dislocation between form and materials. Behind them stand rows of silver shelves with glasses on them, punctuated by mirrors.

Another scene comprises three figures, almost human-sized, dangling on wires from the ceiling in front of a broken mirror (Figure 47). Made from black fibrous materials with white shell-like forms on top – these are not immediately recognizable – so, as with surrealist art, I use my imagination to try and place them. Oversized sci-fi puppets? Wireframes and metal stands sit on a ground of rusty rocks. Broken shells and electronic equipment scattered on the rocks suggest an accident or disaster has happened recently. A row of glasses on shelves bleeds into my zone of vision and I see myself and the shelves fragmented in the mirror.

The store's installation reminds me of post-apocalyptic literature, films or anime. I think of the manga classic *Neon Genesis Evangelion*, then Cormac McCarthy's novel *The Road*. Like these, the store's designers have created a futuristic, dystopian atmosphere. These strange installations destabilize a conventional shopping experience, but the connection to the glasses is not entirely clear. In a luxury eyewear boutique, you expect glossy photographs of glamorous models wearing sunglasses on a beach or embracing under the Eiffel Tower. What's curious is that such associations are desirable, whereas the Gentle Monster store has a distinctly uncomfortable ambience. Who wants to live in a dystopian future world?

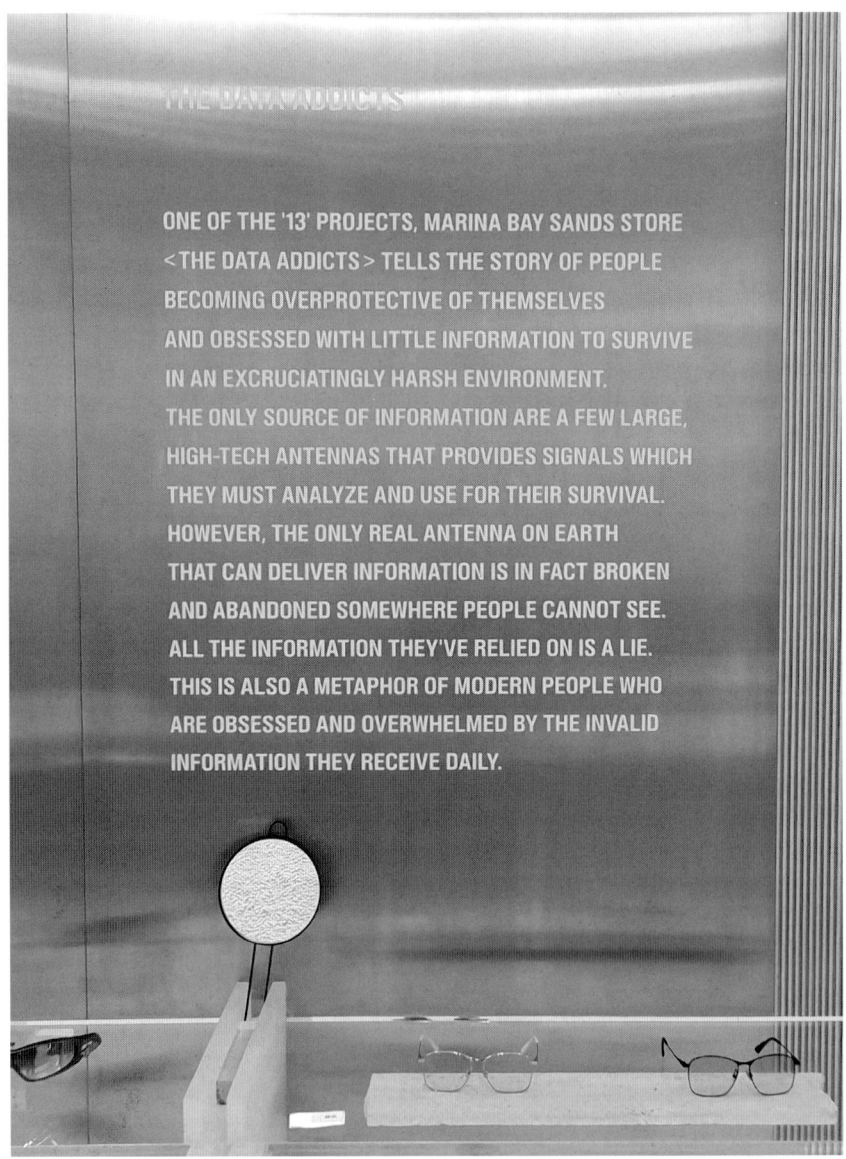

Figure 45 Gentle Monster, Singapore, "The Data Addicts". Author photo.

Figure 46 Gentle Monster, Singapore, satellite dish and crystals. Author photo.

Figure 47 Gentle Monster, Singapore, sunglasses and sculptures. Author photo.

I found out later that Gentle Monster's in-house designers Jihee Lee and Somi Shim created the store in 2018. It followed the brand's strategy of immersive, installation-style stores that engage customers with a futuristic scenario. Strange, surreal and dystopian are not typical retail themes, but, given Gentle Monster keeps opening stores around the world, it must appeal to some customers. Perhaps this is the ideal experience for people "who are obsessed and overwhelmed by the invalid information they receive daily".

Figure 48 Gentle Monster, Soho, New York, The Visitor. Author photo.

A Korean Dystopia: Gentle Monster

Although every Gentle Monster store is different, they share a similar atmosphere. Not long after visiting the Marina Bay Sands store, I visited New York's Soho Gentle Monster store. Based on a scenario titled "The Visitor", this store contains installations that immerse customers in a futuristic, "New Earth" (Figure 48). In this alternate world, environmental chaos reigns due to a tilt in the planet's orbital axis. According to a wall text, a creature born from an egg – The Visitor – has arrived to restore hope. Well, some hope. The text ends: "the 13th month spawns this unceremonious marriage of arcane life and impeding disarray …".

Figure 49 Gentle Monster, Soho, New York, digital screen and sculptures. Author photo.

Like the Singapore store, the Soho store features surreal scenes of strange creatures on stones in between silver shelves filled with sunglasses. A huge screen depicts a digital artwork that continuously generates new, colourful and fluid forms (Figure 49). This store also contains kinetic sculptures. A giant worm undulates on sand, and, in reference to the wall text's story about the birth of The Visitor, a crane draws a clump of crystals from a viscous liquid (Figure 50). Although different to the Singapore store, there is a common ambience to the Gentle Monster experience, created by the mix of high-tech and natural materials, static and kinetic sculptures that combine to evoke an uneasy otherworldliness.

Figure 50 Gentle Monster, Soho, New York, the birth of The Visitor. Author photo.

What Is Gentle Monster?

Entrepreneur Hankook Kim founded Gentle Monster in Seoul in 2011 in response to a perceived gap in the eyewear industry. Kim's idea was that most sunglasses – designed by European or American brands – were engineered to fit a Western facial structure. He set out to design glasses that would better fit Korean faces. As well as redesigning the bridge of the glasses, Kim thought a larger size would appeal as, in Korea, "having a small face is the biggest compliment, there were no competitors for oversize glasses, which make heads look smaller".[1] At first, Kim aimed to break into the Korean market, beginning with high-end women's sunglasses.

An early promotional video stressed the craft-based techniques Gentle Monster began their design process with.[2] It featured a designer drawing on paper, then craftsmen cutting, bending and polishing each frame individually. The message was clear: these were luxury products crafted by hand with care. In an interview, Kim referenced Apple's design approach: "we love Steve Jobs and his craft. We get so much inspiration from his obsession with perfection and beauty."[3] With an initial investment from entrepreneur Jae W Oh, the company began producing sunglasses in 2012 in a Daegu factory which formerly produced frames for Luxottica. Coincidently, due to the dominant position of the Milan-based Luxottica, the sunglasses market was a difficult one to break into at this time.

The Luxottica Group owns well-known brands such as Ray-Ban, Persol and Oakley, but also manufactures sunglasses for brands such as Prada, Chanel, Armani and many others. It also owns retail eyewear businesses, including LensCrafters, Sunglasses Hut and Target Optical, as well as online retailers and vision benefits companies in the United States. One estimate suggested the Group controlled 80 per cent of the major brands in the global eyewear industry (before they became even bigger with the merger with French-based Essilor in 2018).[4] In fact, due to Luxottica's market dominance, in 2012, American critics accused them of anti-competitive practices.[5] But Luxottica's extravagant mark-ups on luxury sunglasses also allowed smaller competitors to enter the market if they could identify a niche.[6]

For Gentle Monster, the niche was discerning customers who would appreciate original designs yet wanted something new, distinctive and futuristic. The brand's debut at Seoul Fashion Week in 2012 featured models wearing oversized sunglasses, most with red- or orange-tinted lenses. Although this was a start, Gentle Monster's reputation took off when Jun Ji-hyun wore several pairs in the popular Korean drama series, *You Who Came from the Stars* in 2013 and 2014. In Korea, such endorsement can result in spectacular sales.

At first, Gentle Monster sold its glasses in Shinsegae, a chain of Korean malls, and online. But Kim soon realized that the Luxottica market dominance would cut them out of many retail stores and make expansion difficult. His solution was to sell directly to customers. So, in 2013, Gentle Monster opened its first store in a luxury shopping district of Seoul. Customers entered the store through a ship, which immediately set the scene for a different type of retail experience. Inside, one floor of the store featured walls covered with moss while another was designed as a desert landscape. Experiential retailing became an essential part of Gentle Monster's differentiation.

Initially, Gentle Monster's store designs in Korea – in collaboration with artists, digital creators and other creatives – changed quickly, with new installations every twenty-five days. They featured sci-fi themes, animatronic robots, animal sculptures, as well as moss, tree trunks and live plants. The brand name itself reinforced such strange juxtapositions. In an interview, Kim explained:

> As in all humans, there exists a certain duality within me: the gentle and the monster. This duality is what makes Gentle Monster unique and unforgettable: it is unpredictable.[7]

By 2016, Gentle Monster opened its first store in Beijing as well as its first store outside Asia, in New York's Soho. A *Vogue* feature that year noted that the new Soho store was "the perfect selfie spot".[8] Gentle Monster followed these with stores in Singapore, Hong Kong, more stores in Korea and China and, with investment from French luxury conglomerate LVMH, further stores in London and Dubai. All were characterized by a distinctive aesthetic. According to American CEO Won Lee:

> Our aesthetic can be described as "Weird Wonder Wow Beauty." Gentle Monster creates anticipation and excitement through our five core focuses: product, space, style, technology and culture. We have also determined that there are shared values between the east and the west—namely the past and future; technology and art.[9]

Through celebrity endorsements, online advertising campaigns and collaborations, Gentle Monster started to become known outside East Asia.

Coincidentally, in 2012, the same year Gentle Monster launched their first collection, Psy's viral hit "Gangnam Style" propelled K-pop into the United States and European mainstream. Although Psy did not wear Gentle Monster sunglasses in that video, he did in later videos. Regardless, while Korean pop culture already had a large following in China, Japan and Southeast Asia, after 2012, it gained fans in the United States and Europe too. As names such as BTS and Blackpink, along with Korean television dramas and films, became known all around the world, Korean fashion brands such as Gentle Monster rode the Korean Wave.

As well as Korean celebrities, Gentle Monster looked to non-Korean collaborations, particularly to expand into the United States and Europe. A collaboration with actor and director Tilda Swinton in 2017 was one of the first with a Western celebrity. For Gentle Monster, Swinton helped design three different oversized sunglasses with rose and pale blue tinted, mirrored lenses. Swinton said the appeal is their "warrior-shield" aspect – providing fierceness "even for the chronically shy".[10] The promotional video, entitled "The End Game", featured two characters, both played by Swinton, fencing to a soundtrack of haunting cello music.[11] Known for her roles in unusual arthouse and cross-over films by directors such as Derek Jarman, Jim Jarmusch and Wes Anderson, Swinton's androgynous, otherworldly look suited a unisex, futuristic brand.

Gentle Monster's more recent celebrity collaborations include a 2020 collaboration with Jennie from Blackpink. Soon after forming in 2016, Blackpink became huge in Korea and beyond, their global fanbase measures video views in the billions. Jennie alone has 81 million Instagram followers.[12] While all four members endorse global fashion brands, Jennie is particularly famous as a fashion icon.[13] Jennie's first Gentle Monster collection sold out immediately, while the second in 2022 included *Jennie's Jentle Garden Game*, a mobile video game that immersed players in a fantasy world of colourful gardens. Promotional photographs featured Jennie in sunglasses against dreamy, flowery backdrops: futuristic and surreal but not – in this case – dystopian.

Wary of too close an association with Korean popular culture, Gentle Monster has also partnered with Chinese celebrities such as actors Li Yifeng and Yang Yang. And the brand has collaborated with established fashion brands, such as New York streetwear brand Hood by Air (2016 and 2022) and luxury fashion brands Alexander Wang and Fendi (both in 2019). As well as celebrities and fashion designers, Gentle Monster also collaborated with Dutch-based Moooi in 2017, an interiors, lighting and furniture brand founded by Marcel Wanders and Casper Vissers. Few of these collaborations last long – on their website, the oldest are two years old. In this way, Gentle Monster follows fast fashion's rapid turnover of styles.

Interestingly, what remains constant in Gentle Monster's branding is the simple, all-caps black font, usually black on white. This type appears above the entrance of its stores, on the all-white shopping bag, the cardboard box that contains the glasses, the glasses pouch and other packaging. Gentle Monster redesigns its packaging for each new collection but always maintains a sparse simplicity that echoes other luxury brands. Its packaging is particularly reminiscent of Apple's and, as with Apple, Gentle Monster fans upload "unboxing" videos to YouTube. In its packaging and graphics, Gentle Monster adopted the conventional minimalism of other luxury brands rather than anything futuristic or dystopian.

Another aspect that remains constant, even in a post-Covid retail landscape, is Gentle Monster's commitment to physical stores. Although the stores are not redesigned as quickly as the original Korean store, the in-store experience is still compelling. In an interview Gentle Monster's Brand Director, Gary Bott, stated that "bricks and mortar" is "in our DNA as we're focused on experimental spatial design. Physical brand storytelling and our own retail make up over 90% of our business worldwide."[14] As of 2021, Gentle Monster employs "more than 100 in-house artists who specialize in spatial art, including architecture, interior design, sculpture, media art, engineering, pottery, robotics, and kinetic art".[15] The company employs far more visual artists to design stores than product designers to design glasses.

As of 2024, Gentle Monster operates over forty retail stores around the world and of these, almost half are in China. Each store is unique and offers customers an immersive, art gallery-like experience. The glasses, manufactured in relatively small batches in China and Korea, include four hundred new models each year, most associated with celebrity promotions and pop culture, film or video games. Gentle Monster's blend of uncanny installations, futuristic glasses and dystopian environments is unique within a relatively safe retail landscape. But not without precedent. First, I want to reflect on the installation aspects of the Gentle Monster store, then in the final section, consider its connections to Korean popular culture.

Artification

Gentle Monster's stores are an unusual hybrid of art installation and fashion boutique. Their designers use a strategy some term "artification": "the transformation of nonart into art – which has been increasingly strategically employed by luxury fashion brands in recent times".[16] Artification describes the process by which art's "magical power" is transferred to mundane products such as sunglasses.[17] While a luxury fashion brand using artification is nothing new, Gentle Monster's implementation is. The company not only uses the language of contemporary art to design stores but at the same time collaborates with pop singers, actors and video game creators to design a coherent, alternative Gentle Monster universe. Rather than appeal to high art's status as intellectual and rarefied, Gentle Monster's designers have created stores that are surreal and mysterious, yet accessible and Instagrammable.

Connections between high fashion, art and theatre have existed since the start of the haute couture system in nineteenth-century France.[18] Associations with art and theatre functioned to legitimate fashion's ephemeral, superficial reputation with art's timelessness and intellectual sophistication. Paul Poiret's 1909 couture house, for example, "employed high culture as a rhetorical tool", and included a stage within the store.[19] Collaborations between fashion designers and artists such as Elsa Schiaparelli and Salvador Dali's projects in the 1930s also suggested that artification was beneficial for both fashion houses and artists.

In the late 1970s and 1980s, Japanese fashion designers, including Issey Miyake, Yohji Yamamoto and Rei Kawakubo of Comme des Garçons, integrated avant-garde artist practices into their clothing, runway shows and boutiques. Comme des Garçons' Tokyo flagship store hosted contemporary art exhibitions.[20] Hermès' Ginza flagship store also hosted regular art exhibitions and Chanel's Ginza flagship store held both exhibitions and concerts. For fashion houses, "substituting themselves for well-respected institutions (i.e., museums), the brands gained credentials and protected themselves".[21] Italian fashion house Prada's foray into art included sponsoring exhibitions and commissioning high-profile architects to design distinctive flagship stores. Koolhaas' 2001 New York Prada flagship store set the scene for "Prada's strategy of redefining shopping as cultural entertainment".[22]

Part of this turn to artification was a response to changes in manufacturing and materials. By the twenty-first century, luxury fashion was less defined by highly skilled, labour-intensive craft production or expensive raw materials. Rather, high fashion maintained its value via symbolic means. Associations with high art proved particularly powerful in maintaining a fashion brand's "aura". For couture houses to survive in a world of low-cost yet designer fast fashion, art and store design became important as "value is increasingly seen to lie in the codes of meaning enshrined in commodities through processes of dematerialization, commodity fetishism and the elevation of the retail store and commodity aesthetic as key creators of value".[23]

In the 2000s, Louis Vuitton launched a slightly different artification strategy. Beginning in 2002, a partnership with artist Takashi Murakami "involved printing Murakami's soft toy images over Louis Vuitton's feted monogram, a logo central to the fashion house's closely protected authenticity".[24] This not only invested Louis Vuitton with artistic cache but reinforced the idea of its products as limited-edition artworks. In 2006, Creative Director Marc Jacobs worked with artist Olafur Eliasson to create the "Eye See You Lamp" installations in Louis Vuitton store windows. This was designed as an "installation that challenges the tropes of retail design and display and actively enrolled the consumer in the production and interpretation of the space – visuality at its most stark".[25] In 2012, Louis Vuitton began a decade-long collaboration with Yayoi Kusama that resulted in limited-edition handbags and other accessories covered in Kusama's signature polka dots.

Fashion boutiques also underwent a process of "artification" in the early twenty-first century.[26] To create both aesthetic distinction and compelling retail experiences, many major fashion houses moved away from standardized global stores (such as the Apple store, for example). Instead, the fashion flagship stores aimed to recreate an experience like that of visiting an art gallery. One fashion scholar argued that Louis Vuitton, for example, "does not use contemporary art as a theme, but, rather, that LV flagship stores are art institutions in their own right, and are experienced as such by enthralled consumers …".[27] By the time Gentle Monster open their first flagship store in 2013, a fashion boutique designed as a type of art gallery experience was well established.

But the Gentle Monster store differs from these earlier high fashion examples. First, there is no significant creative individual responsible for the art. That is, no creative genius (such as Murakami or Kusama) behind a Gentle Monster installation. Gentle Monster's store design team remains anonymous. Second, the store installations are intended as ephemeral. Unlike installation art in a gallery, Gentle Monster does not document these as art practices: there are no catalogues or websites devoted to the stores. For customers, a compelling, intriguing installation in a retail store is something else. It is less rarefied than in an art gallery and involves a more intimate kind of participation.

By the second decade of the twenty-first century, the fashion flagship store was a well-established phenomenon, one typically associated with identity formation:

> Luxury flagships are self-indulgent environments infused with drama which invite self-affirmation and conspicuous consumption. One performs a self in the midst of the excitement of the branded universe of the luxury flagship. This may involve affirming an already held privileged identity or a claim to a desired or aspirational identity. Identity affirmation as well as the affirmation of interpersonal relations is solidified through shopping in ways that hold individual significance for the shoppers. The identity of the brand is also solidified for the customer within the flagship store.[28]

Interestingly, the dramatic environment of the Gentle Monster store is not that of conventional luxury – sipping cocktails on a white-sand beach or posing below the Eiffel Tower – but a distinctly dystopian one. It involves a similar form of escapism as a luxury fashion store but not to a better imaginary world but a worse one.

But the idea of dystopian fashion is not entirely new. A thread of dystopian tendencies in high fashion goes back to at least the 1980s. Some designers, particularly the Japanese avant-garde designers mentioned above, developed collections based on cyberpunk themes or runway shows that referenced nuclear or ecological disasters. In the 1990s, Alexander McQueen's catwalk spectacles and dramatic clothing also contained dystopian themes but strangely, his boutiques were spare and neutral. Other boutiques that sold dystopian fashion –

Darklands in Berlin, for example, or If Soho in New York – were also not especially distinctive in their store design.

In contrast, Gentle Monster uses dystopian themes more holistically. From a customer's perspective, Gentle Monster stores are designed to perform like a contemporary art experience but without the cultural and intellectual baggage of a gallery or museum. Customers experience art stripped of external referents that a gallery would typically provide – the name of an artist, dates and other contextual information. A Gentle Monster store includes only an intriguing, anonymous wall text that sets the scene. Rather than the artist, the glasses are the hero of a Gentle Monster store. Importantly, the customer can participate in this strange world by buying a pair.

The Gentle Monster store also taps into the lineage of installation art, well established by the twenty-first century, as an aesthetic experience that one physically enters. Importantly, an installation is an artwork of which the spectator is an intrinsic part – such art typically plunges the viewer into a theatrical or cinematic set, directly implicating them in an unfamiliar environment.[29] But, unlike exhibitions in galleries or museums, which typically involve an entrance fee, the Gentle Monster store is free. And, while there was formerly a distinction between an art gallery and a retail store, this boundary is no longer so clearly defined.

Artification, while it stimulates browsing and increased time spent in stores, is generally believed to have a positive impact on brand awareness and customer loyalty but not necessarily a direct, immediate impact on sales.[30] For Gentle Monster, the retail stores are part of a broader strategy that includes digital promotion, social media and its website. As a strategic tool, artification also has benefits "as a moral and aesthetical endorsement, uncommercial connotation and reinforcing element renewing brands – images and relevance close to culture justify high prices".[31]

A further separation of the Gentle Monster installation from the contemporary art gallery is a temporal one – while galleries and museums house, store and exhibit "timeless" art, the Gentle Monster store began with a kind of "fast art" model. Hankook Kim's original concept was to redesign stores quickly:

> He changed the display in stores every seven days, at first—finding it extremely difficult, he slowed the pace to every 21 days and continues to keep up with that pace today. Every display has a distinct theme such as: The Artisan, Home and Recovery, Secret Apartment, and Quantum Project.[32]

This rapid pace has slowed even further as the in-store installations have become more elaborate and longer lasting, but designers keep refreshing and redesigning the stores to maintain a sense of newness (and a reason for customers to return).

Gentle Monster's artification, rather than associated with art's timelessness, instead conforms to the accelerated tempo of fast fashion cycles. Art "has historically been exalted as the more noble and intellectual pursuit in comparison to fashion, which was regarded as a primarily commercially motivated form of expression".[33] But in the case of Gentle Monster, the art installation appears as temporal, not especially intellectual, and without named artists or documentation. This positions the customer in a different – more active – role compared to a person viewing installations in an art gallery:

> The collision between the two practices in the spaces of the fashion store reveals the significance of visuality and affective affordance in consumption, framing the consumer in a new role as active participant and interpreter rather than merely passive receiver of prescribed sales messages.[34]

Gentle Monster's convergence of art and fashion extends beyond the in-store installation in a holistic manner. This is apparent if we consider the company's digital promotions and marketing as a complement to the retail experience described above.

The Gentle Monster website and social media feeds contain not only the categories of products – sunglasses, glasses – but collaborations, styles, stories, stores and services. The glasses are presented against neutral backgrounds, on a single model's face, and in close-up. Recent collaborations include not only those with celebrities mentioned earlier, but with the video game *Overwatch 2* and Chinese pop star Cai Xukun. The latter collaboration features videos, still photographs and temporary (physical) pop-ups, all of which feature Kun in the role of a "secret agent". Cinematic videos starring Kun as an action-adventure hero in a futuristic city, always wearing his sunglasses, even at night. The collaboration also included a mobile video game, featuring a Kun avatar, again as an action hero.

Importantly, the website also includes a "Styles" section that comprises a changing feed of fan photos. Here, Gentle Monster fans can submit photographs – some selfies, some shot by others – of themselves or friends wearing Gentle Monster glasses. By sharing photos of themselves online, customers become part of the Gentle Monster website, on the same page as their favourite pop star or actor. This participation highlights Gentle Monster's artification strategy of including customers within its virtual worlds.

In the *Overwatch 2* story, Gentle Monster highlights the nature of this limited-edition collaboration. *Overwatch 2* is a popular multiplayer combat game that takes place in a future world, so aligns with both the Kun videos and the in-store experience. Gentle Monster's *Overwatch* box contains limited-edition sunglasses, a plastic figurine, an in-game item and a gaming skin (via redeemable codes). Beyond the box, customers can purchase a weapon, a weapon charm and a signature pose (whereby the game zooms in on the avatar's face and glasses) for the game.[35] Digital skins, weapons and signature moves allow customers to "dress" their gaming avatar in Gentle Monster glasses. An additional component of the *Overwatch* collaboration is an Instagram filter for fans to use and upload selfies, again encouraging customer participation and slipping between physical and digital realms.

Gentle Monster's link to video games is strong and aligns with the store experience – both involve creative self-expression within an immersive narrative world. Fashion brands have collaborated with video game companies in the past – not always successfully – including H&M and *The Sims 2* (2008), Louis Vuitton and *League of Legends* (2019) and Balenciaga and *Fortnite* (2021).[36] Unlike these random connections, Gentle Monster's collaborations align with their overall narratives. The futuristic, dystopian theme of *Overwatch* is reinforced by Gentle Monster's retail, in-store experience, and vice versa.

Finally, it is worth returning to the narrative nature of Gentle Monster installations. Unlike contemporary installations in art galleries which typically feature a heterogenous array of themes, Gentle Monster's installations have a particular focus. Specifically, the stores focus on the discontents of modern society – the control of data and information, "fake news", anxiety around climate change and the effects of technology – themes that have universal resonance. Poignant yet ambiguous symbols such as a broken satellite or the birth of a clump of crystals are both open enough to spark a customer's imagination, yet also create common threads across Gentle Monster's imaginary worlds.

Singapore's "Data Addicts" and Soho's "The Visitor" scenarios have a similar vibe. Gentle Monster continues this through its short social media videos. Importantly, all these videos, as well as endorsements and collaborations are "placeless" – that is, they feature no recognizable landmarks, symbols or icons associated with specific cities, countries or cultures. All take place in strange, otherworldly spaces such as Kun's secret agent futuristic city. These are reinforced in-store by the wall texts, which provide a backstory to each store's futuristic world. Many of Gentle Monster's online videos include similar narrative texts at the beginning that help situate their strange world.

Gentle Monster's artification process involves using art but without an artist's name to enhance a luxury product by infusing it with the artist's perceived creativity, prestige or intellect.[37] Instead, limited editions and exclusivity are associated with pop stars or film stars, not artists. In this way, Gentle Monster uses art differently from Louis Vuitton's collaborations with Takashi Murakami or Yayoi Kusama. The in-store installations operate like stage sets for customers to participate in Gentle Monster's futuristic universe, centring the experience on the customer rather than the artist. But, while artification helps us understand the appeal of a Gentle Monster store, a brief look at the parallels with Korean pop culture will help illuminate other aspects of its retail experience.

Korean Dystopias

In less than a decade – from Psy's 2012 "Gangnam Style" to Bong Jun-ho's film *Parasite* winning the Cannes Film Festival's Palme d'Or and the Academy Awards' Best Picture in 2020 – Korean pop culture became a global phenomenon. Gentle Monster not only rode this "Korean wave" but collaborated with its biggest stars. When K-pop idol Jimin of BTS wore Gentle Monster's tinted sunglasses at the 2019 Billboard Music Awards, that model immediately sold out. A seemingly trivial detail like which sunglasses someone wore in a three-minute pop song is vitally important for millions of K-pop fans who obsessively comment on – and buy – every item of clothing worn by their idols.

Chinese outlets first used the term "Hallyu" in the 1990s to describe the Korean wave of popular culture, including K-pop, K-drama, Korean films and video games. It swept China and Japan first before moving down to Southeast Asia in the 2000s.[38] Led by K-pop and K-drama, Korean popular culture was characterized by high production values, attractive stars and a handful of huge conglomerates that design, market and micromanage its performers. The Korean government actively supported K-pop, K-drama and Korean films, realizing the export potential of cultural products.[39] Although this first Hallyu wave had a significant impact across Asia, it was not yet a global phenomenon.

But Hallyu's second wave – in the 2010s – was. Importantly, it spread via blogs, fan sites, YouTube, Facebook and Instagram. YouTube, for example, enabled Psy's 2012 video for "Gangnam Style" to reach a billion views. Driven by social media, the new wave of Hallyu combined Korean and Western modes of music, fashion and dance.[40] The new generation of K-pop stars such as Blackpink and BTS, were consciously designed to appeal to a global audience. In the second wave, Korean popular culture was not only the synthetic creation of corporate cultural industries but also a participatory culture whereby millions of online fans were constantly engaged via social media.[41]

K-pop has a slightly different appeal inside compared to outside of Korea. For the Korean state, within Korea its appeal lay in

> the lively and youthful images with which it is associated, the availability of attractive and talented pop stars and idols, innovative cultural genres and formats, and the nation's remarkable capacity to produce well-made, trendy cultural products. In this way, implicit cultural policy is neatly packaged with and fused into entertaining cultural products that are consumed within the realm of personal enjoyment, cultural consumption, media fandom and audience engagement.[42]

This unique blend of corporate-driven, state-supported popular culture, designed both for internal consumption and global export, was also ripe for product endorsements, collaborations and product placements. Even the French-based luxury conglomerate LVMH could see the potential, investing in 2014 in YG Entertainment, one of Korea's biggest companies representing K-pop and K-drama celebrities (including Blackpink).[43] Soon after this, LVMH invested in Gentle Monster.

Within Korea, the connection between the fashion industry and celebrity culture is crucial:

> Korean people purchase things they see worn by popular celebrities on television almost immediately, and the phenomenon is so frequent that there is even a term for celebrities who contribute to fashion items being sold out. "Wanpannyeo" means a female celebrity who wears something with such influence that what she wears gets sold out, and "wanpannam" means a male celebrity who has the same effect.[44]

This was precisely the effect when Jun Ji-hyun wore Gentle Monster sunglasses in the popular drama series *You Who Came from the Stars*. While such an endorsement can instantly sell a particular model of sunglasses, fame in Korean culture is fleeting. Korean celebrities quickly sign up for as many endorsements, advertisements and promotions as possible, knowing their time in the spotlight may be limited. This also helps explain Gentle Monster's constant churn of collaborations, endorsements and appearances with the latest celebrities.

For fans, Hallyu is participatory. Fans have a particular relationship with their celebrity idols, "simultaneously as an object of adulation and familial affection".[45] Korean pop and film stars have a strangely intimate relationship with their fans who copy their dance moves, singing styles and fashion sense. K-pop invites fans to participate in its escapist world of music, dance, fashion and visuals. Endorsing and promoting products, brands and services is central to this world. Particularly among young Koreans, this makes the link between celebrities and brand culture very strong.[46]

Hallyu blurs the boundary between high and low culture. BTS, for example, has endorsed brands from Louis Vuitton and Tiffany to McDonald's and Coca-Cola. One Korean popular culture commentator described this as representative of

> a new middlebrow class that is neither the classic connoisseur of arts (high cultural capital) nor the highly pragmatic "tasteless" average Joes (low cultural capital), but the class that inflates consumerism and advocates status consumption through the cultural currency of "cool".[47]

What remains interesting about Gentle Monster is that, despite numerous K-pop and K-drama collaborations, the Gentle Monster universe, as portrayed in-store and online is a surreal, dystopian one. This seems a long way from the optimistic, shiny world of BTS and Blackpink videos.

Yet part of the Korean wave included some dystopian films and television series. The 2012 film *Doomsday Book*, for example, a sci-fi trilogy directed by Kim Jee-woon and Yim Pi-sung, tells three stories about human self-destruction due to technological and environmental disasters that lead to catastrophic consequences. The first focuses on a robot who is trying to attain enlightenment; the second features a zombie virus generated by genetic modification; the third a Korean family who hide in an underground bunker and emerge seven years later to rebuild civilization after an asteroid collides with earth.

A second example is director Bong Joon-ho's 2013 film *Snowpiercer*. Set in 2031, it features a cast of characters in a high-speed train circling the earth, the only survivors of a new ice age in which people struggle to survive in a hostile environment. Not coincidentally, Tilda Swinton, who featured in Gentle Monster advertisements not long after the film was released, was one of the film's stars. Dystopian narratives such as the Data Addicts and The Visitor from Gentle Monster's stores parallel both *Doomsday Book* and *Snowpiercer*.

The specificity of twenty-first-century Korean society is also worth linking to these dystopian narratives, particularly anxieties around future technologies. After the 1997 Asian Economic Crisis, the Korean government designed policies to enable rapid technological development. This was described as "ubiquitous Korea (u-Korea)", a policy that "emphasizes universal access to information and service as a major precondition for an ideal information society".[48] Such policies led to media stories such as "South Korea, the World's Most Wired Country",[49] from 2006 and claims that robots would soon be inhabiting every Korean home. Such rapid change is bound to result in social anxiety.

In response, dystopian films such as *Doomsday Book* and *Snowpiercer*, as well as Gentle Monster's scenarios of people in a technologically advanced, information-driven society desperately trying to survive, make sense. Further than this, the dystopian strain in Korean culture relates to income inequality (as in the film *Parasite* or the series *Squid Games*) and fear of North Korean invasion or nuclear attack, surveillance, smartphone and gaming addiction. Gentle Monster stores focus on the relationship between humans and technology (in the Data Addicts) and the ongoing crisis of climate change and the destruction of the earth's living systems (in The Visitor).

Yet dystopian worlds in film, video games or retail stores can function in a variety of ways. One is to warn viewers/players/visitors of a possible future generated from apparent or perceivable trends of the present. Another is to reassure them that our present world is not too bad after all. Science-fiction author Kim Stanley Robinson explained dystopias in this way:

A realistic portrayal of a future that might really happen isn't really part of the project—that lens of the science fiction machinery is missing. The Hunger Games trilogy is a good example of this; its depicted future is not plausible, not even logistically possible. That's not what it's trying to do. What it does very well is to portray the feeling of the present for young people today, heightened by exaggeration to a kind of dream or nightmare. To the extent this is typical, dystopias can be thought of as a kind of surrealism.[50]

He also notes that dystopias can be complacent, creating a sense of comparative safety or an expression of detachment and hopelessness.

Staging disasters become a fable of possible future apocalypses that might result as the consequences of present human actions. Ultimately, the Gentle Monster store presents these scenarios as "feelings of the present" to evoke an emotional response. As ambiguous, surreal art, the Gentle Monster installations do not suggest any particular action or solutions to issues such as the climate crisis or information overload. For customers, the situation is perhaps not completely hopeless: you can always buy a pair of sunglasses.

Two final examples reveal Gentle Monster's holistic retail experience. The company's Haus Dosan, a multi-level building that opened Seoul in 2021, included collaborations with artist Frederik Heyman and a soundtrack designed by musician Arca. Both have an interest in cyborgs and post-human, biological-machinic symbiosis. Using photogrammetry (making 3D scans from photographs), 3D scanning of real-world objects and computer-generated imagery (CGI), Heyman creates realistic-looking yet surreal still images, videos and installations. In an interview, he described his practice as creating "a speculative present":

> A photo-real or virtual suggestion towards an altered dimension. What I like about 3D scanning and digital alterations is that I can literally copy elements from our present world and paste them into this alternative reality. This reality depicts a detailed narrative that I've created out of the desire to overcome humanity.[51]

This desire to overcome the human body has a particularly Korean connection. The nation is the world's leader in cosmetic surgery, driven – at least in part – by a desire to look like K-pop or K-drama idols and a fetishization of young celebrities.[52] Cosmetic surgery is encouraged by Korean popular culture which is "ubiquitous in its promotion of aesthetically augmented bodies".[53] Biomedical enhancement fits with Gentle Monster's themes of the relationship between humans and technology, robots with idealized faces and digitally enhanced videos of celebrities featured in their online promotions.

Another recent Gentle Monster store, opened in 2023 in Manila, displayed the refined formula of retail as both a physical store and a Korean pop culture celebration. The opening event starred Korean actor Ahn Hyo-seop and K-pop boy band POW, who posed in sunglasses outside the store for photographs. Inside the store, atop a ruined fragment of a building, sat The Giant. Two storeys tall, this realistic-looking sculpture by Heyman of a man dressed in only white feather trousers, his back to the street, provides a perfect backdrop for selfies. The store also includes a giant winking eye. Gentle Monster's connection between the physical store, K-pop and K-drama's celebrity culture, and art is encapsulated in its Manila store as a holistic theatre mediated by digital interaction and engagement.

The Gentle Monster store is not only an immersive experience like an art installation in a gallery – it both draws upon specifically Korean aesthetics and themes yet remains general enough to appeal to a global audience (particularly one familiar with Korean popular culture). A narrative such as the Data Addicts is a provocative – if none too subtle – "metaphor of modern people who are obsessed and overwhelmed by the invalid information they receive daily". That such statements fit neatly with shiny, positive Korean celebrities is quite a feat. But whether the Gentle Monster store exposes a dark side of Korean culture or leads customers to uncomfortable questions about contemporary culture is questionable. For shoppers accustomed to uniform chain stores, its strangeness at least creates a unique retail experience.

Conclusion

Although a modest collection, I believe these eight cases illustrate many of the significant changes to retail culture over the past two decades. This conclusion will outline common themes and suggest possible retail and research futures. First, I will highlight some shared aspects of these stores and how they design retail experience. In all cases, customers encounter interactions designed to ensure a seamless experience across stores, websites, apps and social media. Second, I will reiterate the environmental and social consequences of this contemporary retail experience. The third and final section reflects on potential futures stemming from this book's case studies.

Led by Apple's example, all of the stores analysed in this book are carefully designed to immerse customers in a sensory, holistic experience. Apple, Zara and Aesop eliminate distractions to focus a customer's attention on their products. Such sparse stores contrast department stores with their competing shelves of products, and discount stores that overflow with abundant bargains. Designed to highlight exclusivity, such minimalism associates Apple, Zara and Aesop with timeless luxury. Reinforced by digital images, videos and advertising, all three continue this unified design language across stores, products and packaging.

While the interiors of Apple, Zara and Aesop are serene, calm spaces, in each case, minimalism evokes slightly different ideals. Beyond timeless luxury, Apple's glass walls and sparse interiors remind us of its transparency. Aesop's calm vibe reminds us to relax and slow down, re-engage with nature and focus on ourselves. Zara's simple arrangement of clothes plus mirrors functions to situate us as the central character in our own fashion world. In each case, the customer is immersed in a sensory environment that reinforces brand values.

Another approach, no less immersive, comprises stores designed to situate the customer in alternate worlds. LEGO, Gentle Monster and IKEA stand out as prominent examples. Although different, both LEGO's surreal universe and Gentle Monster's dystopian installations engage the customer's imagination. In contrast, IKEA's domestic installations mimic the real world. IKEA's ideal lounge rooms, bedrooms and kitchens, infused with Swedish design and social democracy, invite customers to act within them. So too LEGO and Gentle Monster invite customers to suspend their disbelief and participate in their alternate worlds. By actively co-creating these alternate worlds, customers become immersed in an experience before they can critically reflect on it.

Sensations act upon a customer's visual, auditory, olfactory and somatosensory systems. Store designers carefully consider what a customer will hear, smell and touch in-store. Customers are encouraged to handle a product, play with it, feel its weight, texture and curves. In the Apple store, iPhones are carefully positioned for this purpose. The LEGO store's play stations invite customers to build with bricks, make their own minifigure or create their own mosaic. IKEA invites customers to sit on a couch, lie on a mattress and walk around a kitchen. Every physical interaction both encourages spontaneous purchases and embeds the experience in a customer's memory.

Some of these stores generate more obvious sensory experiences than others. The Aesop store is the best example of how a store can be designed to engage a customer's senses of smell, hearing, touch, sight and sound. Yet Nike adopts a similar approach. In the entrance of the Nike store I described at the beginning of Chapter 5, customers are encouraged to touch a new fabric, move around in an interactive installation and swipe on an iPad, all while absorbing high-energy hip-hop. In both Aesop and Nike, customers embed these sensations as emotional connections and memories. A customer remembers the vibe of an Aesop or Nike store, reinforced by later marketing they encounter online: a serene, minimal Aesop advertisement versus a dynamic, high-energy Nike advertisement.

One of the biggest changes in our retail experiences over the past twenty-five years is this connection between the physical and digital realms. Given the pervasive and inescapable nature of online advertising – from browsing news sites to apps – many customers already know something about these brands before entering the store. Customers already know Amazon stands for convenience and speed, for example, so when they first encounter an Amazon Go store, it makes sense. Even a relatively unknown company such as Gentle Monster makes sense for a customer who has already absorbed K-pop or Korean films.

Sports fans already know Nike sponsors their favourite players, teams or sports. Nike's strategy is to encourage in-store customers to interact with its app and website. IKEA, Zara and LEGO also have apps designed to continue the customer relationship before and after visiting their stores. Meanwhile, Amazon and Apple have kept customers continually interacting for decades, integrating customers into their growing digital ecosystems. All have sophisticated means to encourage ongoing digital relationships. All invite customers to like, follow, subscribe and sign up to apps, email lists and social media feeds. All can then push out nudges, prompts and reminders to customers via notifications, posts and emails.

I experienced this recently in New York. It was winter, night, and I was waiting for a friend when I spotted a Starbucks sign. Inside was a Starbucks counter but nowhere to sit down, only barriers to an Amazon Go store. After buying a coffee,

I asked about a seat and the barista directed me to walk through Amazon Go to the Starbucks lounge. I used a credit card to open the Amazon Go barrier, took some photographs (see Figure 12), and then sat in the lounge. The next day, Amazon sent me three emails. The first informed me that my trip time was 9 minutes 21 seconds. The second was a receipt noting that I wasn't charged as I did not buy anything. The third was a request to fill out a survey as part of Amazon's "ongoing effort to provide a great in-store experience" and offered me a $5 gift card if I did.

This is a good example of Pine and Gilmore's "helping the customer learn how to act". For Amazon Go's relatively new, staff-less store, the first step was to partner with Starbucks to funnel new customers through the store. This familiarizes them with the concept of Amazon's "grab and go" retail experience. The second step was the follow-up emails. I'd used a credit card to enter, not an Amazon card or any Amazon-specific information such as an account number. Presumably, I'd used this card to buy something from Amazon or one of its subsidiaries in the past. The emails highlighted how efficient my in-store experience was (or slow, in my case) and an offer with a tempting reward to pick up something next time. For Amazon, even if I only filled out the survey, that's valuable data.

For all the companies profiled in these case studies, such data gathering is essential. More data enables them to build up customer profiles, optimize processes, increase efficiency, better target advertising and promotions, and better predict what customers might want next. Amazon founded its empire on gathering and using customer data. Data gathering across platforms and devices has also been a long-term strategy of Apple. Zara also makes extensive use of data and Nike and IKEA both placed QR codes prominently in-store to encourage customers to download their apps and engage with their websites. Even LEGO has a Chief Data Officer charged with using data for "more effective customer engagement".[1] All of these companies use data not only to better *serve* customers but to better *train* them.

Although inseparable in some ways, physical and digital retail experiences are still fundamentally different in others. A customer's experience in a physical store is shared, while a digital experience is singular. In this way, companies can design the same stores around the world, yet personalize interactions via digital engagement, social media feeds and notifications. That is, while every customer enters the same physical Nike store, an NBA fan may have a different experience to a runner or someone who does a weekly yoga class. Sports fans or amateur athletes, male or female, old or young, Nike can engage with individuals via the app and digital interactions personally within a shared store.

Even more so, the neutral minimalism of the Apple, Zara and Aesop stores aims to appeal to a wide range of customers. Yet if I subscribe to each of these brands' social media feeds, search their websites and receive their notifications,

I get a unique, personalized experience based on previous searches and purchases. Although global, each brand designs regional and national promotions and advertising according to local holidays, seasons or events. In this way, a Zara customer in Madrid receives different digital promotions to a customer in Santiago even though their local stores appear similar and stock the same clothes.

In all cases, in-store experiences situate the customer as the central actor. User-centred design enables smooth interactions for individuals and mediates their shared experience. In this way, a customer becomes part of a community of LEGO fans or Nike athletes. Store designs centred on individual desires encourage customers to pursue self-interest. This is reinforced by an appeal to values – convenience, self-care, simplicity, personalization – taken as fundamental and universal. Within the store, the customer encounters material products that have been transmuted into values – the iPhone as simplicity itself; Nike shoes as the essence of high-performance sports; LEGO's bricks as building blocks of a playful universe.

Ultimately, these stores are designed as theatres for a customer's transformation. In Nike, I can buy shoes and apparel to improve my sporting performance. In LEGO, I buy my children not simply a box of bricks but the gift of creativity. In IKEA, I transform my lifestyle. At Apple, the latest device can simplify my complex life. I grab and go at Amazon Go as my life is so busy. I put on my sunglasses and become a character in the sci-fi world of Gentle Monster. At Aesop, I buy not simply a nice smelling handwash but serenity and self-care. At Zara, I become as fashionable as an Instagram influencer. In these theatres, using these props, I become the star.

Theatres of the Extinction Economy

As in theatre, few customers consider the many backstage activities of their retail experience. In all these cases, the supply chains that create the in-store products are concealed or erased. In-store, the customer encounters material things designed and made far away that simply appear as if by magic. Social media feeds, advertising and promotions have already informed them of the product's usefulness as a tool for a better life. Apple products stamped with "designed in California" or IKEA's in-store references to Swedish-ness reinforce the ideas of Californian tech ingenuity and inherently good Swedish design. But a customer only knows what little the company chooses to tell them about where and how these products were designed and made.

Crucial to the design of retail experience in these cases is to engage customers yet suppress critical reflection. Without thinking, the customer participates in an unsustainable system. From plastic shoes to plastic bricks, composite furniture to composite textiles, fast food to fast fashion: most things for sale in these stores are single-use products that are not designed for reuse or recycling. Obsolescence by design is a defining characteristic of all of these companies. All are founded on a model of growth that requires them to sell more products, increase market share and spread across the globe to anywhere with a middle class large enough to support them. Such retail models are part of a systemic problem.

Humans are currently overshooting critical planetary boundaries.[2] The consequences of this include ecological breakdown, ocean acidification, ozone depletion, deforestation, biodiversity collapse and polluted water, land and air. The acceleration of ecological destruction and pollution is due largely to over-consumption in the Global North. While billionaires are responsible for a large share and attract some media attention from time to time, the global middle classes are equally responsible:

> The world's richest 10% encompasses most of the middle classes in developed countries – anyone paid more than about $40,000 (£32,000) a year. The lavish lifestyles of the very rich – the 1% – attract attention. But the 10% are responsible for half of all global emissions, making them key to ending the climate crisis.[3]

Their biggest carbon emissions come from transport and consuming goods. Media attention on the climate crisis occasionally focuses on transport (debates on electric cars or public transport, for example) but the consumption of clothing, electronic products and personal items are typically overlooked. These are the goods stocked in the stores in this book. The customers referred to throughout this book comprise that 10 per cent of the global middle classes.

Although each chapter touched on the environmental impact of its respective company, it is worth considering this issue holistically. One aspect that surprised me was the overall dependence on fossil fuels. I'd never considered the fact that Nike shoes and clothing are primarily made from plastic. Nor that Zara's clothing and IKEA furniture are mainly composites that combine plastics with other materials. I'd also never considered how many billion LEGO bricks, Nike shoes and Zara garments are produced every year. A single LEGO brick or pair of Nike leggings contains only a little plastic, but if we imagine a customer continually consuming from Nike, IKEA, LEGO and Zara – or Adidas, Williams-Sonoma, Mattel and H&M – this amounts to a lifestyle dependent on single-use plastic products.

In-store, a customer encounters an innocuous, single-use plastic product such as a Nike shoe or an IKEA plastic container in isolation. It is difficult to imagine the process that brought it into being. Plastic begins with oil extraction, refining and transportation. Then factory workers mould and colour raw plastic pellets into a usable product. Fossil fuels drive the trucks, ships or planes that transport and distribute these products around the world. By the time they arrive in-store, even a LEGO brick or a Nike shoe has – for its modest size – a very high carbon emission. And this is only the beginning of the cycle. Few of these plastic products are recycled into anything useful. Most end up in landfills or in the oceans.

While landfills are easy to ignore, huge waste accumulations such as the Great Pacific Garbage Patch, a soupy vortex containing over a million tons of plastic waste floating in an area twice the size of Texas, are harder to ignore.[4] Recent media reports on microplastics have also highlighted tiny plastic particles entering the food chain, water systems and human bloodstreams. There are currently no global treaties aimed at limiting plastic production or pollution, such as caps on production, elimination of single-use plastics or regulations on recycling plastics. Although the process towards designing a United Nations Environmental Program treaty on plastic began in 2022, it has yielded no progress so far.[5]

Design predicated on single use pervades the products on display in my case study stores. This is demonstrated by the absence of design thought going into repair, reuse or recycling. Apple's built-in product obsolescence and Zara's disposable clothes are outstanding examples of this. But the same mentality is also implicit in the products found in Gentle Monster, Nike, IKEA and LEGO stores. All launch hundreds of new products every year and their stores function as showcases for this constant churn. Such an endless parade of novelty not only makes last month's products seem dated but also ensures customers return regularly.

Not surprisingly, the customer in-store rarely encounters any mention of environmental impact. In contrast, greenwashing reigns in the digital realm. Sustainability statements abound on websites and advertising as central to every company's mission. Incremental sustainable additions are promoted as transformational and future innovations are reassuringly just around the corner. LEGO, for example, promotes their experiments in alternatives to ABS bricks and Nike promotes their recycled nylon clothes. Yet both fail to mention these are a tiny fraction of their product lines. In-store, only IKEA highlights its "responsibly sourced wood", ironically presented next to shelves of plastic flowers (Figure 22).

Another element erased from the theatre of retail experience is the reliance on global labour disparities. The magical products the customer encounters in-store were made or assembled by workers in distant factories and workshops. Low pay, long hours, poor working conditions and toxic hazards characterize many of these. Moroccan and Turkish women sew clothes for Zara. Former Uighur farmers assemble Nike shoes in Xinjiang. Polish workers assemble IKEA flatpacks and Chinese workers make Gentle Monster sunglasses. Such labour disparity exists not only globally but also within national borders. Poor factory workers in Guangzhou assemble Apple products for wealthy Shanghainese while poor Americans in Amazon warehouses in Tennessee labour to deliver products to wealthy New Yorkers.

Immersive retail experiences also distract customers from the global operations of these companies. Aesop, with its localization strategy, attempts to fit into local neighbourhoods, even as the company's owners shifted from Melbourne to São Paolo to Paris. As well as avoiding environmental and labour regulations, tax avoidance is another common tactic used by these multinational companies. IKEA, Nike, Zara, Apple and Amazon all offshore profits with complex tax avoidance schemes. But, to reassure customers of their local commitment, Apple organizes in-store community events, IKEA profiles local couples and families in stores while LEGO features sculptures of local icons in every flagship store.

Despite ours being an era of increased transparency – as we saw in Chapter 1 – the customer finds little transparency when it comes to environmental impact, the use of materials, means of production, global labour or tax issues. Is retail experience in the twenty-first century simply an elaborate artifice constructed to not only entertain but to deceive the customer? Perhaps shopping has always been designed to conceal as much as it reveals. In a study of shopping in ancient Rome, historian Claire Holleran noted that "in both Greek and Latin literature retailers are associated with trickery, dishonesty, and greed".[6] In the twenty-first century, perhaps only the means of deception – the physical and digital artifice – has changed.

Of course, alternative, more sustainable retail practices exist. Slow fashion, for example, in which designers use low-impact textiles such as locally sourced and manufactured linen, with fewer annual styles and collections. Or the Dutch-based company Fairphone, dedicated to building smartphones designed "for longevity, easy repair, and modular upgrades".[7] Or Allbirds, a company that designs shoes made from natural materials (wool, eucalyptus and sugar cane) and recycled plastics.[8] There are many other alternative examples in the realms of fashion, phones and shoes, but all have had limited success over the past twenty-five years, particularly compared to Zara, Apple and Nike.

For furniture, recycled and locally sourced timber is an alternative to IKEA's particleboard and plastics, while Farmers' Markets or local maker's markets offer alternatives for food, textiles, ceramics or other homewares. Etsy, founded in 2013, is an alternative platform to Amazon where people can buy home décor, toys or furniture directly from crafters or makers. Facebook Marketplace and eBay are platforms whereby people can resell and recycle household objects. Local swap meets, garage and car boot sales, school and community fetes are also opportunities for recycling and reusing various household products, toys and fashion. All offer alternatives to the stores presented in this book.

Finally, there is a habitual aspect to these retail experiences. Amazon and Apple in particular count on the convenience of staying with a single brand for multiple products and services. They instil in customers patterns of behaviour, expectations and assumptions. Formed through repetition, such habits are also reinforced via automated systems. This applies to all the brands analysed in this book. In the name of convenience or simplicity, customers continue to use the same products and shop in the same stores. As customers are further integrated into digital ecosystems, updating to the latest model is seen as the easiest option.

Retail Futures

Predictions are always fraught but predicting retail futures in an era marked by rapid technological changes, pandemics, wars and climate events seems especially fraught. But it is worth briefly sketching some possible future directions based on the cases studied in the chapters of this book. Thinking about retail futures includes considering the impact of new technologies, expectations of younger generations and shifting global geo-political and economic scenarios. To encapsulate all of these will require new models of scholarship and I hope the synthetic research method used in this book might inspire others to pursue a similar approach.

It is tempting to understand retail history as a linear evolution of technological innovations, each designed to make shopping easier, faster and more efficient. In this progression, the logical endpoint appears to be Amazon Go. Given the increase in self-checkouts and cashless payment stations over the past two decades, this seems possible. Possible but not inevitable. In late 2023, Booths, a small supermarket chain in northern England announced that – in response to customer demands – it would abandon self-checkout machines and reintroduce staff.[9] At the same time, several Canadian stores and two American Walmart stores removed self-checkout machines that had been in operation for over a decade.[10] Clearly, not all customers want a more efficient experience, nor one without human interactions.

But surely younger generations do? The generations who grew up with smartphones, e-commerce and social media – Generation Z (born between 1995 and 2009) and Generation Alpha (born after 2010) – do have different expectations.[11] Nike's store in particular seemed designed to cater to a consumers who expect "new devices and electronic processes to be widely available, thus offering consumers more autonomy and faster transactions".[12] But it is currently unclear whether younger generations prefer online to physical retail. One study that compared Millennial with Generation Z shopping habits concluded, "both generations still prefer shopping in bricks-and-mortar stores

Conclusion

to online shopping".[13] It also noted that, more than previous generations, Generation Z (and beyond) are more inclined to use digital payment methods and better accustomed to searching online for ratings and reviews.[14]

One option for retailers to bridge the digital-physical gap is pop-up or temporary stores. This is a realm of ongoing experiments, with major brands creating temporary stores within existing malls or empty stores, for special events or in temporary locations. In 2022, I visited a large warehouse in lower Manhattan called Showfields (Figures 51 and 52). Opened in 2019, it was a three-storey building that contained dozens of temporary stalls designed by online-only retailers that rotated every four to six months. Showfields was a place where customers could see, touch and smell products that are only available online. But, by the time I wrote this conclusion in late 2023, Showfields in Manhattan had closed (though it still operates in Brooklyn and Miami). Such is the dynamism of twenty-first-century retail.

Figure 51 Showfields, Manhattan, interior 1. Author photo.

Figure 52 Showfields, Manhattan, interior 2. Author photo.

As younger generations grow up enmeshed in social media, it may be that Instagram, TikTok or other digital platforms serve as future retail stores.[15] At the moment, social media feeds serve primarily promotional and advertising purposes rather than as direct sales points, but it is conceivable that this could change soon. Or it may be that, for younger generations, augmented reality (AR) or digital filters on smartphones enhance physical shopping experiences, so that future stores are filled with distinctive digital interactions. Virtual shopping (touched on in the Gentle Monster chapter) may also be a future retail direction as gamers or others who use online worlds may want to customize their avatars.

Interestingly, despite the Covid-19 pandemic's restrictions which accustomed people to online shopping, e-commerce has not grown quickly since. In the United States, for example, online retail accounted for just over 5 per cent of total retail sales in 2012. This increased to 11 per cent by 2019 (before the pandemic), then jumped to 14 per cent during the pandemic in 2020. Since then, online retail rose to just over 15 per cent in 2023.[16] This represents only a modest post-pandemic rise and, overall, online retail represents only a small percentage of total retail. The trajectory points to further future growth but slower than many imagined. Regardless, given that 85 per cent of retail shopping still occurs in-store, physical shopping is not going to disappear anytime soon.

Another future scenario relates to global economic and geopolitical shifts. Except for Aesop and Gentle Monster, the big companies featured in this book hail from the United States and Europe. My sample stores were located primarily in American and European cities. But the rise of China over the past two decades as the world's biggest middle-class market is already impacting global retail with all these brands opening more stores in China. A reasonable assumption, given the size of the Chinese market, is that future retail concepts and brands will emerge from China. Or from other rising economies such as Brazil and India.

Finally, in terms of research and practice, it is worth ending with a final comment on this book. Rather than considering design within the limited scope of a single object, building or a designer and their intention, in compiling these case studies, I have tried to create a model to encapsulate retail experience in a broad context. Although crossing physical and digital realms, I have tried to continually return to the material consequences of design decisions and processes. Ultimately, understanding how retail experiences are designed helps not only designers but all of us to make informed decisions about how, where and why we shop.

Notes

Introduction

1. Derek Thompson, "What in the World Is Causing the Retail Meltdown of 2017?", *The Atlantic*, 10 April 2017, online: https://www.theatlantic.com/business/archive/2017/04/retail-meltdown-of-2017/522384/.
2. Raymond Williams, *Keywords: A Vocabulary of Culture and Society*, revised edn. (New York: Oxford University Press, 1985), p.89.
3. Martin Jay, *Songs of Experience: Modern American and European Variations on a Universal Theme* (Berkeley: University of California Press, 2015), pp.6–7.
4. I took this distinction from Kahneman's 2010 TED talk, "The Riddle of Experience vs Memory": https://www.ted.com/talks/daniel_kahneman_the_riddle_of_experience_vs_memory?language=en. In an earlier paper, Kahneman writes: "Experiences are fleeting", whereas "memories are what we get to keep from our experience". In Daniel Kahneman and Jacob Riis, "Living and Thinking About it: Two Perspectives on Life", in Felicia A. Huppert, Nick Baylis and Barry Keverne, eds., *The Science of Well-Being* (New York: Oxford University Press, 2005), pp.285–304.
5. See Jillian M. Rickly and Elizabeth S. Vidon, eds., *Authenticity and Tourism: Materialities, Perceptions, Experiences* (Bingley, UK: Emerald Publishing, 2018). Their introduction outlines the debates in tourism studies on authentic experiences.
6. See Daniel C. Knudsen, Jillian M. Rickly and Elizabeth Vidon, "The Fantasy of Authenticity: Touring with Lacan", *Annals of Tourism Research*, 58, 2016, pp.33–45; and Jillian M. Rickly and Elizabeth S. Vidon, "Alienation and Anxiety in Tourism Motivation", *Annals of Tourism Research*, 69, 2018, pp.65–75.
7. See Walter Benjamin, "On Some Motifs in Baudelaire", in *Illuminations*, trans. Harry Zohn (New York: Schocken Books, 1968), pp.155–194.
8. John Dewey, *Experience and Nature* (New York: Dover Publications, 1958), p.215.
9. Joan W. Scott, "The Evidence of Experience", *Critical Inquiry* 17:4, 1991, p.793.
10. Scott, "The Evidence of Experience", p.797.
11. B. J. Pine and J. H. Gilmore, "Welcome to the Experience Economy", *Harvard Business Review*, July–August 1998, pp.97–105.
12. B. J. Pine and J. H. Gilmore, *The Experience Economy* (Boston: Harvard Business Review Press, 2011), p.18.

13 Pine and Gilmore, *The Experience Economy*, p.17. See also B. J. Pine and J. H. Gilmore, *Authenticity: What Consumers Really Want* (Boston: Harvard Business School Press, 2007).

14 Albert Boswijk, Thomas J.P. Thijssen and E. Peelen, *The Experience Economy: A New Perspective* (Amsterdam: Pearson, Prentice Hall, 2005); Jon Sundbo and Flemming Sørensen, eds., *Handbook on the Experience Economy* (Cheltenham, UK: Edward Elgar, 2013).

15 Boswijk, Thijssen, and Peelen, *The Experience Economy*, p.6.

16 Bo A. Christensen, "Connecting Experience and Economy – Aspects of Disguised Positioning", *Integrative Psychology and Behavioral Science*, 47, 2013, p.83.

17 Pine and Gilmore, *The Experience Economy*, p.255.

18 Pine and Gilmore, *The Experience Economy*, p.284.

19 Pine and Gilmore, "The Experience Economy: Past, Present and Future", in Sundbo and Sørensen, eds., *Handbook on the Experience Economy*, p.29.

20 See Boswijk, Thijssen and Peelen, *The Experience Economy*.

21 Pine and Gilmore, "The Experience Economy: Past, Present and Future", p.33.

22 Marc Hassenzahl, "User Experience and Experience Design", in *The Encyclopedia of Human-Computer Interaction*, The Interaction Design Foundation, online: https://www.interaction-design.org/literature/book/the-encyclopedia-of-human-computer-interaction-2nd-ed/user-experience-and-experience-design.

23 Donald Norman, *The Design of Everyday Things*, revised and expanded edn. (New York: Basic Books, 2013), p.293.

24 Paul Hekkert and Hendrik N. J. Schifferstein, "Introducing Product Experience", in *Product Experience* (Oxford: Elsevier, 2011), p.4. See also Paul Hekkert and Pieter Desmet, "Framework of Product Experience", *International Journal of Design*, 1:1, 2007, pp.57–66.

25 Brenda Laurel, *Computers as Theatre*, 2nd edn. (Upper Saddle River, NJ: Addison-Wesley, 2014), p. 38. Like Pine and Gilmore, she argued that theatre was not simply a metaphor for human-computer experiences, see p.30.

26 The dominant paradigm in terms of research in the fields of UX and HCI remains cognitive science (and ethnography derived from anthropology).

27 Key texts include Linda Leung, ed., *Design Experience Design: Ideas, Industries, Interactions* (Bristol: Intellect, 2008); Nathan Shedroff, ed., *Experience Design 1.1* (S.l.: Experience Design Books, 2009); Patrick Newbery and Kevin Farnham, *Experience Design: A Framework for Integrating Brand, Experience, and Value* (Hoboken, NJ: Wiley and Sons, 2013); and Peter Benz, ed., *Experience Design: Concepts and Case Studies* (London: Bloomsbury, 2015).

28 Fay Sweet, ed., *Frog: Form Follows Emotion* (New York: Watson-Guptill, 1999); and Tom Kelley with Jonathan Littman, *The Art of Innovation: Lessons in Creativity from IDEO* (London: HarperCollins, 2001).

29 Tim Brown, *Change by Design: How Design Thinking Transforms Organizations and Inspires Innovation* (New York: Harper Business, 2009), p.8.

30 See Marc Hassenzahl, *Experience Design: Technology for All the Right Reasons* (San Rafael, CA: Morgan & Claypool, 2010); and Benz, ed., *Experience Design*.

31 G. Lynn Shostack, "How to Design a Service", *European Journal of Marketing*, 16:1, 1982, pp.49–63; and G. Lynn Shostack, "Designing Services That Deliver", *Harvard Business Review*, 62:1, 1984, pp.133–139. See also Mary Jo Bitner, "Servicescapes: The Impact of Physical Surroundings on Customers and Employees", *Journal of Marketing*, 56:2, 1992, pp.57–71; and Lucy Kimbell, "The Turn to Service Design", in Guy Julier and Liz Moor, eds., *Design and Creativity: Policy, Management and Practice* (Oxford and New York: Berg, 2009), pp.157–173.

32 See, for example, Anna Meroni and Daniela Sangiorgi, eds., *Design for Services* (Farnham: Gower, 2011); Daniela Sangiorgi and Alison Prendiville, eds., *Designing for Service: Key Issues and New Directions* (London: Bloomsbury, 2017); and Lara Penin, *An Introduction to Service Design: Designing the Invisible* (London: Bloomsbury, 2018).

33 Youngsoo Lee and Miso Kim, "The Poetics of Service: Making in the Age of Experience", *Design Issues*, 37:3, 2021, p.57. Their account optimistically highlights customers as co-creators, participants with agency and collective engagement. Unfortunately, the case studies that follow challenge such optimism.

34 In an even broader sense, Anne-Marie Willis refers to "the double movement of ontological designing", that is, we design our world and our world designs us back. Anne-Marie Willis, "Ontological Designing – Laying the Ground", *Design Philosophy Papers*, 4:2, 2006: pp.69–92.

35 See, for example, Prasad Boradkar, *Designing Things: A Critical Introduction to the Culture of Objects* (Oxford and New York: Berg, 2010); and Leslie Atzmon and Prasad Boradkar, eds., *Encountering Things: Design and Theories of Things* (London: Bloomsbury, 2017).

36 Richard Buchanan, "Design and the New Rhetoric: Productive Arts in the Philosophy of Culture", *Philosophy and Rhetoric*, 34:3, 2001, p.194.

37 I am specifically drawing upon the ideas of Roland Barthes, *Mythologies*, trans. Annette Lavers, London: Paladin, 1973. See also D. J. Huppatz, "Reconsidering: Roland Barthes", *Mythologies, Design and Culture*, 3:1, 2011, pp.85–100.

38 Johan Redström and Heather Wiltse, *Changing Things: The Future of Objects in a Digital World* (London: Bloomsbury, 2019).

39 A useful starting point is Dan Zahavi, *Phenomenology: The Basics* (London and New York: Routledge, 2019). More specific for architecture are Jonathan Hale, *Merleau-Ponty for Architects* (London: Routledge, 2017); and Patricia M. Locke and Rachel McCann, eds., *Merleau-Ponty: Space, Place, Architecture* (Athens, Ohio: Ohio University Press, 2015).

40 See Juhani Pallasmaa, "An Architecture of the Seven Senses", in Steven Holl, Juhani Pallasmaa and Alberto Pérez-Gómez, eds., *Questions of Perception: Phenomenology of Architecture* (Tokyo: a+u publishing, 1994), pp.29–37; Juhani Pallasmaa, *The Eyes of the Skin. Architecture and the Senses* (London: Academy Editions, 1996); and Peter Zumthor, *Atmospheres: Architectural Environments, Surrounding Objects* (Basel: Birkhäuser, 2006).

41 Tonino Griffero, *Atmospheres: Aesthetics of Emotional Spaces* (Farnham: Ashgate, 2010); Christian Borch, ed., *Architectural Atmospheres: On the Experience and Politics of Architecture* (Basel: Birkhäuser, 2014); Gernot Böhme, *Atmospheric*

Architectures: The Aesthetics of Felt Spaces, edited and trans. A.-Chr. Engels-Schwartzpaul (London: Bloomsbury, 2017); Alberto Pérez-Gómez, *Attunement: Architectural Meaning after the Crisis of Modern Science* (Cambridge, MA, and London: MIT Press, 2016).

42 Harry Francis Mallgrave, *From Object to Experience: The New Culture of Architectural Design* (London: Bloomsbury, 2018), p.55.

43 See classic anthologies such as Beatriz Colomina, ed., *Sexuality and Space* (Princeton: Princeton Architecture Press, 1991); and Jane Rendell, Barbara Penner and Iain Borden, eds., *Gender, Space, Architecture: An Interdisciplinary Introduction* (London and New York: Routledge, 2000).

44 Sara Ahmed, "A Phenomenology of Whiteness", *Feminist Theory*, 8:2, 2007, p.157.

45 Silvia Stoller, "Phenomenology and the Poststructural Critique of Experience", *International Journal of Philosophical Studies*, 17:5, 2009, pp.712–713.

46 See also D. J. Huppatz, *Design: The Key Concepts* (London: Bloomsbury, 2020).

47 See the in-depth discussion of bricolage in Chapter 3.

48 Sharon Zukin, *Point of Purchase: How Shopping Changed American Culture* (London and New York: Routledge, 2004); Rachel Bowlby, *Carried Away: The Invention of Modern Shopping* (New York: Columbia University Press, 2001); and Pasi Falk and Colin Campbell, *The Shopping Experience* (London: Sage, 1997).

49 See, for example, Geoffrey Crossick and Serge Jaumain, eds., *Cathedrals of Consumption: The European Department Store, 1850–1939* (London and New York: Routledge, 2018); Vicki Howard, *From Main Street to Mall: The Rise and Fall of the American Department Store* (Philadelphia: University of Pennsylvania Press, 2015); Emily M. Orr, *Designing the Department Store: Display and Retail at the Turn of the Twentieth Century* (London: Bloomsbury, 2019).

50 Walter Benjamin, *The Arcades Project*, trans. Howard Eiland and Kevin McLaughlin (Cambridge, MA, and London: Harvard University Press, 1999), A4, 1, p.43.

51 See Anca Lasc, Patricia Lara Betancourt and Margaret Maile Petty, eds., *Architectures of Display: Department Stores and Modern Retail* (London and New York: Routledge, 2018).

52 See, for example, Lisa Scharoun, *America at the Mall: The Cultural Role of a Retail Utopia* (Jefferson, NC: McFarland, 2012). On malls as a global type, see Nicholas Jewell, *Shopping Malls and Public Space in Modern China* (Farnham, Surrey: Ashgate, 2015); and Matthew Bailey, *Managing the Marketplace: Reinventing Shopping Centres in Post-War Australia* (London and New York: Routledge, 2020).

53 See Jeffrey M. Hardwick, *Mall Maker: Victor Gruen, Architect of an American Dream* (Philadelphia: University of Pennsylvania Press, 2003); and Victor Gruen, *Shopping Town: Designing the City in Modern America*, trans. Anette Baldauf (Philadelphia: University of Pennsylvania Press, 2017).

54 See Alexandra Lange, *Meet Me by the Fountain: An Inside History of the Mall* (London: Bloomsbury, 2022).

55 See, for example deadmalls.com and YouTube videos by Dan Bell on empty "dead malls": https://www.youtube.com/playlist?list=PLNz4Un92pGNxQ9vNgmnCx7dwchPJGJ3IQ.

56 For architects, a key text was Chuihua Judy Chung, Jeffrey Inaba, Rem Koolhaas and Sze Tsung Leong, eds., *Project on the City II: The Harvard Guide to Shopping* (Cologne: Taschen, 2001). See also Christopher M. Moore and Anne Marie Doherty, "The International Flagship Stores of Luxury Fashion Retailers", in Tony Hines and Margaret Bruce, eds., *Fashion Marketing: Contemporary Issues*, 2nd edn. (New York: Elsevier, 2007), pp.277–296.

57 Mattias Karrholm, *Retailising Space: Architecture, Retail and the Territorialisation of Public Space* (London and New York: Routledge, 2012).

58 Anna Klingmann, *Brandscapes: Architecture in the Experience Economy* (Cambridge, MA: MIT Press, 2007); and Brian Lonsway, *Making Leisure Work, Architecture and the Experience Economy* (London: Routledge, 2009).

59 Here, I am influenced by George Ritzer's *The McDonaldization of Society* (Thousand Oaks, CA: Sage, 1993). I will return to the most recent edition of Ritzer's book in Chapter 2. See also Natasha Dow Schull, *Addiction by Design: Machine Gambling in Las Vegas* (New York: Princeton University Press, 2012).

Chapter 1

1 Dominic A. Pacyga, *Chicago: A Biography* (Chicago and London: University of Chicago Press, 2009), p.12.

2 McCormick's factory burned down in the 1871 Chicago fire and he rebuilt elsewhere.

3 John N. Low, *Imprints: The Pokagon Band of Potawatomi Indians and the City of Chicago* (Detroit: Michigan State University Press, 2016).

4 Apple had already developed some ideas about its retail experience with white, clean displays for iMacs within other stores before this. See Michael Steeber, "Before the Genius Bar: Behind the Retail Designs that Paved the Way for 20 Years of Apple Stores", 9to5Mac, 20 May 2021, online: https://9to5mac.com/2021/05/20/20-years-apple-retail-stores-compusa-early-designs/.

5 Also used in the "Think Different" campaign, the photo of John Lennon and Yoko Ono resonated in two ways. First, Apple Corps is the company founded by the Beatles in 1968 which included the recording company Apple Records. From 1978 to 2007, Apple Corps and Apple Computer fought numerous legal battles over trademark disputes. Second, in 1966, Ono exhibited "Apple", an artwork featuring an apple on a plexiglass stand, in a London art gallery. At the exhibition's opening, John Lennon allegedly took a bite of the apple.

6 Walter Isaacson, *Steve Jobs* (London: Brown, Little, 2011), p.492.

7 The firm designed over seventy Apple stores from 2001–16.

8 Ryan E. Smith, "Apple Cube Fifth Avenue", *Journal of Architectural Education*, 62:2, 2008, pp.67–69.

9 See Valentina Palladino, "Apple Store receives trademark for 'distinctive design and layout'", *Wired*, 30 January 2013, online: https://www.wired.com/2013/01/apple-store-trademark/. Lawyers have noted the low level of distinction of a store design and the difficulties of potential enforcement. See Jeremy Blum and Amy

Cullen, "The Apple Store and Unconventional Trademarks: How Easy are They to Enforce?", *Journal of Intellectual Property Law & Practice*, 9:12, 2014, pp.1008–1011.

10   Fan Yang, "China's 'Fake' Apple Store: Branded Space, Intellectual Property and the Global Culture Industry", *Theory, Culture and Society*, 31:4, 2014, pp.71–96.

11   Fan Yang, "China's 'Fake' Apple Store", p.83.

12   Carmine Gallo, *The Apple Experience: Secrets to Building Insanely Great Customer Loyalty* (New York: McGraw Hill, 2012), e-book version, section 169.3.

13   Isaacson, *Steve Jobs*, pp.375–376.

14   Reports on the so-called "Secret Training Manual" became public in 2012. See Sam Biddle, "How to Be a Genius: This is Apple's Secret Employee Training Manual", *Gizmodo*, 28 August 2012, online: https://gizmodo.com/how-to-be-a-genius-this-is-apples-secret-employee-trai-5938323.

15   Isaacson, *Steve Jobs*, p.455.

16   Chajoong Kim, James A. Self and Jieun Bae, "Exploring the First Momentary Unboxing Experience with Aesthetic Interaction", *The Design Journal*, 21:3, 2018, p.419. See also Sharif Mowlabocus, "'Lets get this thing open': The pleasures of unboxing videos", *European Journal of Cultural Studies*, 23:4, 2020, pp.564–579.

17   For a detailed map of this process, see David Potente and Erika Salvini, "Apple, IKEA and their Integrated Architecture", *Bulletin of the American Society of Information Science and Technology*, 35:4, 2009, pp.32–42.

18   See Leander Kahney, *The Cult of Macintosh* (San Francisco, CA: No Starch Press, 2004).

19   See Anja Pogačnik and Aleš Črnič, "iReligion: Religious Elements of the Apple Phenomenon", *The Journal of Religion and Popular Culture*, 26:3, Fall 2014.

20   See Leander Kahney, *Tim Cook: The Genius Who Took Apple to the Next Level* (London: Portfolio/Penguin, 2019).

21   Apple press release, 19 October 2017, online: https://www.apple.com/au/newsroom/2017/10/apple-michigan-avenue-opens-tomorrow-on-chicagos-riverfront/.

22   Jennifer Reingold, "What the Heck is Angela Ahrendts Doing at Apple?", *Fortune*, 10 September 2015, online: https://fortune.com/2015/09/10/angela-ahrendts-apple/.

23   Jack Riedy, "Too Big to Pay", *Reader: Chicago's Alternative Nonprofit Newsroom*, 22 May 2019, online: https://chicagoreader.com/music/too-big-to-pay/. A similar report from radio station KQED in the Bay Area suggested the same for the San Francisco Apple store; see Nastia Voynovskaya, "Apple Isn't Paying Artists Who Perform at Its Stores", KQED, 14 March 2019, online: https://www.kqed.org/arts/13852882/artists-today-at-apple-unpaid-exposure-money.

24   On Foster's early work, see Malcolm Quantrill, *The Norman Foster Studio: Consistency Through Diversity* (London: Routledge, 1999); Deyan Sudjic, *Norman Foster: A Life in Architecture* (New York: Overlook Press, 2010); and D. J. Huppatz, "Globalising Corporate Identity in Hong Kong: Redesigning Two Banks", *Journal of Design History*, 18:4, 2015, pp.357–369.

25 See Abigail A. Van Slyck, *Free to All: Carnegie Libraries and American Culture, 1890–1920* (Chicago: University of Chicago Press, 1995).

26 Ironically, Steve Jobs' rival Bill Gates, through the Bill and Melinda Gates Foundation, has contributed far more of his personal fortune than Jobs or Cook.

27 Stephanie Williams, "Can the New Carnegie Library Apple Store Help Boost D.C.'s creative community?", *The Washington Post*, 15 May 2019, online: https://www.washingtonpost.com/express/2019/05/15/can-new-carnegie-library-apple-store-help-boost-dcs-creative-community/.

28 Tom Ravenscroft, "Stockholm Blocks Chipperfield's Nobel Centre, Foster's Apple Store and City's Olympic Bid", *Dezeen*, 8 November 2018, online: https://www.dezeen.com/2018/11/08/stockholm-apple-store-foster-chipperfield-nobel-center-olympic-bid/.

29 Richard Willingham, "Federation Square Apple Store Doomed After Permit Refused by Heritage Authorities", ABC News online, 5 April 2019, online: https://www.abc.net.au/news/2019-04-05/apple-store-federation-square-melbourne-plans-permit-refused/10975938.

30 Isaacson, *Steve Jobs*, p.126.

31 See, for example, Richard Koch and Greg Lockwood, *Simplify: How the Best Businesses in the World Succeed* (London: Piatkis, 2016); and Jin Kang Møller, *The Simplicity Playbook for Innovators: Creating Lovable Experiences in a Complicated World* (Singapore: Marshall Cavendish Business, 2020).

32 Cameron Shelley, "The Nature of Simplicity in Apple Design", *The Design Journal*, 18:3, 2015, p.441.

33 Shane Richmond, "Jonathan Ive Interview: Simplicity Isn't Simple", *The Telegraph*, 23 May 2012, online: https://www.telegraph.co.uk/technology/apple/9283706/Jonathan-Ive-interview-simplicity-isnt-simple.html.

34 Adrian Forty, *Words and Buildings: A Vocabulary of Modern Architecture* (London: Thames and Hudson, 2000), p. 250.

35 A 2011–12 exhibition at San Francisco's Museum of Modern Art, *Less and More: The Design Ethos of Dieter Rams* made clear the connection between Rams and Apple. See also Shelley, "The Nature of Simplicity in Apple Design", *The Design Journal*, 18:3, 2015, pp.439–456.

36 John Maeda, *The Laws of Simplicity: Design, Technology, Business, Life* (Cambridge, MA, and London: MIT Press, 2006); Per Mollerup, *Simplicity: A Matter of Design* (London: Laurence King Publishing, 2015); and Hartmut Obendorf, *Minimalism: Designing Simplicity* (London: Springer-Verlag, 2009).

37 Ken Segall, *Insanely Simple: The Obsession That Drives Apple's Success* (London: Portolio/Penguin, 2012).

38 Jobs' biographer even linked his obsession with simplicity to Jobs' reverence for Japanese Buddhism, encountered on a trip to Japan. See Isaacson, *Steve Jobs*, p. 74.

39 See Adrian Forty, "Simple", in *Words and Buildings: A Vocabulary of Modern Architecture* (London: Thames and Hudson, 2000), pp.249–255.

40 See Brian Merchant, *The One Device: The Secret History of the iPhone* (New York: Little, Brown, 2017). See also this detailed description of the trip of the finished

phones from China: David Barboza, "An Apple iPhone's Journey, From Chinese Factory Floor to Western Retail Store", 3 January 2017, *Australian Financial Review*, online: https://www.afr.com/technology/an-apple-iphones-journey-from-chinese-factory-floor-to-western-retail-store-20161230-gtjnaf.

41 Such a philosophy resonates with Marie Kondo's "tidying up" lifestyle advice. See Marie Kondo, *The Life-Changing Magic of Tidying Up: The Japanese Art of Decluttering and Organizing* (New York: Ten Speed Press, 2014); and the popular 2019 Netflix series "Tidying Up with Marie Kondo".

42 See the detailed analysis by Taehoon Kim's medium page, "'Liquid to Light' – 10 minute summary on iPhone Design Philosophy", 12 June 2016, online: https://medium.com/@taehoonkim_22222/10-minute-summary-on-iphone-design-philosophy-liquid-to-light-892c7d117ff.

43 Klaus Klemp, "Dieter Rams: Ethics and Modern Philosophy: What Legacy Today?" *Docomodo*, 46, 2012. See also the 2018 Gary Huswit documentary, *Rams*.

44 Cameron Shelley, "The Nature of Simplicity in Apple Design", *The Design Journal*, 18:3, 2015, p.453.

45 D. J. Huppatz, *Design: The Key Concepts* (London: Bloomsbury, 2020), pp.70–71.

46 Aaron Perzanowski, *The Right to Repair: Reclaiming the Things We Own* (Cambridge: Cambridge University Press, 2022).

47 David Harvey, "The Fetish of Technology: Causes and Consequences", *Macalester International*: 13:7, 2003, online: http://digitalcommons.macalester.edu/macintl/vol13/iss1/7.

48 Adrian Forty, "Transparency", *Words and Buildings*, p. 286. While he notes transparency as a twentieth-century concept in architectural discourse, examples such as the Crystal Palace and department store architecture suggest a longer history.

49 See, for example, John Stanislav Sadar, *Through the Healing Glass: Shaping the Modern Body through Glass Architecture, 1925–35* (New York and London: Routledge, 2016).

50 On the controversy around transparency, see Sarah M. Dreller, "Curtained Walls: Architectural Photography, the Farnsworth House, and the Opaque Discourse of Transparency", *Arris: The Journal of the Southeast Chapter of the Society of Architectural Historians*, 26, 2015, pp.3–39.

51 Walter Benjamin, "Experience and Poverty", in Michael W. Jennings, Howard Eiland and Gary Smith, eds., *Walter Benjamin: Selected Writings, Volume 2, Part 2, 1931–34* (Cambridge, MA, and London: Harvard University Press, 1999), p.734.

52 I owe a debt here to Freyja Hartzell, "Enemy of Secrets: Transparency and Displacement in Interwar Glass", *Journal of Design History*, 43:3, 2021, pp.227–242.

53 Japanese firm SANAA were also at the forefront of glass innovation in architecture. See Michel Bell and Jeannie Kim, eds., *Engineered Transparency: The Technical, Visual and Spatial Effects of Glass* (New York: Princeton Architectural Press, 2009).

54 See Byung-Chul Han, *The Transparent Society*, trans. Erik Butler (Stanford: Stanford University Press, 2015).

55 Claire Birchall, *Radical Secrecy: The Ends of Transparency in Datafied America* (Minneapolis and London: University of Minnesota Press, 2021), p.69.

56 Emmanuel Alloa, ed., *This Obscure Thing Called Transparency: Politics and Aesthetics of a Contemporary Metaphor* (Leuven: Leuven University Press, 2022), p.28.

57 Bødker for example, used transparency as a goal, in suggesting that digital tools should let users work directly on their tasks, the interface becoming invisible. Bødker, S., *Through the Interface – A Human Activity Approach to User Interface Design* (Hillsdale, NJ: Lawrence Erlbaum Associates, 1990).

58 This report was compiled by three Chinese organizations: the Institute of Public and Environmental Affairs, Friends of Nature and Green Beagle. The original report is online: https://media.business-humanrights.org/media/documents/files/media/documents/it_report_phase_iv_the_other_side_of_apple-final.pdf.

59 Brian Merchant, *The One Device: The Secret History of the iPhone* (New York: Little, Brown, 2017); Jenny Chan, Mark Selden and Pun Ngai, *Dying for an iPhone: Apple, Foxconn, and the Lives of China's Workers* (Chicago: Haymarket Books, 2020).

60 Chan, Selden and Ngai, *Dying for an iPhone*, p.82.

61 Annie Kelly, "Apple and Google Named in US Lawsuit Over Congolese Child Cobalt Mining Deaths", *The Guardian*, 16 December 2019, online:https://www.theguardian.com/global-development/2019/dec/16/apple-and-google-named-in-us-lawsuit-over-congolese-child-cobalt-mining-deaths.

62 Maura Doolan and Victoria Kim, "Apple-FBI Fight Over iPhone Encryption Pits Privacy Against National Security", *Los Angeles Times*, 18 February 2016, online: https://www.latimes.com/business/la-me-fbi-apple-legal-20160219-story.html.

63 See "Paradise Papers: Secrets of the Global Elites" by the International Consortium of Investigative Journalists: https://www.icij.org/investigations/paradise-papers/, particularly Simon Bowers, "Leaked Documents Expose Secret Tale of Apple's Offshore Island Hop", 6 November 2017, online: https://www.icij.org/investigations/paradise-papers/apples-secret-offshore-island-hop-revealed-by-paradise-papers-leak-icij/.

64 Han, *The Transparent Society*, p. vii.

65 See Ryan Mac and Kellen Browning, "Apps and Oranges: Behind Apple's 'Bullying' on Trademarks", *New York Times*, 11 March 2022, online: https://www.nytimes.com/2022/03/11/technology/apple-trademarks.html.

Chapter 2

1 Jeffrey Dastin, "Amazon to Shut Its Bookstores and Other Shops As Its Grocery Chain Expands", *Reuters*, 2 March 2022, online: https://www.reuters.com/business/retail-consumer/exclusive-amazon-close-all-its-physical-bookstores-4-star-shops-2022-03-02/.

2 Various iterations of the Amazon website since 1995 are available at the "Version Museum: A Visual History of your Favorite Technology", online: https://www.versionmuseum.com/history-of/amazon-website.

3 Robert Spector, *Amazon.com Get Big Fast* (London: HarperCollins, 2008), p.168.

4. Though Amazon unboxing videos have not been as popular as Apple's, some feature in the Reviews section of the Amazon website.
5. Richard L. Brandt, *One Click: Jeff Bezos and the Rise of Amazon.com* (New York: Portfolio/Penguin, 2011), p.85.
6. Twenty years later, customer review and ratings sites, such as Rotten Tomatoes and TripAdvisor, are common.
7. Claire Cain Miller and Julie Bosman, "E-Books Outsell Print Books at Amazon", *New York Times*, 19 May 2011, online: https://www.nytimes.com/2011/05/20/technology/20amazon.html.
8. See Jonathan Zittrain, *The Future of the Internet and How to Stop It* (New Haven: Yale University Press, 2008), pp.101–126.
9. Since 2009, Amazon Publishing has launched more than a dozen imprints.
10. Jia Tolentino, "Amazon's Brick-and-Mortar Bookstores Are Not Built for People Who Actually Read", *The New Yorker*, 30 May 2017, online: https://www.newyorker.com/culture/cultural-comment/amazons-brick-and-mortar-bookstores-are-not-built-for-people-who-actually-read.
11. See Emily West, *Buy Now: How Amazon Branded Convenience and Normalized Monopoly* (Cambridge, MA: MIT Press, 2022), pp.100–101.
12. Jeffrey Dastin, *Reuters*, 3 March 2022, online: https://www.reuters.com/business/retail-consumer/exclusive-amazon-close-all-its-physical-bookstores-4-star-shops-2022-03-02/
13. Natalie Berg and Miya Knights, *Amazon: How the World's Most Relentless Retailer Will Continue to Revolutionize Commerce*, 2nd edn. (London: Kogan, 2022), p.130.
14. Katie Tarasov, "Amazon Bought Whole Foods Five Years Ago for $13.7 Billion. Here's What's Changed at the High-End Grocer", CNBC, 25 August 2022, online: https://www.cnbc.com/2022/08/25/how-whole-foods-has-changed-in-the-five-years-since-amazon-took-over.html.
15. Another aspect to the Whole Foods purchase was that it instantly increased Amazon's delivery network and refrigerated warehouse capacity.
16. Shoshana Zuboff, *The Age of Surveillance Capitalism: The Fight for a Human Future at the New Frontiers of Power* (London: Profile Books, 2019), p.v. See also Nick Srnicek, *Platform Capitalism* (Cambridge and Malden, MA: Polity Press, 2017).
17. See Brad Stone, *Amazon Unbound: Jeff Bezos and the Invention of a Global Empire* (New York: Simon and Schuster, 2021).
18. West, *Buy Now*, p.15.
19. See Shep Hyken, *The Convenience Revolution: How to Deliver a Customer Service Experience That Disrupts the Competition and Creates Fierce Loyalty* (Shippensburg, PA: Sound Wisdom, 2018), especially chapter 3, The Six Principles.
20. Bill Gates (with Nathon Myhrvold and Peter Rinearson), *The Road Ahead* (New York: Viking Press, 1995).
21. John E. Crowley, *The Invention of Comfort: Sensibilities of Design in Early Modern Britain and Early America* (Baltimore: John Hopkins University Press, 2001), p.151.
22. See, for example, Frank Trentmann, *Empire of Things: How We Became a World of Consumers from the Fifteenth Century to the Twenty-First* (London: HarperCollins,

23 Elizabeth Shove, *Comfort, Cleanliness and Convenience: The Social Organization of Normality* (Oxford and New York: Berg, 2003), p.171.
24 Ruth Schwartz Cowan, *More Work for Mother: The Ironies of Household Technology from the Open Hearth to the Microwave* (New York: Basic Books, 1983), p.178.
25 Cameron Tonkinwise, "The Practically Living Weight of Convenient Things", in Leslie Atzmon and Prasad Poradkar, eds., *Encountering Things: Design and Theories of Things* (London: Bloomsbury, 2017), p.54.
26 West, *Buy Now*, p.45.
27 Yolande Strengers and Jenny Kennedy, *The Smart Wife: Why Siri, Alexa, and Other Smart Home Devices Need a Feminist Reboot* (London and Cambridge, MA: MIT Press, 2020).
28 See D. J. Huppatz, "Robot Salesmen: Vending Machines and Automated Retail in the United States, 1925–39", *History of Retail and Consumption*, 7:3, 2021, pp.261–276.
29 David Freeland, *Automats, Taxi Dances and Vaudeville: Excavating Manhattan's Lost Places of Leisure* (New York: New York University Press, 2009), p.113.
30 "Self Checkout", NPR podcast, episode 730, 19 October 2016: https://www.npr.org/transcripts/498571623.
31 Video: "Introducing Amazon Go and the world's most advanced shopping technology", YouTube, uploaded 6 December 2016: https://www.youtube.com/watch?v=NrmMk1Myrxc.
32 See Louisa Iarocci, "Bin, Bag, Box: The Architecture of Convenience", in Charlotte Ashby and Mark Crinson, eds., *Building/Object: Shared and Contested Territories of Design and Architecture* (London: Bloomsbury, 2022).
33 Here, I have adopted ideas from Shove, *Comfort, Cleanliness and Convenience*, especially chapter 10, "Convenience, Co-ordination and Convention", pp.169–185.
34 Jenny Huberman, "Amazon Go, Surveillance Capitalism, and the Ideology of Convenience", *Economic Anthropology*, 8, 2021, p.346.
35 See West, *Buy Now*, especially chapter 2, pp.51–80.
36 Shove, *Comfort, Cleanliness and Convenience*, p.180.
37 Vance Packard, *The Waste Makers* (London: Longmans, 1960), p.101.
38 Tim Wu, "The Tyranny of Convenience", *New York Times*, 16 February 2018, online: https://www.nytimes.com/2018/02/16/opinion/sunday/tyranny-convenience.html.
39 Tim Wu, "The Tyranny of Convenience".
40 "About Amazon", online: https://www.amazon.jobs/en/landing_pages/about-amazon.
41 See John Rossman, *The Amazon Way: Amazon's 14 Leadership Principles*, 3rd edn. (Seattle: Clyde Hill Publishing, 2014), especially chapter 2, Customer Obsession. Rossman is a former Amazon executive.
42 See West, *Buy Now*, pp.58–59.

43 Huberman, "Amazon Go, Surveillance Capitalism, and the Ideology of Convenience", p.342.

44 Ben Unglesbee, "Amazon Go Store in NYC is the 1st to Take Cash", *Retail Dive*, 8 May 2019, online: https://www.retaildive.com/news/amazon-go-store-in-nyc-is-the-1st-to-take-cash/554352/.

45 West, *Buy Now*, p.221.

46 Jodi Kantor and David Streitfeld, "Inside Amazon: Wrestling Big Ideas in a Bruising Workplace", *New York Times*, 15 August 2015, online: https://www.nytimes.com/2015/08/16/technology/inside-amazon-wrestling-big-ideas-in-a-bruising-workplace.html.

47 Jake Alimahomed-Wilson and Ellen Reese, eds., *The Cost of Free Shipping: Amazon in the Global Economy* (London: Pluto Books, 2020).

48 Alimahomed-Wilson and Reese, eds., *The Cost of Free Shipping*, p.91.

49 Alessandro Delfanti, *The Warehouse: Workers and Robots at Amazon* (London: Pluto Press, 2021).

50 NELP, "Amazon's Disposable Workers: High Injury and Turnover Rates at Fulfillment Centers in California", *National Employment Law: Data Brief*, March 2020, online: https://s27147.pcdn.co/wp-content/uploads/Data-Brief-Amazon-Disposable-Workers-Injury-Turnover-Rates-California-Fulfillment-Centers3-20.pdf.

51 Alimahomed-Wilson and Reese, eds., *The Cost of Free Shipping*, p.23.

52 Faris Tanyos, "Amazon Go Stores in New York City Didn't Properly Alert Customers They Were Being Biometrically Tracked, Lawsuit Says", CBS News, 18 March 2023, online: https://www.cbsnews.com/news/amazon-go-stores-new-york-city-lawsuit-biometric-tracking/.

53 Nora Draper and Joseph Turow, "The Corporate Cultivation of Digital Resignation", *New Media & Society*, 21:8, 2019, pp.1824–1839.

54 See Shoshana Zuboff, *The Age of Surveillance Capitalism: The Fight for a Human Future at the New Frontiers of Power* (London: Profile Books, 2019).

55 See Joseph Turow, *The Aisles Have Eyes: How Retailers Track Your Shopping, Strip Your Privacy, and Define Your Power* (New Haven and London: Yale University Press, 2017).

Chapter 3

1 This history of LEGO is taken primarily from Sarah Herman, *Building a History: The LEGO Group* (Barnsley, UK: Pen & Sword Books, 2012); Maaike Lauwaert, *Place of Play: Toys and Digital Cultures* (Amsterdam: Amsterdam University Press, 2009); and the LEGO Group history, online: https://www.lego.com/en-us/aboutus/lego-group/the-lego-group-history.

2 See the 1958 patent filed by Godtfred Kirk Christensen for a "toy building element" (granted in 1961): https://patents.google.com/patent/US3005282A/en.

3 Lauwaert, *Place of Play*, p.50.

4 The 1973 version is the logo used today although LEGO redesigned it slightly in 1998 for better digital reproduction.

5 Colin Fanning, "Building Kids: LEGO and the Commodification of Creativity", in Megan Brandow-Faller, ed., *Toys and the Material Culture of Childhood* (London: Bloomsbury, 2018), p.96. Minifigures can also be seen as a reaction to the popularity of the German-designed Playmobil plastic figures and sets, launched in 1975.

6 Stephen Kline, *Out of the Garden: Toys and Children's Culture in the Age of TV Marketing* (London and New York: Verso, 1993), p.158.

7 The story of LEGO's revival is told in David C. Robertson with Bill Breen, *Brick By Brick: How LEGO Rewrote the Rules of Innovation and Conquered the Global Toy Industry* (New York: Crown Business, 2013).

8 Stig Hjarvard, "From Bricks to Bytes: The Mediatization of a Global Toy Industry", in I. B. Bondebjerg and Peter Golding, eds., *European Culture and the Media* (Bristol: Intellect Books, 2004), pp.43–63.

9 Fernando Vianna, Francis Kanashiro Meneghetti and Juliana Vianna, "The Dark Side of LEGO Digitization: From Bankruptcy to Power through Surveillance Capitalism", Conference paper, EGOS Colloquium, Hamburg, July 2020.

10 Alanna Petroff, "Lego Becomes the World's Biggest Toymaker", *CNN online*, 4 September 2014, online: https://money.cnn.com/2014/09/04/news/companies/lego-biggest-toymaker/index.html.

11 The first official LEGO retail store opened in Sydney in 1984 but closed ten years later. Another LEGO store opened in 1992 at Minnesota's Mall of America, but both remained one-off and were different to "LEGO branded stores" of the twenty-first century.

12 See LEGO annual report 2002: https://www.lego.com/cdn/cs/aboutus/assets/blt58b55737b9dfc7cb/Annual_Report_2002_ENG.pdf.

13 Figures are hard to verify. I have based this on the LEGO annual report of 2019, in which 150 new stores opened, and the total was 570, meaning that in 2018 there were 420 stores. According to the 2022 LEGO Annual Report, 155 new stores opened in 2022, 95 of these in China, with a total of 904 globally. See: https://www.lego.com/cdn/cs/aboutus/assets/blt70ef2efdd8d21dc7/LEGO_Annual_Report2022_Final_WEB.pdf.

14 See Jonathan Rey Lee, "The Plastic Art of LEGO: An Essay into Material Culture", in Dennis M. Weiss, Amy D. Propen and Colbey Emmerson Reid, eds., *Design, Mediation and the Posthuman* (Lanham: Lexington Books, 2014), pp.99–102.

15 Lee, "The Plastic Art of LEGO", p.95.

16 Jonathan Rey Lee, *Deconstructing LEGO: The Medium and Messages of LEGO Play* (London: Palgrave Macmillan, 2020), p.47.

17 See Anna Wilson, "Moshe Safdie used 'all the Lego in Montreal' to design Habitat 67", interview with Moshe Safdie, *Dezeen*, 19 December 2014, online: https://www.dezeen.com/2014/12/19/moshe-safdie-movie-interview-habitat-67/.

18 See Kjetil Fallan, *Design History: Understanding Theory and Method* (London: Bloomsbury, 2010).

19 Hjarvard, *From Bricks to Bytes*, p.127.

20. Lee, *Deconstructing LEGO*, p.169.
21. See Hjarvard, *From Bricks to Bytes*, pp.128–130.
22. See the podcast *Bits and Bricks*, episode 8, "LEGO Minifigures: A Conversation", 27 January 2021: https://podcasts.apple.com/au/podcast/lego-minifigures-a-conversation/id1542166642?i=1000506740033.
23. Hjarvard, *From Bricks to Bytes*, p.136.
24. Rosemary J. Coombe and Andrew Herman, "Rhetorical Virtues: Property, Speech, and the Commons on the World-Wide Web", *Anthropological Quarterly*, 77:3, 2004, pp.559–574, p.563. After meeting with Māori leaders and lawyers, LEGO agreed to remove some of the more offensive words and references and agreed to work on a code of conduct on the use of traditional knowledge – but the latter, as far as I can find out, did not eventuate. See also Brian Fitzgerald and Susan Hedge, "Traditional Cultural Expression and Internet World", in C. Antons, ed., *Traditional Knowledge, Traditional Cultural Expressions and Intellectual Property Law in the Asia-Pacific Region* (Netherlands: Kluwer Law International, 2009), pp.245–272.
25. Interestingly, such distinctions are a twenty-first century development, although LEGO had previously tried female-oriented series with LEGO Belville and LEGO Homemaker.
26. Rebecca W. Black, Bill Tomlinson and Ksenia Korobkova, "Play and Identity in Gendered LEGO Franchises", *International Journal of Play*, 5:1, 2016, p.73.
27. See Stephanie M. Reich, Rebecca W. Black and Tammie Foliaki, "Constructing Difference: Lego® Set Narratives Promote Stereotypic Gender Roles and Play", *International Journal of Play*, 5:1, 2016, pp.64–76; and Rebecca C. Hains and Jennifer W. Shewmaker, "'I Just Don't Really, Like, Connect To It': How Girls Negotiate LEGO's Gender-Marketed Toys", in Rebecca C. Hains and Sharon R. Mazzarella, eds., *Cultural Studies of LEGO* (Cham: Palgrave Macmillan, 2019), pp.247–269.
28. M. Fulcher and A. R. Hayes, "Building a Pink Dinosaur: The Effects of Gendered Construction Toys on Girls' and Boys' Play", *Sex Roles*, 79:5–6, 2018, 273–284.
29. Johan Huizinga, *Homo Ludens: A Study in the Play-Element of Culture* (London: Routledge and Kegan Paul, 1949), p.13.
30. David Gauntlett, "The Lego System as a Tool For Thinking, Creativity, and Changing the World", in Mark J. P. Wolf, ed., *LEGO Studies: Examining the Building Blocks of a Transmedia Phenomenon* (London and New York, Routledge, 2014), p.194. Workshop methods are now open source but facilitators need to purchase the physical LEGO blocks: https://www.lego.com/en-au/themes/serious-play.
31. Jacques Ehrmann, trans. Cathy Lewis and Phil Lewis, "Homo Ludens Revisited", *Yale French Studies*, 41, 1968, pp.31–57.
32. Ehrmann, "Homo Ludens Revisited", p.34.
33. Ehrmann, "Homo Ludens Revisited", pp.42–43.
34. Seth Giddings, *Gameworlds: Virtual Media and Children's Everyday Play* (London: Bloomsbury, 2014), p.31.
35. Claude Levi-Strauss, *The Savage Mind* (London: Weidenfeld and Nicholson, 1966).

36 See Mark Amerika, *Remix: The Book* (Minneapolis: University of Minnesota Press, 2011); and Eduardo Navas, Owen Gallagher and xtine burrough, eds., *The Routledge Companion to Remix Studies* (London and New York: Routledge, 2014).

37 Mark Deuze, "Participation, Remediation, Bricolage: Considering Principal Components of a Digital Culture", *The Information Society*, 22:2, 2006, p.70.

38 Dick Hebdige, *Subculture: The Meaning of Style* (London and New York: Routledge, 1979), p.103.

39 Fredric Jameson, *Postmodernism, or the Cultural Logic of Late Capitalism* (Durham, NC: Duke University Press, 1997), p.17.

40 Fredric Jameson, "Postmodernism and Consumer Society", in Hal Foster, ed., *The Anti-Aesthetic: Essays on Postmodern Culture* (Port Townsend, WA: Bay Press, 1983), p.116. He also mentions *Raiders of the Lost Ark* in this respect – perhaps no coincidence that these were two of LEGO's earliest and successful franchises.

41 Roland Barthes, "Toys", in *Mythologies*, trans. Annette Lavers (London: Paladin, 1973), p.59.

42 Miguel Sicart, *Play Matters* (Cambridge, Mass and London: MIT Press, 2014), p.36.

43 Fanning, "Building Kids: LEGO and the Commodification of Creativity", p.96.

44 See LEGO's "Play Well Report", 2018, online: https://education.theiet.org/media/5555/lego-play-well-report-pdf-6-847kb.pdf.

45 See Michael R.W. Dawson, Brian Dupuis and Michael Wilson, *From Bricks to Brains: The Embodied Cognitive Science of LEGO Robots* (Edmonton: Athabasca University Press, 2010).

46 Sicart, *Play Matters*, p.9.

47 Brian Sutton-Smith, *The Ambiguity of Play* (Cambridge, MA, and London: Harvard University Press, 1997), p.155.

48 Lee, *Deconstructing LEGO*, p.139.

49 See Lincoln Geraghty, "(Re-)Constructing Childhood Memories: Nostalgia, Creativity, and the Expanded Worlds of the Lego Fan Community", in E. Wesseling, ed., *Reinventing Childhood Nostalgia: Books, Toys, and Contemporary Media Culture* (London: Routledge, 2018), pp.66–83. The term "rejuvenile" comes from Christopher Noxon, *Rejuvenile: Kickball, Cartoons, Cupcakes, and Reinvention of the American Grown-up* (New York: Crown, 2006).

50 John Baichtal and Joe Meno, *The Cult of LEGO* (San Francisco: No Starch Press, 2011), p.14.

51 The Greenpeace campaign of 2014 is retold in Ashley Hinck, *Politics for the Love of Fandom: Fan-Based Citizenship in a Digital World* (Baton Rouge: Louisiana State University Press, 2019) pp.104–133.

52 Nils Stockmann and Antonia Graf, "'Polluting our kids' imagination'? Exploring the Power of Lego in the Discourse on Sustainable Mobility", *Sustainability: Science, Practice and Policy*, 16:1, 2020, pp.231–246.

53 Andrew Turner, Rob Arnold and Tracey Williams, "Weathering and Persistence of Plastic in the Marine Environment: Lessons From LEGO", *Environmental Pollution*, 262, 2020, online: https://www.sciencedirect.com/science/article/pii/S0269749119364152?via%3Dihub#sec4.

54 See this *Conversation* article: https://theconversation.com/sustainable-lego-plastics-from-plants-wont-solve-a-pollution-crisis-92953.

55 Jem Bartholomew, "Lego Abandons Effort to Make Bricks From Recycled Plastic Bottles", *The Guardian*, 25 September 2023, online: https://www.theguardian.com/lifeandstyle/2023/sep/24/lego-abandons-effort-to-make-bricks-from-recycled-plastic-bottles.

Chapter 4

1 Myths about Kamprad abound. He commissioned a writer to tell his story, which repeats these myths. See Bertil Torekull, *Leading by Design: The IKEA Story* (New York: HarperBusiness, 1999). Details on his early sales are on page 19.

2 See the complete digitalized IKEA catalogue collection: https://ikeamuseum.com/en/explore/ikea-catalogue/.

3 Ingvar Kamprad in Torekull, *Leading by Design*, p.25.

4 Lasse Brunnström, *Swedish Design: A History* (London: Bloomsbury, 2019), p.77.

5 See IKEA history: https://ikeamuseum.com/en/explore/the-story-of-ikea/czesc-polsko/.

6 See IKEA: Made in Poland report, 2020: https://www.ikea.com/pl/pl/files/pdf/9d/c3/9dc30f67/digital_en_project_made_in_poland.pdf. On timber, see IKEA wood report: https://about.ikea.com/en/sustainability/wood-forestry/wood-we-use#woodmap.

7 Rebecca Carrai, "Normalizing the Home: A Synchronic Comparison Between the Ikéa Catalogue and God Bostad", *Studies in History and Theory of Architecture*, 9, 2021, p.35.

8 Kate Connelly, "Ikea to Stop Printing Catalogue After 'Successful Career' That Spanned 70 Years", *The Guardian*, 8 December 2020, online: https://www.theguardian.com/business/2020/dec/07/ikea-to-stop-printing-catalogue-after-70-years-as-customers-move-online.

9 Ingvar Kamprad, "A Furniture Dealer's Testament", 1976, reprinted in Torekull, *Leading by Design*, p.228.

10 Ingvar Kamprad, "A Furniture Dealer's Testament", p.228.

11 Sara Kristoffersson, *Design by IKEA: A Cultural History* (London: Bloomsbury, 2014), p.29.

12 See the exposé by former long-time IKEA employee Johan Stenebo, in which he disputes Kamprad's claims to be dyslexic, alcoholic and a poor English speaker: "My impression is that Kamprad is extremely clever at using exaggerations that border on lies in order to create an image of himself and IKEA that benefits the company." Johan Stenebo, *IKEA: How to Become the World's Richest Family* (London: Gibson Square, 2022), p.31.

13 Kristoffersson, *Design by IKEA*, p.3.

14 The same since the 1980s but the logo was updated in 2018 for digital legibility. See: https://ikeamuseum.com/en/explore/the-story-of-ikea/history-of-the-logotype/.

15 Kristoffersson, *Design by IKEA*, p.55.

16 Stenebo, *IKEA: How to Become the World's Richest Family*, p.140. See also Marc Auerbach, "IKEA: Flat Pack Tax Avoidance" report from 2016, online: https://www.greens-efa.eu/legacy/fileadmin/dam/Documents/Studies/Taxation/Report_IKEA_tax_avoidance_Feb2016.pdf.

17 The book has not been translated into English. See Elisabeth Åsbrink, "On the Far Right Past of Ingvar Kamprad, Founder of Ikea", *Lithub*, 17 October 2019, online: https://lithub.com/on-the-far-right-past-of-ingvar-kamprad-founder-of-ikea/.

18 Sarah Fager, Senior Designer at IKEA, interview, "Democratic Design: Making Great Design Available to Everyone", on the IKEA website: https://www.ikeasocialentrepreneurship.org/sitecore/content/nl/aboutikea/home/life-at-home/how-we-work/democratic-design?sc_lang=en.

19 See Staffan Bengtsson, *IKEA, The Book: Designers, Products and Other Stuff* (Stockholm: Arvinius Förlag, 2010).

20 Despite globalization, the board remains resolutely Swedish and male. See IKANO group Supervisor Board: https://group.ikano/organisation/.

21 Kristoffersson, *Design by IKEA*, p.120.

22 Kamprad, "A Furniture Dealer's Testament", p. 229.

23 Stenebo, *IKEA: How to Become the World's Richest Family*, p.72.

24 See Kristofferson, *Design by IKEA*; Ursula Lindqvist, "The Cultural Archive of the IKEA Store", *Space and Culture*, 12:1, 2009, pp.43–62; and Pauline Garvey, *Unpacking IKEA: Swedish Design for the Purchasing Masses* (London and New York: Routledge, 2018).

25 Designed in collaboration with IKEA's head of design at the time, Lars Engman. Originally the POEM chair, it was given a Nordic name later.

26 See chapter 3 of Kristofferson, *Design by IKEA*, Swedish Stories and Design.

27 Lindqvist, "The Cultural Archive of the IKEA Store", p.44.

28 Life at Home 1960s, IKEA Museum: https://ikeamuseum.com/en/explore/life-at-home/life-at-home-1960s/.

29 Lars Trägårdh, "Introduction", in Lars Trägårdh, ed., *State and Civil Society in Northern Europe: The Swedish Model Reconsidered* (Oxford and New York: Berghahn Books, 2007).

30 Lindqvist, "The Cultural Archive of the IKEA Store", p.59.

31 See Magnus Ryner, "Neoliberal Globalization and the Crisis of Swedish Social Democracy", *Economic and Industrial Democracy*, 201:1, 1999, pp.39–79.

32 Lindqvist, "The Cultural Archive of the IKEA Store", p.52.

33 Garvey, *Unpacking IKEA*, p.32.

34 See Tod Hartman, "The Ikeaization of France", *Public Culture*, 19:3, 2007, pp.483–498; Dana BOȘCOR and Gabriel BRĂTUCU, "Transnational Strategies Adopted by Furniture Manufacturers. Case Study: IKEA", *Pro Ligno*, 5:3, 2009, pp.55–61.

35 Lei Ping, "Advertising Homeownership Through Cultural Capitalism: Neoliberal Making of New Shanghai Middle-Class Dream", *Journal of Chinese Architecture and Urbanism*, 2:1, 2020, p.15.

36 See Ulf Johansson and Asa Thelander, "A Standardized Approach to the World? IKEA in China", *International Journal of Quality and Service Sciences*, 1:2, 2009, pp.199–219; and Steve Burt, John Dawson, Ulf Johansson and Jens Hultman, "The Changing Marketing Orientation Within the Business Model of an International Retailer – IKEA in China Over 10 Years", *The International Review of Retail, Distribution and Consumer Research*, 31:2, 2021, pp.229–255.

37 Tod Hartman, "On the Ikeaization of France", *Public Culture*, 19:3, 2007, p.486.

38 Kyle Chayka, *The Longing for Less: Living with Minimalism* (London: Bloomsbury, 2020).

39 Tomás Errázuriz, "Everything in Place: Peace and Harmony in an Overcrowded Home", *Visual Culture*, 18:4, 2019, p.508.

40 Rania Magdi Fawzy, "Neoliberalism in your Living Room: A Spatial Cognitive Reading of Home Design in IKEA Catalogue", *Discourse, Context and Media*, 31, 2019.

41 Riccardo Biffi, "Exhibiting Nordic Values: A Critical Look at the IKEA Store", in Ingrid Halland, ed., *Ung Uro: Unsettling Climates in Nordic Art, Architecture and Design* (Oslo: Cappelen Damm Akademisk, 2021), p.38.

42 Per Ledin and David Machin, "Forty Years of IKEA Kitchens and the Rise of the Neoliberal Control of Domestic Space", *Visual Communication*, 18:2, 2019, p.178.

43 See IKEA, "Life at Home" report: https://lifeathome.ikea.com/blog/annie-leibovitz-life-at-home/.

44 Stenebo, *IKEA: How to Become the World's Richest Family*, p.156.

45 Biffi, "Exhibiting Nordic Values", p.42.

46 See the figures for 2024: https://about.ikea.com/en/life-at-home/how-we-work.

47 Alexander Sammon, "Ikea's Race for the Last of Europe's Old-Growth Forests", *The New Republic Magazine*, 16 February 2022, online: https://newrepublic.com/article/165245/ikea-romania-europe-old-growth-forest.

48 See the 2020 Earthlink investigative report "Flatpacked Forests: IKEA's illegal timber problem and the flawed green label": https://www.earthsight.org.uk/flatpackedforests-en and the 2021 follow-up, "IKEA's House of Horrors": https://www.earthsight.org.uk/investigation/ikea-house-of-horrors.

49 U.S. Environmental Protection Agency, "Durable Goods: Product-Specific Data", updated 22 November 2023, online: https://www.epa.gov/facts-and-figures-about-materials-waste-and-recycling/durable-goods-product-specific-data#FurnitureandFurnishings.

50 Debra Kamin, "'Fast furniture' Is Cheap and Americans are Throwing It in the Trash", *New York Times*, 31 October 2022, online: https://www.nytimes.com/2022/10/31/realestate/fast-furniture-clogged-landfills.html. Though IKEA started a "Buyback & Resell" scheme in some countries, it does not involve recycling materials. Customers receive an IKEA credit voucher for furniture in reasonable condition that can be resold by IKEA.

51 Stenebo, *IKEA: How to Become the World's Richest Family*, p.93.

52 Stenebo, *IKEA: How to Become the World's Richest Family*, p.90.

53 Kamprad, quoted in Torekull, *Leading by Design*, p.76.

54 Pauline Garvey, "Consuming IKEA and Inspiration as Material Form", in Alison J. Clarke, ed., *Design Anthropology: Object Cultures in Transition* (London: Bloomsbury, 2018), p.111.

55 Christine Harold, *Things Worth Keeping: The Value of Attachment in a Disposable World* (Minneapolis and London: University of Minnesota Press, 2020), p.132.

56 Michael I. Norton, Daniel Mochon and Dan Ariely, "The IKEA Effect: When Labor Leads to Love", *Journal of Consumer Psychology*, 22:3, 2012, pp.453–444.

57 Tiffany Hsu, "IKEA Enters 'Gig Economy' by Acquiring TaskRabbit", *New York Times*, 28 September 2017, online: https://www.nytimes.com/2017/09/28/business/ikea-taskrabbit.html.

58 Stephen Knott, "Design in the Age of Prosumption: The Craft of Design after the Object", *Design and Culture*, 5:1, 2013, p.54.

59 See C. K. Prahalad and Venkat Ramaswamy, "Co-Creation Experiences: The Next Practice in Value Creation", *Journal of Interactive Marketing*, 18:3, 2004, pp.5–14.

60 Harold, *Things Worth Keeping*, p.120.

61 See Pinterest, "Success Stories: IKEA": https://business.pinterest.com/en-au/success-stories/ikea/.

62 See Selcen Ozturkcan, "Service Innovation: Using Augmented Reality in the IKEA Place App", *Journal of Information Technology*, 11:1, 2021, pp.8–13.

63 Pascal Kowalczuk, Carolin Siepmann and Jost Adler, "Cognitive, Affective, and Behavioral Consumer Responses to Augmented Reality in E-Commerce: A Comparative Study", *Journal of Business Research*, 124, 2021, pp.357–373.

64 Rebecca Carrai, "Fiction: IKEA's Saleable Living for Pandemic Life", in Penny Sparke, Ersi Ioannidou, Pat Kirkham, Stephen Knott and Jana Scholze, eds., *Interiors in the Era of Covid-19: Interior Design Between the Public and Private Realms* (London: Bloomsbury, 2023), p.171.

65 Helen Reid, "IKEA Bets on Remote Interior Design as AI Changes Sales Strategy", *Reuters*, 13 June 2023, online: https://www.reuters.com/technology/ikea-bets-remote-interior-design-ai-changes-sales-strategy-2023-06-13/.

66 Harold, *Things Worth Keeping*, p.110.

Chapter 5

1 Daniel A. Vos, "Nike Flagship Façade – Design, Engineering and Testing", in Jens Schneider and Bernhard Weller, eds. *Engineered Transparency: Glass in Architecture and Structural Engineering* (Berlin: Ernst & Sohn, 2018), p.205.

2 For the history of Nike, I have relied predominantly on Phil Knight, *Shoe Dog: A Memoir by the Creator of Nike* (New York: Scribner, 2016); Geoff Hollister, *Out of Nowhere: The Inside Story of How Nike Marketed the Culture of Running* (Maidenhead, UK: Meyer & Meyer Sports, 2008); and J. B. Strasser and Laurie Becklund, *Swoosh: The Unauthorized Story of Nike and the Men Who Played There* (New York: Harcourt, Brace, Jovanovich, 1991).

3. Bowerman also co-authored a 1967 book, *Jogging*, that helped launch running as a recreational activity. See William J. Bowerman and W. E. Harris, *Jogging* (New York: Grosset and Dunlap, 1967).
4. Hollister, *Out of Nowhere*, pp.30–31.
5. Hollister *Out of Nowhere*, p.52.
6. Beyond elite sports, the Cortez went on to become a classic in the 1980s, notably among Los Angeles' gang members, and is still popular today. See Sean Saldana, "An Oral History of the Nike Cortez, 50 Years After Its Release", National Public Radio, broadcast 15 February 2022, online: https://www.npr.org/2022/02/15/1077040201/nike-cortez-50-anniversary-history-los-angeles.
7. On the details of the waffle iron story, see Hollister, *Out of Nowhere*, pp.74–75; and Knight, *Shoe Dog*, p.166.
8. Knight, *Shoe Dog*, p.234.
9. See Hollister, *Out of Nowhere*, p.185. Hollister wrote: "Though Pre's job title was intentionally imprecise, his role was real, and his belief in Nike was authentic as well. He wore Nike T-shirts everywhere he went, and he allowed his foot to be Bowerman's last for all shoe experiments. Pre preached Nike as gospel, and brought thousands of new people into our revival tent."
10. Knight, *Shoe Dog*, p.178.
11. Note Apple's similar counter-cultural marketing during the same era. See Chapter 1.
12. See Yuniya Kawamura, *Sneakers: Fashion, Gender, and Subculture* (London: Bloomsbury, 2016), pp.75–76.
13. Mythologized in the 2023 film, *Air*, directed by Ben Affleck.
14. Douglas Kellner, *Media Spectacle* (London: Routledge, 2003), p.69.
15. Kellner, *Media Spectacle*, p.74.
16. David L. Andrews and Michael Silk, "Sport and the Neoliberal Conjecture: Complicating the Consensus", in David L. Andrews and Michael Silk, eds., *Sport and Neoliberalism: Politics, Consumption, and Culture* (Philadelphia: Temple University Press, 2012), p.20.
17. Ben Carrington, *Race, Sport and Politics: The Sporting Black Diaspora* (London and Thousand Oaks, CA: Sage, 2010), p.114.
18. Such has been my experience in junior sports over the past decade.
19. Richard Mocarski and Andrew C. Billings, "Manufacturing a Messiah: How Nike and LeBron James Co-Constructed the Legend of King James", *Communication and Sport*, 2:1, 2014, pp.3–23.
20. See the "Cultural A-Z of Nike Air Max" by Chris Owen and Jack Grayson for a good summary: https://www.endclothing.com/us/features/the-cultural-a-z-of-nike-air-max.
21. Robert Goldman and Stephen Papson, *Nike Culture: The Sign of the Swoosh* (London and Thousand Oaks, CA: Sage, 1998), p.5.
22. Lisa Penaloza, "Just Doing It: A Visual Ethnographic Study of Spectacular Consumption Behavior at Nike Town", *Consumption, Markets and Culture*, 2:4, 2014, p.379.

23 I visited this store regularly between 2005 and 2007 and had students write about it and other Fifth Avenue flagship stores. That may be the origin of this book.

24 Steve Booth Marston, "The Episodic Kneel: Racial Neoliberalism, Civility, and the Media Circulation of Colin Kaepernick, 2017–2020", *Race and Social Problems*, 13, 2021, pp.205–214.

25 Julie Creswell, Kevin Draper and Sapna Maheshwari, "Nike Nearly Dropped Colin Kaepernick Before Embracing Him", *The New York Times*, 26 September 2018, online: https://www.nytimes.com/2018/09/26/sports/nike-colin-kaepernick.html. See also Alex Abad-Santos, "Why the Social Media Boycott over Colin Kaepernick is a Win for Nike", *Vox*, 6 September 2018, online: https://www.vox.com/2018/9/4/17818148/nike-boycott-kaepernick.

26 Yoon Kyoung Kima, Holly Overton, Nandini Bhallac and Jo-Yun Lid, "Nike, Colin Kaepernick, and the Politicization of Sports: Examining Perceived Organizational Motives and Public Responses", *Public Relations Review*, 46, 2020, p.8.

27 See the fashion collaborations for the Tokyo 2020 Olympics, featured in Vogue, 6 February 2020: https://www.vogue.com.au/fashion/news/5-fashion-designers-on-nikes-new-tokyo-olympicsinspired-collaboration/image-gallery/a5e0c2fef2e85c1baa89e09836c0445f. See also the *GQ* article by Cam Wolf, "'The Vibe of the Times': How Nike Became the Biggest Fashion Brand in the World", 25 September 2018, online:https://www.gq.com/story/how-nike-became-the-biggest-fashion-brand-in-the-world.

28 Jeff Ballinger at the Center for Communication and Civic Engagement created a useful timeline of Nike and labour issues in the 1990s: https://depts.washington.edu/ccce/polcommcampaigns/NikeChronology.htm.

29 Sydney H. Schanberg, "Six Cents an Hour", *Life Magazine*, 28 March 1996, online: https://laborrights.org/in-the-news/six-cents-hour-1996-life-article.

30 Naomi Klein, *No Logo: Taking Aim at the Brand Bullies* (London: Flamingo, 2001).

31 Vicky Xiuzhong Xu and James Leibold, "Your Favorite Nikes Might be Made From Forced Labor", *Washington Post*, 17 March 2020, online: https://www.washingtonpost.com/opinions/2020/03/17/your-favorite-nikes-might-be-made-forced-labor-heres-why/. See the original 2020 report by the Australian Strategic Policy Institute here: https://www.aspi.org.au/report/uyghurs-sale.

32 Breakdown of typical Nike shoes by "The Shoemaker's Academy", online: https://shoemakersacademy.com/what-are-nike-shoes-made-of/. Compare this with Nike's "What are the Parts of a Shoe?": https://www.nike.com/au/a/parts-of-shoe-anatomy.

33 See Nike Manufacturing Map, 2023, online: https://manufacturingmap.nikeinc.com/#.

34 See Michelle Childs and Byoungho Jin, "Nike: An Innovation Journey", in Byoungho Jin and Elena Cedrola, eds., *Product Innovation in the Global Fashion Industry* (New York: Palgrave, 2018), pp.97–98.

35 Anneke Smelik, "Polyester: A Cultural History", *Fashion Practice*, 15:2, 2023, p.294.

36 See Nike Zenvy Leggings online: https://www.nike.com/gb/w/zenvy-tights-leggings-29sh2z8dhfr.

37 Lea M. Elston, "Textiles as a Source of Microfiber Pollution and Potential Solutions", *Fordham Environmental Law Review*, 32:1, 2020, p.118.

38 "Licence to Greenwash: How Certification Schemes and Voluntary Initiatives are Fuelling Fossil Fashion", Report, March 2022, online: http://changingmarkets.org/wp-content/uploads/2022/03/LICENCE-TO-GREENWASH-FULL-REPORT.pdf.

39 Patrick Reichert and Oscar Vosshage, "Heavy (Carbon) Footprints: Can Subscription Shoes Create a Sustainable Footwear Industry", *The European Business Review*, 24 July 2023, online: https://www.europeanbusinessreview.com/heavy-carbon-footprints-can-subscription-shoes-create-a-sustainable-footwear-industry/. See also Tansy E. Hoskins, "Some Soles Last 1000 Years in Landfill: The Truth About the Sneaker Mountain", *The Guardian*, 21 March 2020, online: https://www.theguardian.com/fashion/2020/mar/21/some-soles-last-1000-years-in-landfill-the-truth-about-the-sneaker-mountain. For the US statistics, see Tess DiNapoli, "Global Shoe Waste: The Environmental Impact of Footwear", 30 April 2022, *Unsustainable Magazine*, online: https://www.unsustainablemagazine.com/global-shoe-waste/.

40 Alexander Curtis and Amanda Hansson, "Examining the Viability of Corporate Recycling Initiatives and Their Overall Environmental Impact: The Case of Nike Grind and the Reuse-A-Shoe Program", *Case Studies in the Environment*, 3:1, 2019, p.6.

41 Childs and Jin, "Nike: An Innovation Journey", p.98.

42 Mikolaj Jan Piskorski, *A Social Strategy: How we Profit From Social Media* (Princeton: Princeton University Press, 2014), p.207.

43 See Venkat Ramaswamy, "Co-creating Value through Customers' Experiences: The Nike Case", *Strategy and Leadership*, 36:5, 2008, pp.9–14.

44 Willem Standaert, "Product Digitalization at Nike: The Future Is Now", *Journal of Information Technology Teaching Cases*, 21:1, 2021, p.29.

45 An interesting aside worth noting is that Apple CEO Tim Cook has been on the Nike board since 2005.

46 Ramaswarmy, "Co-creating Value through Customers' Experiences: The Nike Case", p.11.

47 Piskorski, *A Social Strategy*, p.205.

48 See Deborah Lupton, *The Quantified Self: A Sociology of Self-Tracking* (Cambridge and Malden, MA: Polity Press, 2016).

49 Mark McClusky, "The Nike Experiment: How the Shoe Giant Unleashed the Power of Personal Metrics", *Wired*, 22 June 2009, online: https://www.wired.com/2009/06/lbnp-nike/.

50 Katherine Hepworth, "A Panopticon on My Wrist: The Biopower of Big Data Visualization for Wearables", *Design and Culture*, 11:3, 2019, p.337.

51 Hepworth, "A Panopticon on My Wrist", p.337.

52 Piskorski, *A Social Strategy*, p.216.

53 Jennifer R. Whitson, "Gaming the Quantified Self", *Surveillance and Society*, 11:1/2, 2013, p.171.

54 See Cristina García-Magro, María-Luz Martín-Peña and José María Sánchez-López, "Emotional Mechanics of Gamification and Value Co-Creation: The Digital Platform

Nike+ as a B2B2C Ecosystem", *Journal of Business & Industrial Marketing*, 38:2, 2023, pp.414–428.

55 William J. Bowerman and W.E. Harris, *Jogging* (New York: Grosset and Dunlap, 1967), p.7.

56 Mehdi Poornikoo, "Gamification: A platform for Transitioning From Goods-Dominant Logic to Service-Dominant Logic: The Case of Nike+Fuelband", master's thesis, Norwegian School of Economics, 2014, p.6, online: https://openaccess.nhh.no/nhh-xmlui/bitstream/handle/11250/276110/Masterthesis.PDF?sequence=1.

57 Ben Zimmerman, "Why Nike Cut Ties with Amazon and What It Means for Other Retailers", *Forbes*, 22 January 2020, online: https://www.forbes.com/sites/forbesbusinesscouncil/2020/01/22/why-nike-cut-ties-with-amazon-and-what-it-means-for-other-retailers/?sh=39d74d8564ff.

58 "The World's Leading Brands Jump on the Direct-Selling Bandwagon", *The Economist*, 26 July 2020, online: https://www.economist.com/business/2020/07/26/the-worlds-leading-brands-jump-on-the-direct-selling-bandwagon.

59 See Nathaniel Meyersohn, "Nikes are Getting Harder to Find at Stores. Here's Why", CNN Business, 22 March 2021, online: https://edition.cnn.com/2021/03/22/business/nike-independent-shoe-stores/index.html.

60 Khadeeja Safdar, "Meet the New Nike Boss Trading Tech for Air Jordans", *Wall Street Journal*, 8 February 2020, online: https://www.wsj.com/articles/meet-the-new-nike-boss-trading-tech-for-air-jordans-11581166802.

61 Ryan Owen, "Artificial Intelligence at Nike – Two Current Use-Cases", Emerj, 26 October 2021, online: https://emerj.com/ai-sector-overviews/artificial-intelligence-at-nike/.

62 Qing Na, "Why Is Nike and China's Esports Icon Uzi's Partnership Shrewd Esports Marketing?", *Creative Works*, November 1, 2022: https://daoinsights.com/works/nike-and-chinas-esports-icon-uzis/.

63 See Shawn Lim, "Nike Invest in eSports Gamers in South Korea to Allow Them to Just Do It", The Drum, 16 January 2020, online: https://www.thedrum.com/news/2020/01/16/nike-invest-esports-gamers-south-korea-allow-them-just-do-it.

64 Alex Williams, "Nike Sold an NFT Sneaker for $134,000", *New York Times*, 26 May 2022, online: https://www.nytimes.com/2022/05/26/style/nike-nft-sneaker.html.

65 Inside Retail Asia, "Nike Shanghai Marks Brand's First House of Innovation", 8 October 2018, online: https://insideretail.asia/2018/10/08/nike-shanghai-marks-brands-first-house-of-innovation/.

66 Ruth Hogan, "Inside Nike's Latest House of Innovation", *Inside Retail*, 22 September 2020, online: https://insideretail.com.au/stores/inside-nikes-latest-house-of-innovation-202009.

67 Carly Salpini, "Nike Doubles Down on Localization in Nike Rise Concept", *Retail Dive*, 11 August 2021, online: https://www.retaildive.com/news/nike-doubles-down-on-localization-with-nike-rise-concept/604819/.

68 See Tracey Meyers, "Study: Nike Ranked Number One in Social Media Traffic", WWD, 1 September 2017, online: https://wwd.com/business-news/retail/nike-ranked-number-one-in-social-media-traffic-10969406/.

Chapter 6

1. See "The Paris Review and Aesop", online: https://www.aesop.com/us/r/the-paris-review/.
2. Aesop's valuation is now estimated at over $2 billion: https://www.smartcompany.com.au/industries/retail/aesops-journey-to-2-billion-valuation/.
3. Nigel Whiteley, *Design for Society* (London: Reaktion Books, 1993), p.50.
4. Whiteley, *Design for Society*, p.54.
5. Jon Entine, "Caring Capitalism", *The Sunday Times*, 31 December 1995, online: http://archives.jonentine.com/reviews/caring_capitalism.htm. See also Jon Entine's Social and Environmental Audit: https://jonentine.com/a-social-and-environmental-audit-of-the-body-shop-anita-roddick-and-the-question-of-character/.
6. Melissa Aronczyk, "Market(ing) Activism: Lush Cosmetics, Ethical Oil and the Self-Mediation of Protest", *JOMEC: Journalism, Media and Cultural Studies Journal*, 0:4, 2013, online: https://jomec.cardiffuniversitypress.org/articles/abstract/10.18573/j.2013.10256/.
7. The European Union regulations on cosmetic testing began in 1993 and by 2004 animal testing for finished products was completely banned. See European Commission, "Ban on Animal Testing", online: https://ec.europa.eu/growth/sectors/cosmetics/ban-animal-testing_en. This issue is complex because raw materials used in finished cosmetics may have already been tested on animals.
8. Anthony Kent and Dominic Stone, "The Body Shop and the Role of Design in Retail Branding", *International Journal of Retail and Distribution Management*, 35:7, 2007, p.536. The Body Shop today has over three thousand stores globally, though most are operated by franchisees.
9. From 2020, flagship Body Shop stores have been redesigned with "Activist Maker Workshops" which combine personalized makeovers and bodycare demonstrations with information stations where customers can read about The Body Shop's environmental and social campaigns. Marianne Wilson, "First Look: The Body Shop Unveils New Concept Store", *Chain Store Age*, 3 June 2020, online: https://chainstoreage.com/first-look-body-shop-unveils-new-concept-store. These new stores also contain refill stations so customers can refill shower gel bottles as well as recycling stations.
10. Dominic Powell, "How Aesop Chief Executive Michael O'Keeffe Helped Craft a $250 Million Business Model", *Smart Company*, 9 September 2016, online: https://www.smartcompany.com.au/entrepreneurs/influencers-profiles/how-aesop-chief-executive-michael-okeeffe-helped-craft-a-250-million-business-model/.
11. The company's global success after the launch of their retail strategy led to Brazilian giant Natura buying a majority share in the company in 2012. Natura attained full ownership in 2016. Natura then sold Aesop to L'Oreal in 2023.
12. See also D. J. Huppatz, "Aesop's Sensory Experience Design", in John Potvin, Marie-Ève Marchand and Benoit Beaulieu, eds., *The Senses and Interior Design* (Manchester: Manchester University Press, 2023), pp.232–247.
13. On the design process for creating the Flinders Lane store, see: "Aesop's Design Team: Q+A with Kian Yam and Tim Mather", *Australian Design Review*, 2015,

online: https://www.australiandesignreview.com/architecture/aesops-design-team-qa-with-kian-yam-and-tim-mather/

14   Marcus Fair, "Interview with Dennis Paphitis", *Dezeen*, 10 December 2012, online: https://www.dezeen.com/2012/12/10/dennis-paphitis-aesop-interview/.

15   James Baron, "The End for a Cleaners Where Little but the Name Has Changed", *New York Times*, 14 April 2016, online: https://www.nytimes.com/2016/04/15/nyregion/the-end-for-a-cleaners-where-little-but-the-name-has-changed.html.

16   See D. J. Huppatz, "Fashion Branding: Staging Identities", in G. Riello and P. McNeil, eds., *The Fashion History Reader: Global Perspectives* (Routledge: London, 2010); D. J. Huppatz, "The Spaces of Interiors: Staging Fantasies", in T. Vaikla-Poldma, ed., *Meanings of Designed Spaces* (New York and London: Fairchild Books, 2013).

17   Marcus Fair, "Interview with Dennis Paphitis", *Dezeen*, 10 December 2012, online: https://www.dezeen.com/2012/12/10/dennis-paphitis-aesop-interview/.

18   In the UK, for example, Aesop has seventeen stores in London, two in Edinburgh and one in Bath.

19   Work&Co website: https://work.co/clients/aesop/.

20   Pine and Gilmore, *The Experience Economy* (Boston: Harvard Business Review Press, 2011), p.18.

21   Cameron Shelley, "The Nature of Simplicity in Apple Design", *The Design Journal*, 18:3, 2015, p.441.

22   Katy Hall, "A Post-It Ban and No Weather Talk: The Weird and Wonderful Secrets of Working at Aesop", Mamamia, 1 March 2017, online: https://www.mamamia.com.au/working-for-aesop.

23   David Vernet and Leontine de Wit, eds., *Boutiques and Other Retail Spaces* (New York and London: Routledge, 2007), p.xi.

24   On Prada, see Chuihua Judy Chung, Jeffrey Inaba, Rem Koolhaas and Sze Tsung Leong, eds., *Project on the City II: The Harvard Guide to Shopping* (Cologne: Taschen, 2001). On Louis Vuitton's architectural programme, see Frederic Edelmann and Ian Luna, *Louis Vuitton: Architecture and Interiors* (New York: Rizzoli, 2011).

25   Mark Pimlott, "The Boutique and the Mass Market", in Vernet and de Wit, eds., *Boutiques and Other Retail Spaces*, p.4.

26   Juhani Pallasmaa, "Space, Place, and Atmosphere: Peripheral Perception in Existential Experience", in Christian Borsch, ed., *Architectural Atmospheres: On the Experience and Politics of Architecture* (Basel: Birkhauser, 2014), p.19.

27   Christian Norberg-Schultz, *Genius Loci: Towards a Phenomenology of Architecture* (New York: Rizzoli, 1979), pp.10–11.

28   Juhani Pallasmaa, *Eyes of Skin* (Chichester, UK: Wiley and Sons, 2012), p.21.

29   See Rob DeSalle, *Our Senses: An Immersive Experience* (New Haven and London: Yale University Press, 2018). In relation to architecture, see also Harry Francis Mallgrave, *From Objects to Experience: The New Culture of Architectural Design* (London: Bloomsbury, 2018).

30   See Tam Gim Ean's interview with Aesop retail architectural manager Denise Neri, "Aesop Store Speaks Sensitively to Local Surroundings, Honouring Neighborhoods

31. Walter Benjamin, "Some Motifs in Baudelaire", in W. Benjamin, *Selected Writings, Volume 4, 1938–1940* (Cambridge, MA, and London: Harvard University Press, 2006), p.335.
32. Lucy Moyse Ferreira, "'A Seductive Weapon … a Necessary Luxury': Shopping for 'Designer Perfume' During the Interwar Period", in Serena Dyer, ed., *Shopping and the Senses, 1800–1970: A Sensory History of Retail and Consumption* (Cham, Switzerland: Palgrave/Macmillan, 2022), p. 179.
33. See Linda Tischler, "Smells Like Brand Spirit", *Fast Company*, 1 August 2005, online: https://www.fastcompany.com/53313/smells-brand-spirit. And Martin Lindstroem, *Brand Sense: Build Powerful Brands Through Touch, Taste, Smell, Sight, and Sound* (New York: Free Press, 2005).
34. *Time Magazine*, "Samsung Gets Sensual", 2 October 2005, online: https://content.time.com/time/subscriber/article/0,33009,1112831,00.html.
35. A. S. Barwich, *Smellosophy: What the Nose Tells the Mind* (Cambridge, MA, and London: Harvard University Press, 2020), p.127.
36. Barwich, *Smellosophy*, p.125.
37. Barwich, *Smellosophy*, p.265.
38. See Christian Borsch, ed., *Architectural Atmospheres: On the Experience and Politics of Architecture* (Basel: Birkhäuser, 2014).
39. Peter Zumthor, *Thinking Architecture* (Basel, Birkhäuser, 1998), p.13.
40. Tonino Griffero, *Atmospheres: Aesthetics of Emotional Spaces*, trans. Sarah de Sanctis (Farnham, Surrey: Ashgate, 2010), p.6.
41. Juhani Pallasmaa, "Space, Place, and Atmosphere: Peripheral Perception in Existential Experience", in Christian Borsch, ed., *Architectural Atmospheres*, p.19.
42. Pallasmaa, "Space, Place, and Atmosphere", p.19.
43. Marc Augé, *Non-Places: Introduction to an Anthropology of Supermodernity*, trans. John Howe (London: Verso, 1995), p.118.
44. Kate Bezar, "Suzanne Santos is the Brains behind Aesop", *Dumbo Feather*, 31 March 2013, online: https://www.dumbofeather.com/conversations/suzanne-santos-brain-behind-aesop-brand/.
45. Pine and Gilmore, "The Experience Economy", p.33.
46. See A. Boswijk, J. P. T. Thijssen and E. Peelen, *The Experience Economy: A New Perspective* (Amsterdam: Pearson, Prentice Hall, 2005).
47. Bezar, "Suzanne Santos is the Brains behind Aesop".
48. Julianna Preston, "In the Midst of", in "Interior Atmospheres", *Architectural Design*, 78:3, 2008, p.8.
49. Teresa Brennan, *The Transmission of Affect* (Ithaca and London: Cornell University Press, 2004), p.1.
50. Colleen Derkatch, *Why Wellness Sells* (Baltimore: Johns Hopkins University Press, 2022), p.188.

51 Derkatch, *Why Wellness Sells*, p.200.

52 This was on the Aesop website in 2015. It now seems to have disappeared. See *Guardian* article by Ana Andjelic, "Luxury Brands Are Failing in Their Storytelling", 23 November 2015, online: https://www.theguardian.com/media-network/2015/nov/23/luxury-brands-marketing-failing-storytelling.

53 Paolo Chua and Amanda Herrera, "Q&A: Aesop's Suzanne Santos on the New Rockwell Store, Sustainability and More", *Esquire*, 25 April 2022, online: https://www.esquiremag.ph/style/grooming/suzanne-santos-aesop-interview-a00297-a2741-20220425-lfrm.

54 See Inna Micheali, "Self-Care: An Act of Political Warfare or a Neoliberal Trap?", *Development*, 60, 2017, pp.50–56.

55 Cheryl Wischhover, "The Fable of Aesop's Hand Soap", *Racked*, 17 October 2013, online: https://www.racked.com/2017/10/13/16452460/aesop-hand-soap.

56 In contrast, imagine a skincare brand called "Aristotle".

57 See "The Athenaeum": https://www.aesop.com/au/r/the-athenaeum/view-from-above/.

58 The Aesop Foundation, the brand's charity arm, has long been dedicated to literacy and storytelling. The literary emphasis now seems less prominent, as it is squashed in with sustainability, see https://www.aesop.com/au/r/sustainability/.

59 See Aesop's website, "On Literature": https://www.aesop.com/au/r/the-athenaeum/pride/. This assumes, of course, that the customer's bookshelf does not already contain queer literature.

60 Wenzhuo Wu, "Long Queues Form at Aesop's Pop-up Library for International Women's Day", *Jing Daily*, 11 March 2023, online: https://jingdaily.com/aesop-pop-up-womens-day-library/.

61 From Aesop's Athenaeum: https://www.aesop.com/au/r/the-athenaeum/radiomatique/podcasts/#ath-podcasts-episode-three-butterfly-man.

62 Daniel Upward, "Magic Sponge Interview 14: Michael O'Keefe CEO of Aesop", *Magic Sponge*, 18 April 2020, online: https://www.linkedin.com/pulse/magic-sponge-interview-14-michael-okeeffe-ceo-aesop-daniel-upward/.

63 Natura Brasil, About Us: https://www.naturabrasil.com/pages/about-us.

64 Founder Dennis Paphitis stepped down from active business operations in 2012 but continued to work as an advisor and consultant.

65 See, for example, Kati Chitrakorn, "Forget the Indie Locations, Aesop is Going Mainstream", *Vogue Business*, 5 August 2022, online: https://www.voguebusiness.com/beauty/forget-the-indie-locations-aesop-is-going-mainstream-can-it-keep-its-edge.

Chapter 7

1 "Zara Presents its Latest Brand Image in Porto, in One of the Most Emblematic Commercial Spaces in Portugal", *Attitude: Interior Design Magazine*, 9 September 2022, online: https://www.attitude-mag.com/en/blog/shops/2022-09-09-primeira-zara-de-portugal-reabre-apos-profunda-ampliacao-e-remodelacao/.

2. A Portugal-based study of Zara's social media engagement concluded that Zara fans "skewed quite young: most belonged to the 18–24 demographic (70%) while an incredible 91.2% were less than 35 years old. Zara's fans were predominantly women (92.2%) …". Ana Margarida Gamboa and Helena Martins Goncalves, "Customer Loyalty Through Social Networks: Lessons From Zara on Facebook", *Business Horizons*, 57, 2014, p.716.

3. For the history of Zara, I am primarily drawing upon Enrique Badia, *Zara and Her Sisters: The Story of the World's Largest Clothing Retailer* (London: Palgrave Macmillan, 2009); and Jon P. Howell and Isaac Wanasika, "Amanico Ortega: Fast Fashion Entrepreneur", in *Snapshots of Great Leadership* (London and New York: Routledge, 2018), pp.94–100; and Stephanie O. Crofton and Luis G. Dopico, "Zara-Inditex and the Growth of Fast Fashion", *Essays in Economic and Business History*, 25, 2007, pp.41–53.

4. Badia, *Zara and Her Sisters*, p.170.

5. Badia, *Zara and Her Sisters*, p.114.

6. Stephanie O. Crofton and Luis G. Dopico, "Zara-Inditex and the Growth of Fast Fashion", *Essays in Economic and Business History*, 25, 2007, p.45.

7. See, for example, Michal Addady, "12 Artists are Accusing Zara of Stealing Their Designs", *Fortune*, 21 July 2016, online: https://fortune.com/2016/07/20/zara-stealing-designs/. Zara faced some social media backlash in the wake of this case, which spread to forty artists accusing Zara of plagiarism.

8. Hala Abdel-Jaber, "The Devil Wears Zara: Why the Lanham Act Must Be Amended in the Era of Fast Fashion", *Ohio State Business Law Journal*, 15:2, 2021, p.238.

9. Eleonora Rosati, "Milan Court Applies Nintendo vs Big Ben in Fast Fashion Lawsuit Against ZARA", *Journal of Intellectual Property Law & Practice*, 13:11, November 2018, pp.856–885.

10. Crofton and Dopico, "Zara-Inditex and the Growth of Fast Fashion", p.45.

11. Badia, *Zara and Her Sisters*, p.124.

12. Badia, *Zara and Her Sisters*, pp.121–122.

13. Andrew McAfee, Vincent Dessian and Anders S. Jöman, "Zara: IT for Fashion", *Harvard Business School Studies*, 9-604-081, 17 December 2004, p.4.

14. Joaquin Adell, "Tiendas Zara: Nueva Imagen, Nueva Iluminacion", *Luces*, October 1997, pp.43–45.

15. Anne-Marie Schiro, "Two New Stores That Cruise Fashion's Fast Lane", *New York Times*, 31 December 1989, p. 46.

16. Dana Thomas, *Fashionopolis: The Price of Fast Fashion and the Future of Clothes* (New York: Penguin, 2019), p.30.

17. Howell and Wanasika, "Amanico Ortega: Fast Fashion Entrepreneur", p.95.

18. McAfee, Dessian and Jöman, "Zara: IT for Fashion", p.3.

19. Alex Macheras, "The Spanish Air Cargo Boom Driven by Zara", *Aviation Analyst*, 18 December 2018, online: https://aviationanalyst.co.uk/2018/12/18/the-spanish-air-cargo-boom-driven-by-zara/.

20. Graham Keeley and Andrew Clark, "Zara Overtakes Gap to Become World's Largest Clothing Retailer", *The Guardian*, 11 August 2008, online: https://www.theguardian.com/business/2008/aug/11/zara.gap.fashion.

21 See Inditext Annual Report 2022, online: https://static.inditex.com/annual_report_2022/en/2022-milestones/.

22 Jo Ellison, "The Zara Woman: An Exclusive Interview With Marta Ortega Pérez", *Financial Times*, 29 March 2023, online: https://www.ft.com/content/f5e10605-3c9d-4517-86f5-2e7570bf16f0.

23 George Simmel, "Fashion", *The American Journal of Sociology*, 62:6, 1957, p.451. See also Zygmunt Bauman, "Perpetuum Mobile", *Critical Studies in Fashion and Beauty*, 1:1, 2010, pp.55–63.

24 Judy Wajcman, *Pressed for Time: The Acceleration of Life in Digital Capitalism* (Chicago and London: University of Chicago Press, 2014), p.2. It is worth remembering that some aspects of life have slowed down (traffic, for example), and other aspects stayed the same (pregnancy still lasts nine months).

25 Hartmut Rosa, *Social Acceleration: A New Theory of Modernity*, trans. Jonathan Trejo-Mathys (New York: Columbia University Press, 2013), p.xxxviii.

26 Hartmut Rosa, *Social Acceleration*, p. 231. This is also the thesis outlined in Zygmunt Bauman, *Liquid Life* (Cambridge, Polity Press, 2005).

27 Zygmunt Bauman, "On Fashion, Liquid Identity and Utopia for Today: Some Cultural Tendencies in the Twenty-First Century", in Zygmunt Bauman, *Culture in a Liquid Modern World*, trans. Lydia Bauman (Cambridge and Malden: Polity Press, 2011), p.25.

28 Sam Binkley, "Liquid Consumption", *Cultural Studies*, 22:5, 2008, p.602.

29 Amanda Koontz Anthony and Ian Taplin, "Sustaining the Retail Pilgrimage: Developments of Fast Fashion and Authentic Identities", *Fashion, Style and Popular Culture*, 4:1, 2017, p.41.

30 Anthony and Taplin, "Sustaining the Retail Pilgrimage", p.44.

31 Aline Buzzo and Maria José Abreup, "Fast Fashion, Fashion Brands & Sustainable Consumption", in Subramanian Senthilkannan Muthu, ed., *Fast Fashion, Fashion Brands and Sustainable Consumption* (Singapore: Springer Nature, 2019), p.6.

32 See Karen de Perthuis and Rosie Findlay, "How Fashion Travels: The Fashionable Ideal in the Age of Instagram", *Fashion Theory*, 23:2, 2019, pp.219–242.

33 Haile Lesavage, "This Bubblegum Pink Zara Slip Dress Is Taking Over TikTok", *Harper's Bazaar*, 2 March 2022, online: https://www.harpersbazaar.com/fashion/trends/a39266460/zara-pink-slip-dress/.

34 According to one 2022 survey, Zara was the second most popular brand by influencer after Instagram itself: https://www.statista.com/statistics/1250712/leading-instagram-brands-worldwide-mentions/. Another site suggested Zara was the most popular in 2023: https://focusonbusiness.eu/en/technology/zara-most-popular-brand-on-instagram-with-mentions-from-66-4k-influencers/5244. See also Gyöngyvér Erika Tőkés, "The Digital Brand Identity of Fast-Fashion Brand Zara. A Case Study", Acta Univ. Sapientiae, *Social Analysis*, 12, 2022, pp.131–154.

35 See Karen de Perthuis and Rosie Findlay, "How Fashion Travels: The Fashionable Ideal in the Age of Instagram", *Fashion Theory*, 23:2, 2019, pp.219–242.

36 Veronica Gabrielli, Ilaria Baghi and Vanni Codeluppi, "Consumption Practices of Fast Fashion Products: A Consumer-Based Approach", *Journal of Fashion Marketing and Management*, 17:2, 2013, p.216.

37 Gabrielli, Baghi and Codeluppi, "Consumption Practices of Fast Fashion Products", p.218.
38 Bauman, *Liquid Life*, p.84.
39 Mark C. Taylor, *Speed Limits: Where Time Went and Why We Have So Little Left* (London and New Haven: Yale University Press, 2014), p.161.
40 Caroline Evans and Alessandra Vaccari, eds., *Time in Fashion: Industrial, Antilinear and Uchronic* (London: Bloomsbury, 2020), p.19.
41 Rachel Monroe, "Ultra-Fast Fashion is Eating the World", *The Atlantic*, March 2021, online: https://www.theatlantic.com/magazine/archive/2021/03/ultra-fast-fashion-is-eating-the-world/617794/.
42 US-based fast fashion retailer, Forever 21, for example, filed for bankruptcy in 2019 (though struggled on with greatly reduced presence).
43 On Simmel's "perpetuum mobile", see Bauman, "Perpetuum Mobile".
44 Ali Manik and Jim Yardley, "Building Collapse in Bangladesh Leaves Scores Dead", *New York Times*, 25 April 2013, online: https://www.nytimes.com/2013/04/25/world/asia/bangladesh-building-collapse.html.
45 Sarah Butler and Thaslima Begum, "Abuses 'Still Rife': 10 Years on From Bangladesh's Rana Plaza Disaster", *The Guardian*, 24 April 2023, online: https://www.theguardian.com/world/2023/apr/24/10-years-on-bangladesh-rana-plaza-disaster-safety-garment-workers-rights-pay. See also Sanchita Banerjee Saxena, ed., *Labor, Global Supply Chains, and the Garment Industry in South Asia: Bangladesh After Rana Plaza* (London and New York: Routledge, 2020).
46 Daisy Buchanan, "The Zara Workers' Protest Shows Why Fast Fashion Should Worry All of Us", *The Guardian*, 8 November 2017, online: https://www.theguardian.com/commentisfree/2017/nov/08/zara-workers-protest-fast-fashion-worry-all-of-us.
47 Imane Allam, Simone Scagnelli and Laura Corazza, "Sustainability Reporting, a New Type of Companies' Hypocrisy: Zara and Volkswagen Cases", in Belén Díaz Díaz, Nicholas Capaldi, Samuel O. Idowu and René Schmidpeter, eds., *Responsible Business in a Changing World: CSR, Sustainability, Ethics & Governance* (Cham: Springer, 2020), p.207. This chapter provides a thorough summary and analysis of various scandals.
48 See Clean Clothes Campaign, "Fashion Checker: Zara Brand Profile", April 2020, online: https://cleanclothes.org/file-repository/zara.pdf/view.
49 Impact International, "Fast Fashion at a Human Cost – Zara Fashion Retailer Chooses Sales Over Ethics", 5 July 2021, online: https://impactpolicies.org/news/226.
50 Ewelina U. Ochab, "French Prosecutors to Investigate Retailers' Involvement in Crimes Against Humanity in Xinjiang", *Forbes*, 6 July 2021, online: https://www.forbes.com/sites/ewelinaochab/2021/07/06/french-prosecutors-to-investigate-retailers-involvement-in-crimes-against-humanity-in-xinjiang/?sh=17319d495022.
51 AFR, "France Drops Fashion Groups Probe Over Uyghur Forced Labour", Business and Human Rights Resource Center, 17 May 2023, online: https://www.business-humanrights.org/en/latest-news/france-investigating-judge-to-examine-connection-between-fashion-groups-and-uyghur-forced-labour/.

52　Nikolay Anguelov, *The Dirty Side of the Garment Industry: Fast Fashion and its Negative Impact on Environment and Society* (Boca Raton: CRC Press, 2016), p.183.

53　Sana Khan and Abdul Malik, "Environmental and Health Effects of Textile Industry Wastewater", in Abdul Malik, Elisabeth Grohmann and Rais Akhtar, eds., *Environmental Deterioration and Human Health* (Dordrecht: Springer Science, 2014), pp. 55–71.

54　Anguelov, *The Dirty Side of the Garment Industry*, p.x.

55　Intidex Annual Report, 2023, p.214.

56　Rachel Bick, Erika Halsey and Christine C. Ekenga, "The Global Environmental Injustice of Fast Fashion", *Environmental Health*, 17:92, 2018, p.3.

57　Martina Igini, "10 Concerning Fast Fashion Waste Statistics", Earth.Org, 21 August 2023, online: https://earth.org/statistics-about-fast-fashion-waste/ and Marc Gunther, "Fast Fashion Fills our Landfills", *JSTOR Daily*, 27 September 2016, online: https://daily.jstor.org/fast-fashion-fills-our-landfills/.

58　Dielle Lundberg and Julia Devoy, "The Aftermath of Fast Fashion", 22 September 2022, Boston university School of Public Health, online: https://www.bu.edu/sph/news/articles/2022/the-aftermath-of-fast-fashion-how-discarded-clothes-impact-public-health-and-the-environment/.

59　Nor in Zara stores I visited in New York, Vienna and Melbourne during 2023.

60　Natalie Obiko Pearson, Ekow Dontoh and Dhwani Pandya, "Fast Fashion Waste Is Choking Developing Countries With Mountains of Trash", *Bloomberg*, 2 November 2022, online: https://www.bloomberg.com/news/features/2022-11-02/h-m-zara-fast-fashion-waste-leaves-environmental-impact#xj4y7vzkg.

61　Annamma Joy, John F. Sherry Jr, Alladi Venkatesh, Jeff Wang and Ricky Chan, "Fast Fashion, Sustainability, and the Ethical Appeal of Luxury Brands", *Fashion Theory*, 16:3, 2012, p.288.

62　Lisa McNeill and Rebecca Moore, "Sustainable Fashion Consumption and the Fast Fashion Conundrum: Fashionable Consumers and Attitudes to Sustainability in Clothing Choice", *International Journal of Consumer Studies*, 39, 2015, pp.212–222.

63　See Silvia Blas Riesgo, Mónica Codina and Teresa Sádaba, "Does Sustainability Matter to Fashion Consumers? Clustering Fashion Consumers and Their Purchasing Behavior in Spain", *Fashion Practice*, 15:1, 2023, pp.36–63; and Micael-Lee Johnstone and Lay Peng Tan, "Exploring the Gap between Consumers' Green Rhetoric and Purchasing Behavior", *Journal of Business Ethics*, 132:2, 2015, pp.311–328. On the "Fashion Paradox", see Sandy Black, *Eco Chic: The Fashion Paradox* (London: Black Dog Publishing, 2008).

64　Carmen Adriana Gheorghe and Roxana Matefi, "Sustainability and Transparency – Necessary Conditions for the Transition from Fast to Slow Fashion: Zara Join Life Collection's Analysis", *Sustainability*, 13, 2021, 11013.

65　G. Birtwistle and C. M. Moore, "Fashion Clothing – Where Does It All End Up?" *International Journal of Retail & Distribution Management*, 35:3, 2007, pp.210–216.

66　Kate Fletcher, "Slow Fashion", *The Ecologist*, 37:5, June 2007, p.61, online: https://theecologist.org/2007/jun/01/slow-fashion.

67 See Hazel Clark, "SLOW + FASHION – an Oxymoron – or a Promise for the Future …?", *Fashion Theory*, 12:4, 2008, pp.427–446.

68 See Louise Crewe, *The Geographies of Fashion: Consumption, Space and Value* (London: Bloomsbury, 2017), especially chapter 3, Fast Fashion, Global Spaces, and Bio-commodification, pp.37–64.

69 Nevenka Popović Šević, Anja Jeremić, Milica Slijepčević and Milena Ilić, "Marketing Focused on The Online Brand Community – The Example of Zara", *Marketing*, 52:1, 2021, p.39.

Chapter 8

1 Michelle Jimin Lee, "Gentle Monster Sunglasses: How a Korean Luxury Brand Rose to Global Fame", Best of Korea, 10 July 2023, online: https://bestofkorea.com/gentle-monster-korean-luxury-brand/.

2 See Gentle Monster, "Making Process", 2011 video, Vimeo: https://vimeo.com/28134926.

3 Roman Espejo, "Gentlemonster", *Cool Hunter*, 3 August 2012, online: https://coolhunting.com/style/gentlemonster/.

4 Jonathan Tepper with Denise Hearn, *The Myth of Capitalism: Monopolies and the Death of Capitalism* (Hoboken, NJ: Wiley, 2019), p.124.

5 See "Sticker Shock: Why Are Glasses So Expensive?" (summary of *60 Minutes* special, 7 October 2012), online: https://www.cbsnews.com/news/luxottica-eyewear-why-are-glasses-expensive/#lngtezhvpxegafl058m.

6 Warby Parker entered the United States market in 2012, quickly moving from production to direct retail sales.

7 Chekii Harling, "Gentle Monster", *Selfridges Magazine*, online: https://www.selfridges.com/AU/en/features/articles/selfridges-meets/gentle-monster/.

8 Emily Farra, "Introducing Gentle Monster, the Korean Eyewear Brand You Need to Know Now", *Vogue*, 4 April 2016, online: https://www.vogue.com/article/gentle-monster-korean-eyewear-brand-new-york-store-opening-ceremony.

9 Barry Samaha, "How Independent Luxury Brands Are Disrupting the Eyewear Industry", *Forbes*, 7 November 2017, online: https://www.forbes.com/sites/barrysamaha/2017/11/07/best-independent-luxury-eyewear-brands-pared-gentle-monster-krewe/?sh=25a8a6d456f3.

10 Hannah Goldfield, "Rose-Colored Glasses", *New York Times*, 19 February 2017, online: https://www.nytimes.com/2017/02/16/t-magazine/fashion/gentle-monster-glasses-tilda-swinton.html.

11 The film was inspired by Ingmar Bergman's *The Seventh Seal*. Violet Conroy, "Tilda Swinton Collaborates with Gentle Monster", *Sleek*, 17 March 2017, online: https://www.sleek-mag.com/article/gentle-monster-tilda-swinton/.

12 As at 10 November 2023.

13 Jennie is also currently the face of Chanel and the body of Calvin Klein underwear.

14 Katarina Djoric, "Gentle Monster Interview with Brand Director Gary Bott", *Design Scene*, 9 July 2019, online: https://www.designscene.net/2019/07/gentle-monster-interview.html.

15 Juliana Neira, "Interview with Gentle Monster", *Design Boom*, 18 November 2021, online: https://www.designboom.com/technology/gentle-monster-interview-the-giant-face-robot-11-18-2021/.

16 Marta Massi and Alex Turrini, "When Fashion Meets Art: The Artification of Luxury Fashion Brands", in Marta Massi and Alex Turrini, eds., *The Artification of Luxury Fashion Brands: Synergies, Contaminations, and Hybridizations* (Cham, Switzerland; Palgrave Macmillian, 2020).

17 Delphine Dion and Eric Arnould, "Retail Luxury Strategy: Assembling Charisma through Art and Magic", *Journal of Retailing*, 87:4, 2001, pp.502–520.

18 See Nancy J. Troy, *Couture Culture: A Study in Modern Art and Fashion* (Cambridge, MA, and London: MIT Press, 2003).

19 Valerie Steele, "Fashion," in *Art and Fashion*, Adam Geczy and Vicki Karaminas, eds., *Fashion and Art* (London and New York: Berg, 2012), p.16.

20 Adam Geczy and Vicki Karaminas, "Fashion and Art: Critical Crossovers", in Geczy and Karaminas, eds., *Fashion and Art* (London and New York: Berg, 2012), p.8.

21 See Jean-Noël Kapferer, "The Artification of Luxury: From Artisans to Artists", *Business Horizons*, 57, 2014, pp.371–380.

22 Nicky Ryan, "Patronage: Prada and the Art of Patronage", *Fashion Theory*, 11:1, p.17.

23 Louise Crewe, "Placing Fashion: Art, Space, Display and the Building of Luxury Fashion Markets Through Retail Design", *Progress in Human Geography*, 40:4, 2015, p.518.

24 Crewe, "Placing Fashion", p.519.

25 Crewe, "Placing Fashion", p.519.

26 Gilles Lipovetsky and Veronica Manlow, "The 'Artialization' of Luxury Stores", in Jan Brand, Jose Teunissen, Catelijne de Muijnck and Jos Arts, eds., *Fashion and Imagination – About Clothes and Art* (Arnhem, the Netherlands: ArtEZ Press, 2009), pp.154–167.

27 Annamma Joy, Jeff Jianfeng Wang, Tsang-Sing Chan, John F. Sherry Jr. and Geng Cui, "M(Art)Worlds: Consumer Perceptions of How Luxury Brand Stores Become Art Institutions", *Journal of Retailing*, 90:3, 2014, p.349.

28 Victoria Manlow and Karinna Nobbs, "Form and Function of Luxury Flagships: An International Exploratory Study of the Meaning of the Flagship Store for Managers and Customers", *Journal of Fashion Marketing and Management*, 17:1, 2013, p.61.

29 On the variations of installation art, see Claire Bishop, *Installation Art* (London: Tate Gallery, 2005).

30 Ana Vukadin, Jean-François Lemoine and Olivier Badot, "Store Artification and Retail Performance", *Journal of Marketing Management*, 35:7–8, 2019, pp.634–661.

31 Julia-Sophie Jelinek, "Art as Strategic Branding Tool for Luxury Fashion Brands", *Journal of Product & Brand Management*, 27:3, 2018, pp.294–307, 303.

32. Qin Qian, "The Secrets to Luxury Eyewear Brand Gentle Monster's Rapid Rise", *Jiang Daily*, 17 July 2017, online: https://jingdaily.com/the-secrets-to-strange-luxury-eyewear-brand-gentle-monsters-quick-road-to-success/.
33. Mitchell Oakley Smith and Alison Kubler, *Art/Fashion in the 21st Century* (London: Thames & Hudson, 2013), p.12.
34. Crewe, "Placing Fashion", p.523.
35. See Gentle Monster × Overwatch 2: https://www.gentlemonster.com/int/stories/overwatch2.
36. See Thomas Makryniotis, "Fashion and Costume Design in Electronic Entertainment – Bridging the Gap between Character and Fashion Design", *Fashion Practice*, 10:1, 2018, pp.99–118; and Emma Reay and Vanissa Wanick, "Skins in the Game: Fashion Branding and Commercial Video Games", in Eirini Bazaki and Vanissa Wanick, eds., *Reinventing Fashion Retailing Digitalising, Gamifying, Entrepreneuring* (Cham, Switzerland: Palgrave Macmillan, 2023), pp.73–90.
37. Vicente Marin, Cristobal Barra and Jorge Moyano, "Artification Strategies to Improve Luxury Perceptions: The Role of Adding an Artist Name", *Journal of Product & Brand Management*, 31:3, 2022, pp.496–505.
38. Kyung Hyun Kim and Youngmin Choe, eds., *The Korean Popular Culture Reader* (Durham and London: Duke University Press, 2014), p.1. See also Yasue Kuwahara, ed., *The Korean Wave: Korean Popular Culture in Global Context* (New York: Palgrave Macmillan, 2014).
39. This followed the earlier success with electronics brands such as LG and Samsung and automobile brands such as Hyundai and Kia. See D. J. Huppatz, *Modern Asian Design* (London: Bloomsbury, 2018), pp.158–160.
40. Ju Oak Kim, "The Korean Wave and the New Global Media Economy", in Dal Yong Jin, ed., *The Routledge Handbook of Digital Media and Globalization* (New York and London: Routledge, 2021), p.79.
41. Sangjoon Lee, "Introduction. A Decade of Hallyu Scholarship: Toward a New Direction in Hallyu 2.0", in Sangjoon Lee and Abé Mark Nornes, eds., *Hallyu 2.0: The Korean Wave in the Age of Social Media* (Ann Arbor: University of Michigan Press, 2015), p.16.
42. Hye-Kyung Lee and Xiyu Zhang, "The Korean Wave as a Source of Implicit Cultural Policy: Making of a Neoliberal Subjectivity in a Korean Style", *International Journal of Cultural Studies*, 24;3, 2021, pp.522–523.
43. Colin Stutz, "Louis Vuitton to Invest $80 Million in K-Pop Culture Factory YG Entertainment", 20 August 2014, *Billboard*, online: https://www.billboard.com/pro/louis-vuitton-invest-80-million-k-pop-yg-entertainment-psy/.
44. Judy Park, "Star Power in Korean Fashion: The Win-Win Relationship between Korean Celebrities and Designers", *Fashion Practice*, 7:1, 2015, pp.125–133.
45. Joanna Elfving-Hwang, "K-Pop Idols, Artificial Beauty, and Affective Fan Relationships in South Korea", in Anthony Elliott, ed., *Routledge Handbook of Celebrity Studies* (London and New York: Routledge, 2018), p.190.
46. Park, "Star Power in Korean Fashion", p.128.
47. Valentina Marinescu, ed., *The Global Impact of South Korean Popular Culture: Hallyu Unbound* (Lanham, Maryland: Lexington Books, 2014).

48 Hyeonju Son, "Images of the Future in South Korea", *Futures*, 52, 2013, p.7.
49 Norimitsu Onishi, "Seoul's Vision: A Robot for Every Home", *New York Times*, 2 April 2006, online: https://www.nytimes.com/2006/04/02/technology/02iht-robots.html.
50 Kim Stanley Robinson, "Dystopias Now", *Commune*, 11 February 2018, online: https://communemag.com/dystopias-now/.
51 Grace Powell, "In Conversation with Frederik Heymans", *Glamcult*, 29 January 2021, online: https://www.glamcult.com/articles/in-conversation-with-frederik-heyman/.
52 See So Yeon Leem, "The Dubious Enhancement: Making South Korea a Plastic Surgery Nation", *East Asian Science, Technology and Society: An International Journal*, 10:1, 2016, pp.51–71.
53 Joanna Elfving-Hwang, "Media, Cosmetic Surgery and Aspirational Beauty Aesthetics of the Ageing Body in South Korea", *Asian Studies Review*, 45:2, 2021, p.250.

Conclusion

1 David DeLallo, "How LEGO Plays With Data: An Interview With Chief Data Officer Orlando Machado", *Quantum Black: AI by* McKinsey, 21 December 2022, online: https://www.mckinsey.com/capabilities/quantumblack/our-insights/how-lego-plays-with-data-an-interview-with-chief-data-officer-orlando-machado.
2 See Steven J. Lade, Will Steffen, Wim de Vries, Stephen R. Carpenter, Jonathan F. Donges, Dieter Gerten, Holger Hoff, Tim Newbold, Katherine Richardson and Johan Rockström, "Human Impacts on Planetary Boundaries Amplified by Earth SYSTEM INTERACTIONS", *Nature Sustainability*, 3:2, 2020, pp.119–128.
3 Damian Carrington, "Revealed: The Huge Climate Impact of the Middle Classes", *The Guardian*, 20 November 2023, online: https://www.theguardian.com/environment/2023/nov/20/revealed-huge-climate-impact-of-the-middle-classes-carbon-divide. See also Tim Gore, "Confronting Climate Inequality", *Oxfam Briefing*, 21 September 2021, online: https://oxfamilibrary.openrepository.com/bitstream/handle/10546/621052/mb-confronting-carbon-inequality-210920-en.pdf.
4 See Laura Perdew, *The Great Pacific Garbage Patch* (Minneapolis: Abdo Publishing, 2018); and more recent figures from The Ocean Clean Up, online: https://theoceancleanup.com/great-pacific-garbage-patch/.
5 See Nicola Jones, "Progress on Plastic Pollution Treaty Too Slow, Scientists Say", *Nature*, 20 November 2023, online: https://www.nature.com/articles/d41586-023-03579-1.
6 Claire Holleran, *Shopping in Ancient Rome: Retail Trade in the Late Republic and the Principate* (Oxford: Oxford University Press, 2012), p.5.
7 See Fairphone website: https://www.fairphone.com/en/impact/.
8 See Kathryn Pavolvich, Stephen C. Bowden, Thomas Simnadis, Heather Connolly, Eva Collins and Jenny Gibb, "Allbirds: Sustainable Innovation Disrupting the Casual Shoe Industry", Sage Business Cases Originals, 2020, online: https://sk.sagepub.com/cases/allbirds-sustainable-innovation-disrupting-the-casual-shoe-industry;

and Myles Ethan Lascity, "Anti-Fashion Branding: Framing Technology in Uniqlo and Allbirds", *Fashion Theory*, 26:6, 2022, pp.881–898.

9. Daniel O'Donoghue and Paul Burnell, "Self-Service: Booths Supermarket Puts Staff Back Behind Its Tills", BBC, 10 November 2023, online: https://www.bbc.com/news/uk-england-lancashire-67373472.

10. Sophia Harris, "Why Several Big-Box Stores Have Ditched Their Self-Checkouts", CBC News, 22 November 2023, online: https://www.cbc.ca/news/business/some-retailers-scaling-back-self-checkouts-1.7034047.

11. See Roberta Katz, Sarah Ogilvie, Jane Shaw and Linda Woodhead, *Gen Z Explained: The Art of Living in a Digital Age* (University of Chicago Press, 2021).

12. Constantinos-Vasilios Priporas, Nikolaos Stylos and Antestis K. Fotidis, "Generation Z Consumers' Expectations of Interactions in Smart Retailing: A Future Agenda", *Computers in Human Behavior*, 77, December 2017, p.374.

13. Dan-Cristian Dabija and Lavinia Lung, "Millennials Versus Gen Z: Online Shopping Behaviour in an Emerging Market, Applied Ethics for Entrepreneurial Success: Recommendations for the Developing World", in Sebastian Văduva, Ioan Fotea, Lois P. Văduva and Randolph Wilt, eds., *Applied Ethics for Entrepreneurial Success: Recommendations for the Developing World*, 2018 Griffiths School of Management Annual Conference (GSMAC) on Business, Entrepreneurship and Ethics (Cham, Switzerland: Springer, 2019), p.1.

14. See Durgesh Kumar Agrawal, "Determining Behavioural Differences of Y and Z Generational Cohorts in Online Shopping", *International Journal of Retail & Distribution Management*, 50:7, 2022, pp.880–895.

15. See Aida Molina-Prados, Francisco Muñoz-Leiva and M. Belén Prados-Peña, "The Role of Customer Brand Engagement in the Use of Instagram as a 'Shop Window' for Fashion-Industry Social Commerce", *Journal of Fashion Marketing and Management*, 26:3, 2021, pp.495–515.

16. See Mischa Young, Jaime Soza-Parra and Giovanni Circella, "The Increase in Online Shopping During COVID-19: Who is Responsible, Will It Last, and What Does It Mean for Cities?" *Regional Science Policy & Practice*, 14:1, 2022, pp.162–178. See also US Census Bureau, "Quarterly Retail E-Commerce Sales: 3rd Quarter 2023", 17 November 2023, online: https://www.census.gov/retail/mrts/www/data/pdf/ec_current.pdf.

Index

Abloh, Virgil 113
ABS (acrylonitrile butadiene styrene) 65, 78–9, 194
Adidas 2, 109, 193
Aesop 1, 125–45, 157, 189, 190–2, 195, 199
AI (Artificial Intelligence) 51, 99, 100, 121
Amazon 1, 37–57, 117, 120, 121, 143, 190–2, 195, 196
App 18, 39, 81, 96, 99–100, 118–20, 121–2, 190, 191
Apple 1, 2, 15–35, 47, 48, 57, 75, 95, 99, 106, 110, 117–9, 136–7, 140, 149, 155, 157, 175, 177, 179–80, 189, 190–6
AR (Augmented Reality) 99–100, 198

Barthes, Roland 76
Bauman, Zygmunt 158
Benetton 147, 154, 162
Benjamin, Walter 3–4, 12, 31, 34, 144
Bezos, Jeff 40, 44, 48
Blackpink 176–7, 184, 185
Bohlin Cywinski Jackson 22
Body Shop 130–2, 145
Braun 29–30
BTS 176, 184, 185–6
Burberry 25, 113

Calvin Klein 154, 155
Carlson, Andrea 15–8
Chanel 137, 139, 158, 175, 179
Christensen, Godtfred 65, 78
Christensen, Ole Kirk 65
Comme des Garcons 155, 179
Cook, Tim 24–6, 34

COVID–19 pandemic 1, 40, 55, 95, 100, 120, 161, 166, 178, 198–9
Crawford Ilse 132

Davidson, Carolyn 109
Dewey, James 3–4
Disney 12, 13, 59, 70
eBay 120, 195

Eliasson, Olafur 179
Etsy 195
Experience Design 7–8, 13
Experience Economy 4–5, 73, 136, 141

Facebook 34, 117, 121, 123, 184, 195
FIFA World Cup 112, 117
Fitbit 117–8
Foster+Partners 25–7, 29–32
Ford, Henry 29

Gap 22, 156
Gates, Bill 48–9
Gentle Monster 1, 167–88, 189, 190, 192, 194, 198, 199
Gilmore, James (see Pine and Gilmore)
Global North 118, 141, 157, 159, 193
Google 33, 34, 57, 117
GPS 56, 118
Greenpeace 78, 94
Gropius, Walter 31

H&M 155, 156, 161, 183, 193
Hallyu 184–5
Han, Byung–Chul 34
Hard Rock Café 13, 112
Herzog and de Meuron 13
Huizinga, Johan 72–4, 78
Human–Computer–Interaction (HCI) 6, 7

Index

IDEO 7
IKEA 1, 10, 69, 81–101, 149, 153, 154, 162, 165, 189, 190–5
Instagram 99, 100, 117, 121, 123, 135, 142, 159–60, 177, 183, 184, 192, 198
Issey Miyake 155, 179
Ive, Jonathan 24–5, 28

Jameson, Fredric 75
Jobs, Steve 22–5, 28, 30, 175
Jordan, Michael 106, 110–3, 123

Kamprad, Ingvar 87–90, 94, 96
Kawakubo, Rei 113, 179
Kim, Hankook 175–6
Knight, Phil 109–10, 114
Koolhaas, Rem 13, 137, 179
K–Pop 176, 178, 184–8, 190
Kusama, Yayoi 180, 183

Laurel, Brenda 7–8
LEGO 1, 2, 10, 59–79, 93, 100, 103, 189–195
Loos, Adolf 28, 93
Louis Vuitton 137, 153, 179, 183, 185
Lundgren, Gilles 87, 91
Lush 131–2

March Studio 132, 133, 138
Mattel 67, 193
Merleau–Ponty, Maurice 9
Microplastics 115, 194
Murakami, Takashi 121, 179–80, 183

Nike 1, 2, 48, 103–23, 190–6
Niketown 106, 112
Norberg–Schultz, Christian 138
Norman, Donald 6

O'Keeffe, Michael 131, 144
Ortega, Amancio 152–5

Pallasmaa, Juhani 9, 138, 140
Paphitis, Dennis 130–2, 135, 143
Pine, Joseph and James Gilmore 4–6, 7, 73, 136, 141, 191
Pinterest 99, 121
Prada 13, 137, 175, 179

QR code 39, 81, 103, 105, 106, 121, 151, 191

Rams, Dieter 28–9, 30
Roddick, Anita 130, 145

Samsung 139
Shostack, G. Lynn 8
Simmel, Georg 157
Spotify 120, 136
Starbucks 13, 190–1

TikTok 75, 121, 159–60, 198

Unboxing 24, 177
User Experience (UX) 6–7, 28, 137

Van der Rohe, Mies 19, 31, 32

Walmart 57, 91, 162, 196
Whole Foods 40, 47–8
Williams, Raymond 3

Yohji Yamamoto 155, 179
YouTube 24, 117, 121, 177, 184

Zara 1, 103, 147–66, 167, 189–95
Zumthor, Peter 9, 138, 140